Lasting Wealth Is
A Matter Of Timing

Advance Praise For

Lasting Wealth Is A Matter Of Timing

...I recommend it for anyone interested in learning how to maintain their purchasing power during bull and bear markets.

Skip Viragh, Founder and President
Rydex Series Trust

..."Lasting Wealth Is A Matter Of Timing" is a must read for all mutual fund investors and every baby boomer looking for a well financed retirement. John's message dispels the myths of timing and gets to the truth of the matter.

Marshall L. Schield, President
Schield Management Company

...I applaud your collective efforts in producing a well documented, well organized, and clearly illustrated presentation.... This book is must reading for every serious investor seeking to secure his or her financial future.

Walter J. Loick,
Founder and Chairman
LBS Capital Management

...In "Lasting Wealth Is A Matter Of Timing," John Sosnowy exposes the fallacy of the buy-and-hold investment strategy and shows the value of market timing. The disciplined approach to risk management that John presents will enable investors to follow this advice through both bull and (the inevitable) bear markets.

Robert R. Champion, President
Champion Securities Corporation

Lasting Wealth Is A Matter Of Timing

John K. Sosnowy

WITH
RICHARD J. MATURI

21st Century Publishers

Library of Congress Catalog Card Number: 96-61386

Sosnowy, John K.
     Lasting Wealth is a Matter of Timing   /   John K. Sosnowy
          p.   cm
     Includes index.
     ISBN 0-9607298-3-6
     1. Investments-United States 2. Investment Analysis 3. Finance,
Personal. 4. Mutual Funds. I. Title. II. Title: Lasting Wealth is a
Matter of Timing

2 3 4 5 6 7 8 9 0

Neither the author nor the publisher is engaged in rendering financial, legal, or accounting services to the reader through the sale of this book. Since individual situations do vary, the reader should consult a competent professional on questions specific to the individual. The author and the publisher disclaim any liability for any loss incurred, directly or indirectly, as a consequence of the use or application of any information contained in this book.

21st Century Publishers
1320 Curt Gowdy Drive
Cheyenne, Wyoming 82009
307-635-5511

To LaGayle: My best friend as well as a super wife and mother

To Kori: The best daughter a dad could ever have and quite a young lady

Contents

"...You've gotta know when to hold'em, know when to fold'em, know when to walk away, know when to run..."

— Kenny Rogers

Preface

Lasting Wealth Is A Matter Of Timing! What does this title really mean? The key word here is *lasting*. Ideally, I would bet that you would like to accumulate a financial nest egg that could guarantee you an income stream that you could never outlive...no matter how long you live, no matter how high inflation rises, no matter how high tax rates become, no matter how the economy performs, no matter if the stock market crashes, and no matter what unforeseen events occur. I know I would like that guarantee.

Unfortunately, accumulating wealth and retaining wealth (having lasting wealth) are two different matters. Look at the entertainers and athletes who earn millions and millions and have nothing to show for it after their careers have ended. I learned about retaining wealth firsthand in 1987 as some of my clients with a 60 percent allocation in equities suffered significant drawdowns from large nest eggs built during the late 1970s and 1980s. Fortunately, the setback proved only temporary. But what if there had not been a quick rebound? What if the market decline had only been the beginning of a prolonged bear market like that experienced during 1973-74 or 1929-33? Likewise, what if during that extended period of low stock prices, those investors were retired and making regular withdrawals to meet living expenses? While it would have been tough for these clients who were only partially allocated in stocks, it would have been an absolute disaster for millions of investors who were 100 percent invested in the stock market.

In my opinion, many well-known financial advisors are setting up their clients for a financial massacre by selling the notion that the longer you own stocks, the lower the risk. In plain terms, this is nothing but hogwash! The truth is, the longer you own equities, the higher the probability that you are going to own equities during the next great stock market debacle and lose your financial rear end in the process.

I believe we received a warning shot across the bow in 1987, one we should ignore only to the detriment of our financial well-being. That warning signal made me realize that simple asset allocation strategies and techniques will not save us from financial disaster during a full blown bear market. If asset allocation fails to provide adequate protection in the face of a bear market, where should you turn to safeguard your financial wealth? In *Lasting Wealth is a Matter of Timing*, you will discover how only a total commitment to a disciplined risk management strategy such as market timing or tactical asset allocation is likely to save our generation and future generations from irreparable financial damage.

"Out of every adversity comes the seed of an equivalent or greater benefit." While I don't know the author of that quote, I have seen it come true many times in my lifetime. More recently, the 1987 market correction planted the seeds for better protecting my clients' wealth during the next bear market fiasco, whenever it arrives. Due to my involvement in founding SAAFTI (The Society of Asset Allocators & Fund Timers, Inc.), I believe that many thousands of investors have been exposed to the concept of risk reduction that is helping to secure their financial future. Refer to Chapter 1 for more information on SAAFTI. My goal with this book is to spread the risk management gospel to many more thousands of investors in time to protect and save their wealth. Read this book now before it is too late.

I have been blessed to have been born in this great country of freedom and free enterprise, to have wonderful parents who sacrificed mightily so that my two sisters and I could have a good education, and to have a wonderful wife and daughter who love me and support my endeavors such as writing this book.

I have also been taught to give back to the community, my church, and my fellow man in like proportion to how I have been blessed. Through this book and years of investment experience, I hope I can give back some of how I prospered from investing since 1969 and help you avoid some of the painful lessons learned along the way.

The purpose of this book is not to tout me as the world's greatest money manager, nor is it to try to sell you on the idea of hiring my firm to manage your money. Instead, I want to foster a real understanding of risk management in the securities markets and how it can protect your financial well-being. Whether you call it market timing, tactical asset allocation, dynamic asset allocation, or some other name, the important point is to get you to understand how risk management strategies can safeguard your portfolio. Chapter 3 will explain the subtle differences in these terms.

This book is not for everyone. If you are a speculator looking to get rich overnight, or a gambler willing to risk all of your chips on one roll of the dice, this book is not for you. On the other hand, if you are an investor who wants to build real wealth over time and keep it — while avoiding unnecessary and unreasonable levels of risk — then I believe that this book can help you immensely.

If I am successful in spreading the word via this book, you will *not* see a lifetime of hard-earned savings go down the drain in one catastrophic bear market. Accumulating wealth may be a matter of time, but I strongly believe that lasting wealth is a matter of timing.

I have organized *Lasting Wealth Is A Matter of Timing* in a logical fashion with Chapters 1-5 "Setting the Stage" for market timing and Chapters 6-10 providing you with practical steps to use in "Securing Your Financial Future." However, feel free to study the Table of Contents and jump right into topic material that piques your interest. The end of each chapter also includes a "Major Point Summary" for your benefit. Likewise, a comprehensive glossary at the end of the book is a handy quick reference source of terms and definitions. All of these will help you understand market timing and how it can be put to work to safeguard your financial nest egg.

As you read this book and develop a sense of my personality and passions, I believe you will appreciate how outraged I can become when I see you, the investing public, being fed misinformation that could endanger your financial well-being. For example, it is clear to me that uneasiness in the financial markets is usually accompanied by an increase in the number of articles by academia, mutual fund companies, and financial gurus proclaiming that market timing doesn't work and urging investors to stick with a buy and hold strategy. It is easy to refute the academicians because they often expound theories from their "Ivory Towers" without any real-world investment experience. When academicians say "market timing does not work," I firmly believe what they are really saying is, "I can't make it work," or "I don't understand how it works." Well, I really don't understand how electricity powers or why airplanes fly, but I don't go around making a fool of myself saying that they don't work! Mutual funds, on the other hand, promote buy and hold strategies because it is in their own best interest to keep the investing public in equities where they earn the highest fees.

Turning to the financial gurus who down play the importance of market timing. I believe that the real problem lies in the definition of terms. At one time or another, John Bogle, Warren Buffet, Peter Lynch, and a number of other investment heroes have urged ordinary investors not to attempt to time the market, but I contend that their own words and actions reflect what I define as market timing. We will clear up this confusion and provide some interesting insight in Chapter 4. My personal belief is that every successful investor employs market timing. The only real difference is that some investors' asset class exchange cycles are longer than others.

The bottom line of *Lasting Wealth is a Matter of Timing* is that market timing is a legitimate strategy for reducing the risks of stock market investing. It's not voodoo, it's not black magic, it's not black box complicated, and it's not perfect. No investing strategy is perfect, and anyone who tries to sell you on a perfect investment strategy is not being honest with you.

However, market timing, when employed properly by a professional within a disciplined strategy, reduces the drawdowns in account values during adverse market periods. This allows investors to stay committed to equity investing and benefitting from the market's superior returns over time, resulting in a higher risk-adjusted return. See Chapter 6.

Market timing may not work for amateur investors because they let their emotions get in the way and short-circuit their long-term investment strategy. While common stocks have historically provided sufficient returns to beat taxes and inflation, it's rare that you can get real people to buy and hold common stocks through major market declines. They usually buy late in the market cycle and then cut and run after the market drops. This fact has been documented in recent years in studies by Dalbar Financial and Fidelity Investments, both of which concluded that actual investor results were substantially less than the investment results of the underlying securities being studied.

I don't know what that tells you, but it points out to me that investors are going to practice some form of timing no matter what the Ibbotson statistics say about common stock returns, no matter what the mutual fund companies say, and no matter what their stock broker says. The only real question is whether they are going to practice 'emotional' market timing (buy at the top, sell at the bottom) or 'disciplined' market timing (with the assistance of a professional market timer). Whether you are a young adult starting out (Chapter 9 is especially for you), a baby boomer reaching middle age, or are already in your golden years, the fact that you have chosen to read this book now shows you possess good timing!

If, after reading this book, you either implement your own disciplined risk management strategy, or, to improve your probabilities of success, hire a professional advisor to help you, I believe you can accumulate and preserve your nest egg with the capacity to generate an income stream you cannot outlive. If what you learn from this book saves your capital from the ravages of the next big bear market, consider giving back a portion of your savings to your community through a donation to your church or favorite charity to improve other people's lives. It's a great investment in mankind. You will be glad you donated a portion of what this book has saved you!

Because I know from personal experience that some of you will find it difficult to maintain the discipline necessary to be consistently successful, I'd like to make you a no-strings-attached offer for a free annual update on the concepts and strategies presented in this book and how they are working for actual investors in the real world. All you need to do is send me a stamped, self-addressed envelope each year.

Good reading and may you accumulate and preserve lasting wealth!

John K. Sosnowy
502 N. Travis
Cameron, TX 76520-2563

Acknowledgments

Compared to the effort expended and the lessons learned in my investment research and daily experiences since 1969, compiling the information for this book was fairly easy. I firmly believe its message and put it to good use every day in my investment management business.

Therefore, most of my obligations and indebtedness are to those who first urged me to enter the investment management field and provided me opportunities along the way, those whose counsel sparked the ideas that formed the foundation of my investment philosophy, and those who encouraged me to persevere in the face of traditional skepticism. If you wonder if I was thinking of you when you read this, I was and I sincerely thank you.

I would, however, like to single out the following for special mention: The members of the old Union Carbide P.I.C. Investment Club; Paul Hayes, who first gave me a chance at Merrill Lynch in the late 1960s; A. Gary Shilling, former chief economist at Merrill Lynch; my soulmates on the ground floor of SAAFTI, Corey Colehour, Hays Glover, Carl Kludt; and members of the mutual fund and annuity industry, most notably Ed Tessmer, Bruce Avery, and Ellen Bradley, who took a chance on a new concept many years ago and still support us today. Most of all, I am grateful to the loyal clients who possessed the discipline and patience to stick with me through the years. Without you, there would be no story to tell.

I also owe a debt of gratitude to Marjorie Maxfield, who first encouraged me years ago to write a book; to Linda Ferentchak, who has put many of my ideas on paper through *The Investment Advisor* newsletter; and Rick Maturi, my coauthor, a true professional and a really nice guy.

Investment professionals Gerald Appel, Tom Basso, Bob Champion, Bruce Katz, Walt Loick, Joe Ludwig, Peter Mauthe, Marshall Schield, Steve Shellans, David Solo, Jim Stack, and Skip Viragh were kind enough to review portions of the manuscript, spot errors, and offer constructive comments and suggestions. The errors that remain are, of course, my own.

Sandy Hanel, Celine Sanderson, my wife LaGayle, and my daughter Kori all shared the excitement, labor and tension of this project...and still had encouraging words to offer. To each of you...my heartfelt thanks!

John K. Sosnowy
Cameron, Texas

About the Author

JOHN K. SOSNOWY

John K. Sosnowy is the chairman and CEO of Sosnowy Investment Management Company, Inc. (SIMCO), a registered investment advisor and member of the National Association of Securities Dealers, Inc. During his decades of investment management experience, Sosnowy has been a nationally recognized pioneer in tactical asset allocation/risk management strategies. He is the founder and a past president of the Society of Asset Allocators and Fund Timers, Inc. (SAAFTI), an industry national trade association.

Sosnowy is a member of the American MENSA Society and holds a Bachelor of Science in Mathematics and a Master of Science in Industrial Engineering. His investment philosophy has been featured in *Forbes, Financial Planning, Investment Advisor, Newsweek, Research, Technical Analysis of Stocks & Commodities*, and many other national and regional publications. He has been a guest on Dan Rather's CBS Evening News and hosted "Money Talks," an investment radio show.

His office is on the grounds of the historic Magnolia House in Cameron, Texas. He resides just outside of Cameron with his wife, LaGayle.

With Richard J. Maturi

Richard J. Maturi is a well-respected business and investment journalist with eight investment books and over 1,000 articles in such publications as *Barron's, Investor's Business Daily, Institutional Investor, Kiplinger's Personal Finance, Physician's Financial News, Research and Your Money.* Previous books include *Wall Street Words, Stock Picking, Divining the Dow, Money Making Investments, The 105 Best Investments for the 21st Century, Main Street Beats Wall Street, The Hometown Investor,* and *Investors' Guide for Making MegaBucks on Mergers.* He also publishes three investment newsletters: *Utility and Energy Portfolio, Gaming & Investments Quarterly,* and *21st Century Investments.*

Maturi is a member of the American Society of Journalists and Authors, the Society of American Business Editors, and the Denver Press Club.

PART I

Setting The Stage

> "For age and want save while you may. No morning sun lasts a whole day."
>
> — *Ben Franklin*

CHAPTER 1

Saving Boomers from Bust

BABY BOOMERS COME OF AGE

The first of the baby boom generation officially reached 50 years of age in 1995. Retirement looms for many of the boomer generation in the next decade and by the year 2010 at the latest. The big question is whether boomers have adequately planned for their retirement years and implemented investment strategies designed to deliver returns which will allow them to live their golden years in comfort.

Financial experts estimate that to live well you must be able to generate at least 70 percent of your pre-retirement income. Boomers are faced with the reality that their retirement funds must last longer. With improved health care and more healthy diet and life styles, boomers will likely outlive their parents by a significant margin. According to life expectancy actuary calculations, the United States average life expectancy for men is over 71 years and over 78 years for women. Moreover, when a man reaches age 75, he has a fifty-fifty probability of reaching age 84 while a woman age 75 is expected to reach age 86.

To be sure, in many cases social security benefits and company pension plans will not be able to deliver the required retirement funds. In fact, many baby boomers have opted to work outside of the corporate world without the benefit of company pension plans. Corporate downsizing plus mergers and takeovers have also cast doubt on the certainty that retirement benefits will be there when needed. Likewise, the level of social security benefits remains clouded as Congress wrestles with budget deficits and the large number of retiring baby boomers outstrips the number of active workers paying into the social security program.

Therefore, it is crucial that additional savings and investments make up the shortfall between expected retirement benefits and the amount of capital needed to ensure a comfortable retirement. You may retire but **you cannot afford to let your money retire!**

Will baby boomers be financially ready for retirement? Will their investment plans for retirement be likely to generate an income stream they cannot outlive? From my perspective, the answer to both of those critical questions is an emphatic "No!"

Use Table 1-1, Retirement Savings Calculator, to help determine your own level of savings needed to achieve your retirement goals. It represents the first step in achieving financial independence. Unless you first know where you are headed and then institute an investment plan to get you there, you will not succeed.

Fortunately, there is still time to save boomers from bust, but it is going to take tremendous missionary zeal on the part of us in the investment management business to help this generation develop some new investment habits and to teach them to understand the importance of a **disciplined risk reduction** strategy to their financial security. That's one of the reasons I founded our national trade association, the Society of Asset Allocators and Fund Timers, Inc. (SAAFTI) back in 1989. I believe that we can save an entire generation from financial ruin during the next bear market if we can get the critical message of the importance of disciplined risk reduction out to and accepted by middle America. If we are successful in this endeavor, one of my life's major goals will have been accomplished.

SAAFTI is a non-profit industry trade group. It serves registered investment advisors who manage client mutual fund and variable

Table 1-1
RETIREMENT SAVINGS CALCULATOR

Age at Retirement	Retirement Factor	# of Years to Retirement	Investment Factor	Savings Factor
55	23.3	5	1.09	.192
57	22.6	6	1.11	.159
59	21.8	7	1.13	.135
60	21.4	8	1.15	.117
61	21.0	9	1.17	.103
62	20.5	10	1.19	.092
63	20.1	15	1.29	.059
64	19.6	20	1.41	.043
65	19.2	25	1.53	.033
67	18.2	30	1.67	.026

1. Annual income needed per year after you retire (70% of current income) $_____

2. Guaranteed retirement income (total from social security, pension plans) $_____

3. Annual income required from savings (line 1 minus line 2) $_____

4. Amount you must save before you retire (line 3 times the factor at which age you plan to retire. For example, if you're going to retire at age 60, use the appropriate retirement factor of 21.4.) $_____

5. Amount you already saved, including IRAs & SEPs. $_____

6. Projected value of your savings at the time you retire (line 5 times the investment factor representing the number of years until your retirement. For example, if you're 35 and plan to retire when you're 60, use the investment factor of 1.53 which corresponds to 25 years until your retirement.) $_____

7. Amount you still need (line 4 minus line 6) $_____

8. Amount of annual savings needed to reach your goal (line 7 times the savings factor corresponding to the number of years until you retire. For example, if you have 25 years until retirement use the savings factor of .033) $_____

annuity assets through the use of market timing, tactical asset allocation, dynamic asset allocation, active asset allocation, fund timing,
fund conversion, fund switching, and/or related risk management strategies. We will define and discuss these risk management investment
strategies in detail in Chapter 3. You may also refer to the comprehensive glossary at the end of the book for a definition of these and
other investment terms.

SAAFTI members range in size from small firms managing less
than $1 million to firms managing more than $1 billion. Combined,
over 130 SAAFTI registered investment advisor firms manage in
excess of $10 billion in portfolio assets for their clients. SAAFTI has
adopted a code of ethics to develop and encourage the practice of
high standards of personal and professional conduct among members in their dealings with the investing public. SAAFTI performance
reporting standards help promote consistency, fairness, and complete-
ness in the dissemination of investment return data. For more
information, you can contact SAAFTI at the following address or
call 303-989-5656.

>**SAAFTI**
>**C/O Financial Communications Associates, Inc.**
>**7112 W. Jefferson Ave., Suite 300**
>**Lakewood, CO 80235**

As in any industry, it goes without saying that some members of
SAAFTI are better managers than others, some are more experienced
than others, and some will have an investment philosophy and operating style that you will like better than others. Take the time to check
out a prospective advisor carefully. There is more information on
selecting an advisor in Chapters 6 and 9.

One of the major purposes of SAAFTI lies in making the investing
public aware of the underlying concepts and benefits of asset allocation and market timing. In founding SAAFTI, I wanted those of us in
the industry to join forces with one voice to deliver the following
messages:

1. This is not a new era in which we will never again experience another bear market. This time it's NOT different.

2. In fact, between now and 2010, it is likely that we will undergo at least one terrible recession, maybe even a depression and a cataclysmic bear market during which stock prices drop 50 percent or more. See Chapter 7.

3. If you fail to develop a disciplined risk management strategy for your portfolio; whether you call it market timing, dynamic asset allocation, or some other title; you may suffer a financial disaster from which you can never recover in your lifetime.

For those who heed my message and develop their own risk management strategy or, better still, hire a professional risk manager, there can be lasting riches beyond your wildest dreams. If this book helps deliver this important message and helps save the typical American investor from ruin, it will be well worth the considerable time and effort expended in this project.

If you are a member of the baby boom generation or younger, there is still ample time to save yourself from financial ruin. For those of you nearing or in retirement already, read fast and act quickly. Your financial time bomb is already ticking. Those who ignore history are doomed to repeat it. With that in mind, our first step in helping you achieve financial independence lies in reviewing history by examining the retirement years of three people from an earlier generation. The people are fictional, however, the figures and the financial message are real.

TALE OF THREE INVESTORS

You will meet three individuals, all of whom retired in 1973 with a nest egg of $100,000 to invest. Each needed to withdraw $8,000 (adjusted for inflation) annually for living expenses and as a supplement to their social security benefits.

Connie Conservative chose to invest $50,000 in a portfolio of safe Treasury Bills and $50,000 in long-term government bonds. For analysis purposes she could have easily invested in certificates of deposit and money market funds. Her primary concern was for the safety of her hard-earned money, remembering that her parents had lost everything during the Depression. No event in American history has worried more people over a longer period of time than the Crash of 1929 and the Great Depression. As Connie's actions reveal, the Depression still affects investors' attitudes today, and not in a beneficial way, as we will see later. While Connie truly believed her actions were prudent, she was setting herself up for financial disaster.

As the amount withdrawn each year increased due to the inflation adjustment, the value of her portfolio decreased. By 1983, her bond nest egg disappeared. By 1986, the T-Bills followed suit, and she was completely broke and forced to move in with her daughter's family to live out her golden years.

As stated by William E. Donoghue in *Donoghue's Mutual Fund Super Stars*, "America simply does not have time to play it safe with retirement savings, and with the changes in the investment markets; 'playing it safe' may be the riskiest strategy of all. The risk of not only having insufficient savings but of losing those savings to the 'safety' of the fixed-income markets is dramatic..."

BUY AND HOLD BONDS
January 1, 1973 through January 6, 1984

Chart 1-1 Year	Yearly Return	$ 50,000 Inv. Now Worth *
1973	-1.1%	45,471
1974	4.3%	42,915
1975	9.1%	42,032
1976	16.7%	44,031
1977	-0.7%	38,330
1978	-1.1%	32,031
1979	-1.3%	24,984
1980	-4.0%	16,532
1981	1.8%	8,702
1982	40.4%	3,774
1983	0.2%	— 0 —

Legend: LT Gvt Bds

* Includes systematic withdrawal of $ -4000 at the end of the 1st year and increasing annually to keep up with inflation.

Chart 1-1 Courtesy of SIMCO

BUY AND HOLD MONEY MARKET/T-BILLS
January 1, 1973 through January 2, 1987

Chart 1-2 Year	Yearly Return	$ 50,000 Inv. Now Worth *
1973	6.9%	49,434
1974	8.0%	48,916
1975	5.8%	46,961
1976	5.0%	44,271
1977	5.2%	41,198
1978	7.3%	38,342
1979	10.3%	35,640
1980	11.2%	32,183
1981	14.8%	28,801
1982	10.5%	23,375
1983	8.9%	16,685
1984	9.8%	9,216
1985	7.7%	472
1986	6.0%	— 0 —

Legend: U.S. Treasury Bills

* Includes systematic withdrawal of $ -4000 at the end of the 1st year and increasing annually to keep up with inflation.

Chart 1-2 Courtesy of SIMCO

Charts 1-1 and 1-2 illustrate the decline in value of the bond and T-Bill investments as their earnings fail to keep up with inflation.

Peter Hope employed a buy and hold investment strategy. He invested $50,000 in a diversified stock portfolio and $50,000 in an aggressive growth stock mutual fund. He held on hoping that a bear market would not come along during his retirement years and devour his money. Unfortunately, a big bad bear market lurked right around the corner, rearing its ugly head in 1973 and 1974.

The one/two punch of market depreciation of his portfolios and increased withdrawals due to inflation wiped out his aggressive growth stock fund entirely by 1978. His diversified stock portfolio suffered the same fate, declining to a zero balance by 1984. See Charts 1-3 and 1-4. Peter was last sighted in a Houston soup kitchen line. He resides nearby under a freeway underpass. Refer to the discussion of buy and hold strategies later in this chapter.

AGGRESSIVE GROWTH FUND
January 1, 1973 through December 31, 1978

Chart 1-3 Year	Yearly Return	$ 50,000 Inv. Now Worth *
1973	-39.4%	26,308
1974	-43.9%	10,282
1975	35.6%	9,135
1976	30.0%	6,843
1977	2.1%	1,615
1978	24.7%	— 0 —

An illustration using S4 as Stock fund. Legend: S4=Keystone Small Co. Fund

* Includes systematic withdrawal of $ -4000 at the end of the 1st year and increasing annually to keep up with inflation.

Chart 1-3 Courtesy of SIMCO

DIVERSIFIED STOCK PORTFOLIO
January 1, 1973 through December 31, 1984

Chart 1-4 Year	Yearly Return	$ 50,000 Inv. Now Worth *
1973	-26.9%	32,572
1974	-28.7%	18,728
1975	51.5%	23,563
1976	46.3%	29,450
1977	5.3%	25,627
1978	18.2%	24,420
1979	16.5%	21,803
1980	32.6%	21,438
1981	6.3%	14,651
1982	40.7%	12,162
1983	32.9%	7,395
1984	-1.1%	— 0 —

An illustration using NYSE as Stock fund. Legend: NYSE=NYSE Total Return Index

* Includes systematic withdrawal of $ -4000 at the end of the 1st year and increasing annually to keep up with inflation.

Chart 1-4 Courtesy of SIMCO.

Sammy Savvy also invested $50,000 in a diversified stock portfolio and $50,000 in an aggressive growth stock mutual fund, however he took a different investment tact than Peter Hope. Instead of using a buy and hold strategy, Sammy hired a risk manager (market timer or tactical asset allocator) to monitor his portfolio on a daily basis and protect him from the full consequences of debilitating bear markets. It made all the difference in the world. When we caught up with Sammy on the beach in Hawaii, his tan and sunny disposition exuded success.

Sammy's annual withdrawal now totaled over $30,000 compared with the initial $8,000. More importantly, his original $100,000 investment had grown to in excess of $1.3 million, despite withdrawals exceeding $450,000 over the years and paying advisory fees. See Charts 1-5 and 1-6, for the performance of the two market timing managers Sammy met in 1973. Although he hired Manager A, whose timing model turned out to produce the lesser results of the two, Sammy is a very happy (and wealthy) investor.

Some of you might question the fairness of me choosing 1973 as the retirement date for our three mythical investors and for using an

AGGRESSIVE GROWTH FUND
Signals Generated by the Timing Models
January 1, 1973 through December 29, 1995

Chart 1-5	TIMING MODEL 'A'		TIMING MODEL 'B'	
Year	Yearly Return Net Of Maximum Fee	$ 50,000 Inv. Now Worth *	Yearly Return Net Of Maximum Fee	$ 50,000 Inv. Now Worth *
1973	7.7%	49,850	6.3%	49,167
1974	-5.8%	42,483	11.3%	50,213
1975	45.2%	56,888	43.0%	67,024
1976	23.0%	64,964	28.0%	80,774
1977	-2.4%	58,040	-1.6%	74,091
1978	46.3%	79,068	43.5%	100,472
1979	7.1%	78,065	15.4%	109,325
1980	60.4%	117,752	58.1%	165,367
1981	12.5%	124,309	14.2%	180,567
1982	49.1%	176,794	55.9%	272,573
1983	54.7%	263,986	29.0%	341,784
1984	-4.9%	241,102	-14.2%	283,521
1985	22.5%	284,750	42.2%	392,480
1986	13.6%	312,635	11.5%	426,477
1987	5.1%	317,169	38.2%	577,221

Chart 1-5	**TIMING MODEL 'A'**		**TIMING MODEL 'B'**	
Year	Yearly Return Net Of Maximum Fee	$ 50,000 Inv. Now Worth *	Yearly Return Net Of Maximum Fee	$ 50,000 Inv. Now Worth *
1988	-7.3%	282,383	10.5%	625,215
1989	7.3%	290,656	19.0%	730,408
1990	-13.0%	240,158	21.2%	870,429
1991	67.4%	388,122	68.7%	1,451,988
1992	21.5%	456,716	9.8%	1,578,183
1993	-0.3%	440,193	30.0%	2,035,385
1994	4.5%	444,131	5.6%	2,131,561
1995	41.4%	611,665	41.7%	3,002,617

An illustration using S4 as Stock fund, B1 as BOND fund, BILL as M/Market fund, and SPTR as market index and after all fees

See Appendix A for Disclosure Statement.

* Includes systematic withdrawal of $ -4000 at the end of the 1st year and increasing annually to keep up with inflation

Legend: S4=Keystone Small Co Stock Fund   B1=Keystone B1 Bond Fund   BILL=U.S. Treasury Bills
SPTR=S&P 500 Total Return Index

Chart 1-5 Courtesy of SIMCO.

DIVERSIFIED STOCK PORTFOLIO
Signals Generated by the Timing Models
January 1, 1973 through December 29, 1995

Chart 1-6	**TIMING MODEL 'A'**		**TIMING MODEL 'B'**	
Year	Yearly Return Net Of Maximum Fee	$ 50,000 Inv. Now Worth *	Yearly Return Net Of Maximum Fee	$ 50,000 Inv. Now Worth *
1973	5.7%	48,836	6.3%	49,167
1974	-1.3%	43,719	14.8%	51,944
1975	54.4%	62,694	58.0%	77,244
1976	35.5%	79,904	47.0%	108,484
1977	1.2%	75,480	0.8%	103,975
1978	30.2%	92,452	26.3%	125,463
1979	8.3%	93,470	9.0%	130,113
1980	45.7%	128,681	36.6%	170,231
1981	12.5%	136,602	17.0%	190,941
1982	41.2%	184,344	50.7%	278,932
1983	32.3%	234,640	31.2%	356,299
1984	8.8%	245,534	5.7%	366,572
1985	29.8%	308,281	47.8%	530,662
1986	14.6%	342,350	17.4%	611,299
1987	-1.3%	326,420	36.0%	818,589
1988	-2.6%	306,386	25.2%	1,011,419
1989	11.1%	328,014	19.8%	1,197,032

	TIMING MODEL 'A'		TIMING MODEL 'B'	
Year	Yearly Return Net Of Maximum Fee	$ 50,000 Inv. Now Worth *	Yearly Return Net Of Maximum Fee	$ 50,000 Inv. Now Worth *
1990	-10.5%	280,850	8.5%	1,284,019
1991	52.2%	413,476	52.1%	1,937,125
1992	21.7%	488,047	22.9%	2,365,571
1993	16.4%	552,343	18.9%	2,796,577
1994	3.8%	557,294	5.2%	2,924,296
1995	27.9%	696,868	28.2%	3,732,379

An illustration using NYSE as Stock fund, GBTP as BOND fund, BILL as M/Market fund, and SPTR as market index and after all fees

See Appendix A for Disclosure Statement.

* Includes systematic withdrawal of $ -4000 at the end of the 1st year and increasing annually to keep up with inflation.

Legend: NYSE=NYSE Total Return Index   GBTP=LT Gvt Bds   BILL=U.S. Treasury Bills
SPTR=S&P 500 Total Return Index

Chart 1-6 Courtesy of SIMCO.

Table 1-2 shows the fate of our three investors.

Table 1-2
FATE OF THREE INVESTORS

Connie Conservative
Amount Invested: $ 100,000

Total Amount Withdrawn
    through 12-31-86: $ 154,915

Portfolio Value
    as of 12-31-86: $ —0—

Financial Status: Flat Broke

Sammy Savvy
Amount
    Invested: $ 100,000

Total Amount
    Withdrawn thru
    12-31-95: $ 450,800

Portfolio Value as of
    12-31-95: $1,308,533 *

Financial
    Status: Independently
    Wealthy

* Would be $6,734,996 if we
    used the results from Timing
    Model 'B'

Peter Hope
Amount Invested: $ 100,000

Total Amount Withdrawn
    through 12-31-84: $ 102,773

Portfolio Value
    as of 12-31-84: $ —0—

Financial Status: Destitute

8% withdrawal rate, especially for Connie Conservative. I did this purposely, to get your attention!

I believe that we are long overdue for at least a 1973-74 type bear market. Furthermore, as I said earlier in this chapter, there is good reason to believe that we could even have another Great Depression during the lifetime of the Baby-boomer generation. This will likely occur after most boomers are retired and taking withdrawals.

I can also tell you from experience that people tend to base their withdrawal rate on what they need, not what is necessarily reasonable based on the expected return on the investment. As you will see in Peter Hope's case, even reducing the withdrawal rate to 5% won't save you if you happen to retire at an unfortunate period in market history.

You can see from our tale of these three investors why we titled this book *Lasting Wealth is a Matter of Timing*. Yes, accumulating wealth is a matter of time, IF you have the resources and discipline to invest regularly and the emotional fortitude to hang in there through thick and thin. The younger you are when you begin investing, the more time you have to build wealth and recoup from eventual losses.

However, once you are at or close to retirement age and you plan to begin making withdrawals from your investment portfolios to supplement social security benefits, pension plan benefits and/or other financial resources, conventional investment wisdom goes out the window. Traditional fixed income investments, as chosen by Connie Conservative, or equity buy and hold strategies, as pursued by Peter Hope, can be dangerous and even suicidal to your financial health.

The investment misadventures of Peter Hope clearly point out the dangers of ignoring timing as a key component in the risk management of your investment strategies. On the other hand, Sammy Savvy showed us how proper timing can build and conserve lasting wealth, even if you don't choose what turns out to be the best professional market timing advisor.

Some might contend that if ill-fated Peter Hope had reduced his withdrawal rate from 8 percent (adjusted for inflation), everything would have been okay and he would have avoided the soup kitchen line. If so, what withdrawal rate would be the cure-all to prevent Peter's financial debacle? Former Fidelity Magellan Manager and investment guru Peter Lynch proposed in the April 1996 issue of *Worth* magazine that a 5 percent withdrawal rate (he had previously proposed a 7 percent withdrawal rate) would be the magic panacea for the buy and hold investor. However, Lynch ignored one important fact of life in his 5 percent solution. His calculations fail to take into account inflation. It's obvious that retirement withdrawals must be increased over time to account for inflation in order to compensate for the loss of purchasing power. Either the withdrawal rate must be increased or the retiree's standard of living must be lowered. There is no other realistic scenario.

Even with reducing the withdrawal rate to 5 percent and living a more spartan existence, Peter's (Hope, not Lynch) future would have been determined by the "timing" of his retirement. Retiring in 1973 at that lower withdrawal rate, he would have been OK, but if his retirement date was 1966, he would have been completely broke by 1987 even at the reduced 5 percent withdrawal rate as shown in Chart 1-7. Employing a buy and hold, more appropriately called a buy and hope, strategy with a diversifed stock portfolio is **not** the answer. You are just hoping that a prolonged bear market does not strike. The real answer lies in reducing your risk exposure!

What set Sammy Savvy apart from Peter, who went broke, is the same thing that distinguishes a good comedian from a bad one — Timing!

"To everything there is a season, a time for every purpose under heaven"

—*Bible*
Ecclesiastes 3:1

DISPROVING THE 5 PERCENT WITHDRAWAL SOLUTION
February 1, 1966 through February 1, 1988

Chart 1-7 Year	Yearly Return	$100,000 Inv. Now Worth *
1966	-9.0%	85,967
1967	37.3%	112,852
1968	25.1%	135,743
1969	-22.5%	99,537
1970	-8.1%	85,477
1971	20.6%	96,807
1972	5.0%	95,192
1973	-26.9%	62,605
1974	-28.7%	36,742
1975	51.5%	47,218
1976	46.3%	60,265
1977	5.3%	54,004
1978	18.2%	53,521
1979	16.5%	50,681
1980	32.6%	54,077
1981	6.3%	43,189
1982	40.7%	45,921
1983	32.9%	45,629
1984	-0.8%	29,271
1985	36.7%	23,414
1986	19.3%	11,155
1987	-2.3%	— 0 —

An illustration using NYSE as Stock fund. Legend: NYSE=NYSE Total Return Index

* Includes systematic withdrawal of $ -5000 at the end of the 1st year and increasing annually to keep up with inflation.

Chart 1-7 Courtesy of SIMCO.

THE FALLACY OF "IT'S DIFFERENT THIS TIME"

Very few investors, with the exceptions of the Connie Conservatives of the world, need counseling on how to participate in a bull market. Even the Peter Hopes did well in a bull market. Too many investors with no particular talent have deluded themselves into thinking that they are the proverbial "Wall Street Wizards" when the real secret of their success lies in their good fortune of having participated in a bull market. The real value of investment advice comes into play when the market cracks. Just about any fool can make money in a bull market. It is the unique challenge of bear markets that separates the true wizards from the "wannabies."

When today's investment heroes are discussed, one of the first names to come to mind is Warren Buffett. Since 1974, Buffet has enjoyed the best investment environment imaginable to fit his "value" style of investing, in the form of the greatest bull market of all time. Buffet purchases stocks he determines are undervalued and typically holds on to them almost forever. Since a traditional secular bear market has not visited since 1974, many market pundits have expounded the theory that market timing should be avoided. They may be eating those words while the bear is eating their lunch with sharp drops in the market and the value of their investment portfolios.

If my analysis is correct, sometime between now and when the last of the baby boomers retires, we are going to move away from Buffet's popular investment theory (which even Buffet has not always followed, see Chapter 4) and will reward those investors who have the ability to time the markets as bullish forces ebb and flow. I expect a reincarnation of investors who fit the mold of the investment heroes of the 1960s and early 1970s such as Edson Gould and Jim Hurst. The roster of SAAFTI is prime territory for seeking out members of this new crop of investment heroes.

Unfortunately, most "how-to" investment books avoid messy details such as surviving bear markets. It is much more pleasant to write about bull markets and the profits to be gained from them. This book is written for all the Peter Hopes out there — those who have never experienced a real bear market first hand. Lacking bear market experience, they mistakenly believe (or fervently hope) there will never be another bear market. Thus, they are ill-prepared to position their portfolios and institute risk management strategies designed to tame the bear. Our aim is to show the average investor how to survive bear markets and generate a retirement income stream he or she cannot outlive.

Historically, bear markets arrive with relative frequency — about every five years. With the last bear market dating back to 1990, buy and hold investors and those baby boomers nearing retirement have plenty about which to worry. Equally, if not more importantly, the average decline incurred during a bear market is 33 percent. Can you stand to suffer a 33 percent loss in your investment portfolio, especially if you are depending on it to generate an adequate income stream on which you plan to live comfortably?

With the Dow Jones Industrial Average trading near 5800 in late September 1996, that translates into a better than 1900 point decline in the Dow. Other indices and certain market segments may be decimated even more. The loss could be even more dramatic considering that a large advance, averaging 117 percent, follows every bear market. Shell-shocked investors mauled by the bear on the way down understandably react timidly on the way back up and may miss a good share of the subsequent price rise. Likewise, investors whose portfolios were devastated by a sharp decline in value have relatively little investment capital to work with when compared with market timers who exited the market before the full force of the debacle took place. Thus the buy and hold investors get whipsawed by the market losing on both the downside and upside movements.

For a perspective on the severity of bear market crashes and their subsequent upswings take a look at Chart 1-8. The bear can and will rear its ugly head again. It definitely is **not** different this time.

S & P Bear Market Study

Chart 1-8 Bear Market	Duration	% Decline	% Advance Following Decline
July 1933 — Mar 1935	20 months	-33.93	+ 131.27
Mar 1937 — Mar 1938	12 months	-54.47	+ 62.24
Nov 1938 — Apr 1942	41 months	-45.83	+ 157.70
May 1946 — Mar 1948	22 months	-28.10	+ 259.39
Aug 1956 — Oct 1957	14 months	-21.63	+ 86.35
Dec 1961 — Jun 1962	6 months	-27.97	+ 79.78
Feb 1966 — Oct 1966	8 months	-22.18	+ 48.05
Nov 1968 — May 1970	18 months	-36.06	+ 73.53

Bear Market Duration		% Advance % DeclineFollowing Decline	
Jan 1973 — Oct 1974	21 months	-48.20	+ 125.63
Nov 1980 — Aug 1982	21 months	-27.11	+ 228.81
Aug 1987 — Dec 1987	4 months	-33.51	+ 64.77
July 1990 — Oct 1990	3 months	-19.92	+ 84.37
Average decline of bear market:	-	33.24	
Average advance following decline: +		116.85	

Note: To avoid a negative bias we have excluded the Crash of 1929, when the S&P 500 fell 86.74 %

Chart 1-8 Courtesy of Fabian Investor Resource

A LOOK AT ECONOMIC CYCLES/
VOLATILITY WILL INCREASE

In his book, *The Great Boom Ahead: Your Complete Guide to Personal and Business Profit in the New Era of Prosperity*, economist Harry S. Dent Jr. starts out his discussion of investment strategies for the '90s with a bulletin signalling that he believes that inflation will not be a factor in the coming economy and that this new cycle will favor growth stocks and long-term bonds...provided you use the proper timing.

Ironically, Dent predicts that this new era of economic prosperity will also include a period between the years of 2006 and 2010 with the probability of speculation and volatility increasing as we move toward what Dent estimates may become "the biggest depression of all time." That's precisely when the majority of baby boomers will be heavily dependent on their withdrawals to support their retirement life styles. This debacle could literally wipe out a lifetime of savings for those who do not read and heed the message in this book.

> **"Passive investing will fail again...as it did in the '30s and '70s...and an entire generation may never recover."**
>
> —*John K. Sosnowy*

DEBUNKING BUY AND HOLD STRATEGIES

True or false? Over the long run, the stock market has outperformed virtually all other investments, so buying and holding stocks represents the best investment strategy?

Don't be fooled by this faulty assumption based on a fact. Stock market investments have outperformed all other classes of investment alternatives over the long-run, however, sitting on stocks while a bear market erodes the value of your investment portfolio can be catastrophic to your financial well-being, especially if you don't have time to wait for a market rebound to recapture ground lost during the decline.

> **"We find buy and hold to be highly overrated as an investment approach, perhaps due to false confidence based on hindsight analysis and underestimation of the risks associated with long and severe drawdown periods."**
>
> — *Robert W. Colby and Thomas A. Meyers*
> **The Encyclopedia of Technical Market Indicators**

Employing a buy and hold strategy takes time to work, sometimes extraordinary amounts of time. It takes a strong stomach and tremendous emotional discipline that the vast majority of investors don't possess. Buy and hold is definitely a young person's game and may not even represent the best strategy for them.

If you are at or near retirement a buy and hold strategy may be one of the riskiest approaches to the market you could take. Assume you invested $100,000 in the S & P 500 in January 1973. Within 21 months your portfolio would have shrunk to $51,800, a loss of over 48 percent.

In 1973, the market lost ground nine out of twelve months, closing out the year with a 21.5 percent loss for large company stocks. The following year accelerated the decline with a loss of 34.4 percent in the value of large company stocks. October was the only month to deliver a positive return in 1974. It would have taken seven and one-half years to recoup your bear market loss, over 12 years when you factor in the effects of inflation. I don't know many retirees who could withstand a seven year period, much less 12 years, without earnings on their investments and still enjoy the quality of life they desire.

Academics, including Nobel laureate economist Paul Samuelson at the Massachusetts Institute of Technology, argue that the longer you have your money invested in the stock market, the greater the probability you will suffer devastating losses in a crash or series of crashes. Therefore, the buy and hold strategy makes your retirement funds susceptible to such crashes. Market timing aims to help you miss the brunt of those crashes.

There's another major fallacy in the buy and hold strategy expounded by so-called market pundits. Despite the proclamation and even the determination of investors to stick to their buy and hold guns, in practice many bail out as dramatic stock price plunges become simply unbearable. A recent Dalbar study showed that the individual investor earned an average annual return of only 4.3 percent over the past ten years compared with an average return of 13.6 percent for the underlying stock market investments they owned. That indicates that the individual did not stick to his or her buy and hold strategy.

Mutual fund sales/redemption statistics also point to the same conclusion. One of the largest redemption periods in the last decade followed the crash of 1987 when the market was down. Many of these so-called buy and hold investors then missed out on the market rebound. Likewise, some of the largest mutual funds sales periods consisted of the months leading up to recent market highs. Other high/low periods reveal the same pattern.

Would-be buy and hold investors listen to CNBC reports of stock price plunges and record stock market declines and head for the doors. Emotions take over the reins from rationally thought out long-term investment plans. They become emotional asset allocators instead of tactical asset allocators. Savvy investors would be wise to forget the buy and hold strategy with its accompanying emotional seesaw and employ risk management market timing strategies in its place. While market timing may not work for amateurs without discipline, it does work at the hand of a **professional market timer**!

Money manager Paul Merriman points out the psychology at work today. While many profess to be dedicated buy and hold investors, they lack the true commitment to stick with it. This behavior reflects today's society. Merriman uses marriage as an excellent example. Both people enter into a contract or commitment believing that they won't change their minds later. Yet marriage, like investing, goes through some difficult times over the years. When the pain reaches a certain threshold, many people bail out as testified by the divorce statistics for the United States. Despite most people's honest intentions, many will also abandon the buy and hold strategy when the pain level gets too high.

Bears are no fun to be around and they require a long time to get over. After the 86 percent market drop that began in 1929, twenty years later the market still stood a full 58 percent below its 1929 peak. More recently, sixteen years after the 45 percent drop in the Dow Jones Industrial Average that began in 1966 the Dow still traded 22 percent below its peak.

THE MANAGED RISK ADVANTAGE

Remember how Peter Hope fared? The scenario is quite a bit different for a risk managed investment portfolio. Charts 1-9 and 1-10

RESULTS OF ACTUAL SWITCHING SIGNALS
USING AN AGGRESSIVE GROWTH STOCK FUND

Chart 1-9   **January 1, 1973 to December 31, 1978**

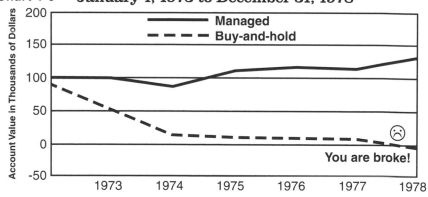

An illustration using the Keystone S4 Fund. The Keystone S4 Fund is a mutual fund, whose goal is long-term growth of capital. Income is not an objective. The fund invests primarily in common stocks which are expected to experience wide fluctuations in price during both rising and declining markets. Ask for and examine a fund prospectus before you invest. Be sure you understand all costs, fees and risks. Past performance is no guarantee of future results. Account begins with $100,000 and includes systematic withdrawals of $8,000 at the end of the first year increasing annually to keep up with inflation.

See Appendix A for Disclosure Statement.

Chart 1-9 Courtesy of SIMCO

RESULTS OF ACTUAL SWITCHING SIGNALS
USING THE NYSE TOTAL RETURN INDEX

Chart 1-10   January 1, 1973 to December 31, 1984

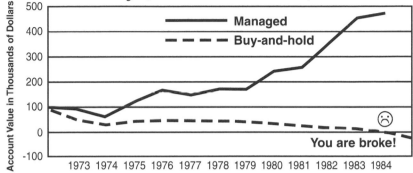

An illustration using NYSE Total Return Index as the Stock Fund. The NYSE Total Return Index represents all stocks on the New York Stock Exchange, with dividends reinvested. It is an unmanaged index. You cannot invest in the NYSE TR Index. Account begins with $100,000 and includes systematic withdrawals of $8,000 at the end of the first year, increasing annually to keep up with inflation. Past performance is no guarantee of future results

See Appendix A for Disclosure Statement.

Chart 1-10 Courtesy of SIMCO

show the results of actual buy and sell signals generated by a timing model in use during the periods shown.

Instead of being fatally mauled by the bear, the risk managed investment portfolio sidesteps most of the steep decline and goes on to post healthy investment gains.

It's critical to look at the performance of any investment strategy over a full market cycle of both bull and bear market environments. Market timing is very much a risk management approach to investing with the preservation of your capital a key priority. It strives to deliver higher returns on a risk-adjusted basis.

MAJOR POINT SUMMARY

— When you retire, you cannot afford to let your money retire too!

— The longer you own stocks the higher the probability you will own stocks during the next great stock market debacle.

— Baby-boomer retirees can ill-afford to suffer a bear market.

— SAAFTI educates the public on risk reduction techniques.

— Only a total commitment to a disciplined risk management strategy will save you from financial disaster.

— Investment conservatism can lead to catastrophe.

— Buy and hold translates to buy and hope.

— Market timing has historically kept bear market losses low enough to keep investors committed to equities and, as a by-product, given investors a superior risk-adjusted return.

— Passive investing will fail again — preserving wealth is a matter of timing.

— Bear markets make or break investment strategies.

— Bear markets are a part of investing life — it's <u>not</u> a new era.

— Market timing is a legitimate strategy for reducing the risks of stock market investing.

— Market timing works in the hands of an investment professional.

— Emotions often short circuit the plans of amateur investors.

— The roster of SAAFTI is prime territory for finding the next great investment hero, i.e. the next Warren Buffet.

> **"I'm not nearly so concerned about the return on my capital as I am the return of my capital."**
>
> — *Will Rogers*

CHAPTER 2
How Does Your Return Measure Up?

AN ANALYSIS OF RISK

In today's volatile and uncertain economic environment, more than ever before, investors must employ an investment strategy firmly grounded in risk management. Without a doubt, the biggest errors most investors make fall into two major categories:

1. Seeking the highest possible return without taking into account the underlying risks involved with each investment alternative.

2. Being overly concerned with the risk of losing money, so that selected investments earn too little, resulting in a loss of buying power when inflation is taken into account.

Every investor naturally desires the highest return possible. However, much too often investors have flocked to high return investments without consideration of, or a plan to control risk, only to lose a large part, if not all, of their investment principal. A good example was the real estate speculation driven savings and loan debacle in the eighties. Greed overshadowed sound investment judgement as investors sought high returns without considering the additional risk undertaken. Not until millions of people lost billions of dollars as savings and loan associations closed their doors did people understand the higher risk they assumed while chasing higher returns.

Comparing investment returns without taking into account the risk associated with investment alternatives is like betting on horses without knowing their odds of winning. Your investment portfolio must be designed to deliver an expected return within acceptable risk tolerance parameters. Commodity futures can sometimes deliver impressive returns but may keep you up all night as commodity prices fluctuate wildly. Each investor has his or her own level of acceptable risk they are willing to take in order to achieve a certain return. If you want to invest wisely, and sleep at night, you need to recognize and understand the relationship between risk and return.

INVESTMENT RISK PYRAMID

Chart 2-1 illustrates a traditional investment risk pyramid.

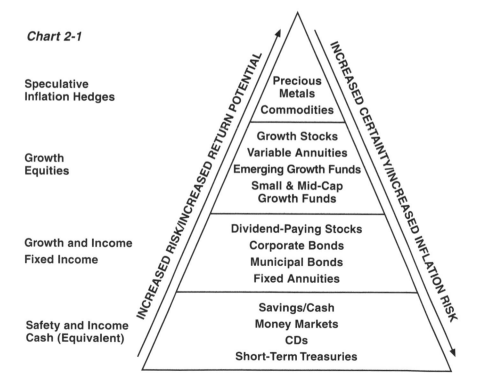

Chart 2-1

Speculative
Inflation Hedges

Growth
Equities

Growth and Income
Fixed Income

Safety and Income
Cash (Equivalent)

INCREASED RISK/INCREASED RETURN POTENTIAL

INCREASED CERTAINTY/INCREASED INFLATION RISK

Precious
Metals
Commodities

Growth Stocks
Variable Annuities
Emerging Growth Funds
Small & Mid-Cap
Growth Funds

Dividend-Paying Stocks
Corporate Bonds
Municipal Bonds
Fixed Annuities

Savings/Cash
Money Markets
CDs
Short-Term Treasuries

As you move up from the base of the pyramid toward the peak, the degree of potential return and the degree of risk rise. For example, U. S. Treasury Bills typically deliver the lowest yields and exhibit the least price volatility due to their safety factor. Treasury securities are predictable. They have never failed to pay despite recent talk of the government defaulting during the budget impasse between President Clinton and the Congress. Therefore, they are virtually riskless.

In comparison, CDs (Certificates of Deposit) represent a slightly higher risk posture since you are now depending on the financial industry and the insurance program backing it. Accordingly, CDs pay a higher yield than T-Bills (Treasury Bills) in order to compensate the investor for the higher risk. As indicated above, too many investors were blinded by higher yields offered on savings and loan CDs and failed to analyze the higher risk status of these investments or chose to ignore it. Moving further up the pyramid, precious metals and other commodities can deliver significant returns coupled with increased risk and higher price volatility.

The level of risk you are willing to assume depends on many factors such as your age, financial status, need for liquidity, tax situation, financial commitments, investment goals and risk tolerance. To illustrate, a young couple has time on their side and can afford to invest a higher portion of portfolio assets in growth equities while a couple nearing retirement may need to shift some investment assets to lower risk fixed income securities that will deliver the current cash flow they need to maintain their desired life style.

RISK RETURN TRADEOFF

Obviously, a relationship exists between the expected return of a given investment and the level of risk assumed to achieve that return. Chart 2-2 graphically illustrates the relationship between risk and return. The young couple discussed above would probably be situated at Point A along the risk/return line while the retirees would assume a more conservative risk posture at Point B. Our philosophy is to take the lowest risk that will give you enough return.

RISK/RETURN RELATIONSHIP

Chart 2-2

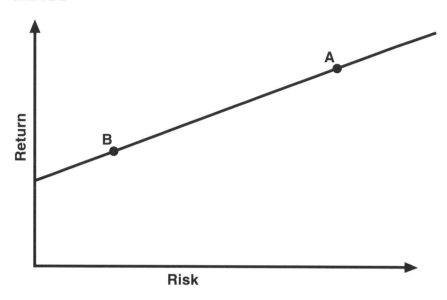

TYPES OF RISK

Overall, you can sum up risk as follows:

"Risk is the chance you take that you won't have your money when you need it."

In the realm of investing, eight basic types of risk or uncertainty need to be understood. Combined, they represent what is unpredictable about an investment and/or the investment environment which can impact the return on the investment.

BUSINESS/INDUSTRY RISK

Business/industry risk stems from the line of business or industry in which the company operates. Economic cycles and changes in other aspects of the business environment pose risks that can impact the firm's ability to deliver expected earnings, dividend payouts and interest payments.

Business/industry risk can take a variety of forms such as domestic and global competition, fiscal and monetary policy, government regulation, management policy, product obsolescence and technological change. Likewise, the level of business risk may increase with the type of investment. For example, initial public offerings (IPOs) are inherently more risky than investing in veteran industry companies with established markets and a history of profitable operations.

Standard & Poor's Corporation and other ratings services have devised rating systems for companies and their stock and fixed income securities to quantify the degree of business or credit risk of the companies' securities. Obviously, investing in a company with a B rating takes on more risk than investing in an A+ rated company. Likewise, investing in junk bonds represents an entirely different investment strategy than investing in AAA bonds.

MARKET RISK

Market risk occurs when the general market or economic environment causes an investment to lose value. Market prices rise or fall for a number of reasons, regardless of the particular security. External events such as interest rate hikes, investor sentiment, sector rotation and economic uncertainty can put downward pressure on the price of a given security despite good prospects for the underlying company.

Market prices can rise and fall for a number of reasons not directly related to the economic fortunes of the company or the industry in which it operates. In the precious metals and commodities arena prices can fluctuate wildly based on raw materials shortages, labor unrest, natural disasters, outbreaks of wars and predictions of shortages or surpluses.

You may have heard about the young fellow considering trading pork belly futures. His broker warned him that this was a very risky strategy. "One day pork belly futures could be up big only to drop down the limit the next day," explained his broker.

"Oh, no problem," said the young man. "I only plan to trade every other day."

Obviously, this young investor does not really understand the nature of market risk.

LIQUIDITY RISK

The inability to sell an investment at a reasonable price during a reasonable time period comprises liquidity risk. To illustrate, private placements offer opportunities for substantial gains which must be tempered by the fact that the security may have limited marketability. The firm may not plan to go public for another three years and the investment may not be able to be liquidated easily until that time. Even then, there is no guarantee that the investing public will greet the initial public offering with enthusiasm three years in the future.

On the other hand, real estate investment trusts (REITs) have gained popularity in recent years because they provide investors with a way to take a position in the real estate market and still have a high degree of liquidity. While individual properties may take months or years to sell, the shares of REITs trade on the stock exchanges just like the shares of other companies and are highly liquid.

CURRENCY RISK

Investments can lose value when the currency in which they are held declines in value relative to other currencies. Obviously, direct investments in foreign currencies run the risk of declining in value against a strong dollar. Holders of the Mexican peso lost money as Mexico devalued the peso in response to that nation's financial crisis.

Holdings in foreign stocks or mutual funds which invest in overseas securities can be positively or negatively impacted by a rise in one currency relative to another. Company earnings can be hurt after adjustments for currency translations are taken into account. An otherwise strong year can end with a decline in earnings due to currency losses. It is important to determine the amount of international operations and the potential impact currency losses can have on company earnings.

POLITICAL RISK

Changes on the political scene, both domestic and global, carry a degree of risk to investments. Tougher legislation can create higher costs for companies in certain industries, negatively impacting their ability to deliver expected returns. Political unrest in both South Africa and Mexico sent investors fleeing those countries until more stable times returned both economically and politically. Despite a trend toward free markets, a number of American companies have lost significant facilities and operations in the past as foreign countries nationalized industries.

Shifts in the controlling political party's approach to economic challenges can create an unfavorable business environment and investor worries that translate into volatile market swings. Deregulation can favorably impact some companies while creating greater competition and possibly lower earnings for others.

INTEREST RATE RISK

Rising interest rates can severely impact the market value and total return of specific investments as their yields suffer in comparison to new securities or those with higher payouts. As a general rule, when interest rates rise, the value of existing fixed income investments decrease and vice versa. The longer the maturity, the greater the degree of interest rate risk and the more volatile the price of the security in a changing interest rate environment. As mentioned earlier, fixed income securities with longer maturities typically pay higher yields to compensate the investor for the higher risk involved. Chart 2-3 illustrates the interest rate/risk relationship for various kinds of investment options while Chart 2-4 shows how the length of maturity impacts the yield on an investment.

INTEREST RATE/RISK RELATIONSHIP

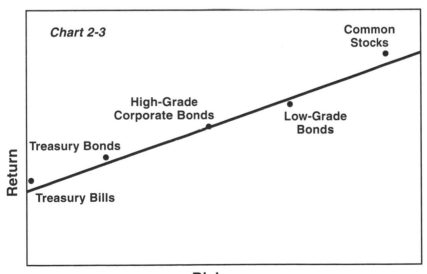

Risk

Chart 2-3 Courtesy of Richard J. Maturi, *Divining the Dow*

Rising interest rates can also prove detrimental to stocks as common stock dividends lose ground to higher yielding fixed income investments. On a macro scale, rising interest rates can trigger a market decline.

NORMAL YIELD CURVE

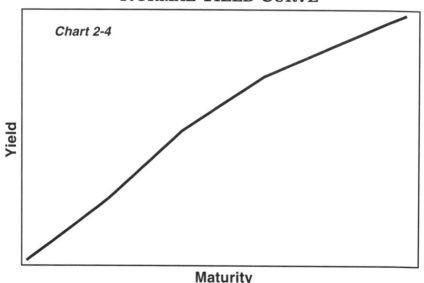

Chart 2-4

Yield

Maturity

Chart 2-4 Courtesy of Richard J. Maturi, *Divining the Dow*

REINVESTMENT RISK

Reinvestment risk derives from the possibility of having to reinvest your capital at an inopportune time at rates substantially less than those offered by the expiring investment. Laddering maturities helps avoid having all of your funds maturing at the trough of interest rates. Laddering is accomplished by purchasing fixed income securities with different maturity dates.

On the other side of the coin, an investment may contain call provisions which result in the investor being cashed out of a security position before anticipated. Call provisions must be taken into account when considering the potential return and risk of a specific investment alternative.

INFLATION RISK

Inflation risk represents the loss in purchasing power when the rate of inflation outstrips your investment return. If your investment return, after taxes, is less than the rate of inflation, the rising cost of goods and services means that you will be able to purchase less with your money.

With certificate yields so low, and inflation threatening to rear its ugly head again, conservative investors could actually lose ground despite their investment return. In other words, they will be less well off after their investment return than they were before they made the investment.

IMPACT OF INFLATION ON PURCHASING POWER

> **"Building your personal wealth without considering inflation risk represents a head-in-the-sand attitude. It's not how many dollars you have but what those dollars will purchase that's important."**
>
> *—Paul Merriman*

All of us are aware of rising costs and their impact on purchasing power. You need only to look back to the gasoline lines of the seventies and early eighties to remember rampant inflation and how it eroded your ability to purchase goods and services. In recent years inflation has taken a more subtle approach, slowly eating away at your wealth. A more robust economy than anticipated and a surge in some commodity prices during the second quarter of 1995 sent warnings of a possible resurgence of inflation and sent nervous shivers through investment markets.

As you no doubt remember, the price of a first-class postage stamp increased to 32 cents on January 1, 1995. I've found that for me, the price of a stamp represents my own personal, real-life, true gauge of what is happening on the inflation front. My postage benchmark price dates back to September 1959 when I left home for the first time to enroll in college. In the true tradition of motherhood, my mother sent me off with a supply of writing paper, envelopes and a roll of 4 cent postage stamps so I would have absolutely no excuse for not writing home. In the true tradition of young sons away from home, I was not the most diligent writer and still had a few 4 cent stamps in my possession when the price was raised to 5 cents in 1963. While a penny may not be much money, even in 1963, that one cent rise in price represented a 25 whopping percent increase in cost. Over the years, each rise in the price of stamps—to 10 cents in 1974, 20 cents in 1981 and now 32 cents—served as my personal reminder that inflation and its impact on my purchasing power is real, not just an economist's term.

Seeing the price of a stamp more than triple from 10 cents to 32 cents in the past twenty years clearly points out that if one of my clients were to retire today on $2,500 a month, we need to have a strategy in place that has a high probability of growing his or her capital enough to provide $8,000 per month of income in twenty years. Unless we put such an investment plan into effect, my client will not be able to pay for the increased costs of clothing, food, gasoline, insurance, utilities and the $1.00 postage stamp that seems inevitable.

I have found that many investors, especially as they near retirement, tend to seek so-called "safe" investments such as bank CDs, Treasury Bills, money market funds and government bonds. What these investors fail to realize is that they pay dearly for these "safe" assets in terms of lost purchasing power. It is nearly impossible, at least in money terms, to end up with less than one puts in, if held to maturity. While these financial assets provide security in the form of certainty of principal, the historical evidence clearly shows they have not preserved purchasing power. In other words, they have not kept up with the rising costs of postage stamps and other necessities of daily life. Chart 2-5 shows the effects of inflation on purchasing power since 1967. As illustrated, a 1967 dollar is worth less than 20 cents in terms of purchasing power today. If inflation continues at that pace, your purchasing power will be cut in half every eleven years. Saying it another way, an item that cost $1.00 in 1967 now costs more than $5.00 to purchase today.

EFFECTS OF INFLATION
ON PURCHASING POWER OF DOLLAR

Chart 2-5

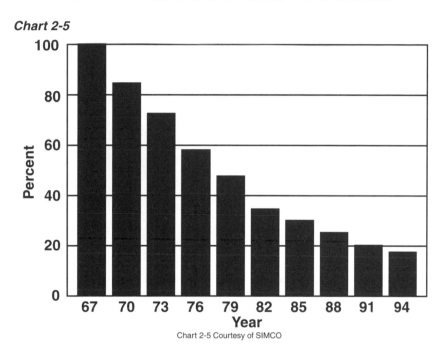

Chart 2-5 Courtesy of SIMCO

Table 2-1 points out some startling facts about how inflation erodes the value of your wealth. It uses 1959, the year I ventured out into the world for the first time, as a benchmark for comparison. People still in the workplace can earn raises and cost of living increases to help offset the ravages of inflation over time. But you can't let your money "retire" at low returns. If you plan to keep ahead of inflation and preserve your purchasing power, you must keep it working to outpace inflation and continue to build your wealth after taking into consideration the effects of taxes and inflation.

Table 2-1
COST OF LIVING COMPARISON

	1959	1996
First Class Postage Stamp	$ .04	$ .32
Bread, 1 pound	.20	.73
Gasoline, 1 gallon	.30	1.23
Milk, 1 gallon	1.02	2.86
New Ford	2,143.00	14,046.00
3-Bedroom Home	13,350.00	112,984.00
Average Income	5,417.00	37,526.00

Throughout the rest of this chapter, we will show you the projected costs of the above items in the year 2022, twenty six years from now, when most baby boomers will be well into retirement. Prices for 1996 are adjusted based on the assumption that we will experience the same rate of inflation over the next twenty six years that we did during the past twenty six years.

OUTPACING INFLATION

COST OF ONE
FIRST CLASS STAMP

1996	**$**	**.32**
2022	**$**	**1.32**

The following story illustrates the impact of inflation on investment decisions. Alice, Bob, and Cathy each purchased a house for $100,000 and sold it a year later. During Alice's year, she experienced 25 percent deflation. In other words, the cost of goods and services declined an average 25 percent during the year. Alice sold her house for $77,000, 23 percent less than she had paid a year earlier. During

Bob's year, prices of goods and services on average rose 25 percent. Bob sold his house for $123,000, 23 percent higher than his purchase price. Prices held steady during Cathy's year and she sold her house for $98,000, 2 percent less than she had paid for the home.

How did the three come out on their house investments? A study conducted by Princeton University psychology professor Eldar Shafir found that approximately 60 percent of people believed that Bob fared the best and Alice fared worst. In fact, after taking inflation into account, Alice was the only house owner who made any money with a 2 percent gain in buying power. With the increase in purchasing power, Alice can trade up on her next house. Unfortunately, both Bob and Cathy will each be forced to trade down on their next house.

The reason most people were mistaken about who fared better in the above scenarios stems from what is called "money illusion." People confuse "nominal" changes in money (more or fewer dollars) with "real" changes (greater or lesser purchasing power). Real change takes inflation or deflation into account.

The moral of this story is that you must think in terms of real value of purchasing power instead of dollar terms. When you track the change in the price of postage stamps over the years as I have, you begin to understand how you will need significantly more dollars years in the future to purchase the goods and services you desire. The challenge is to design and implement an effective investment strategy to earn, after taxes, in excess of the expected inflation rate and have those dollars in place when you need them. Yields must be analyzed in relation to the economic and inflation environment. While a better than 15% yield appears attractive today, it was not a good investment back in 1981. After consideration of the high tax environment of the eighties, a 15.77% CD provided an after-tax yield of 6.46%. However, inflation roared ahead at 8.9%, making the investor worse off despite high CD interest rates. The investor's purchasing power actually diminished after calculation of the real rate of return by factoring in tax and inflation elements. It is important to build a reasonable expected rate of inflation into your investment decision making process.

HOW MUCH RETURN IS ENOUGH?

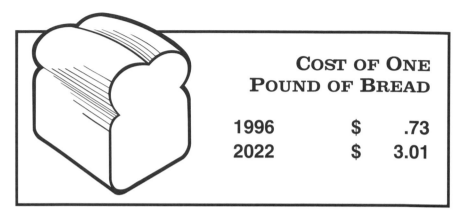

COST OF ONE
POUND OF BREAD

1996	$ .73
2022	$ 3.01

Over the past twenty-six years inflation has averaged almost 6 percent per year. Assuming that rate to be a reasonable average over the next twenty plus years and if total taxes rise as expected, then you will need to earn a return in excess of 10 percent per year compounded annually on your total investment portfolio just to maintain your purchasing power. Have you accomplished that level of return during the past twenty-six years, and more importantly, is your portfolio positioned to have that much return potential over the next twenty-six years?

A recent study commissioned by Twentieth Century Mutual Funds found that two-thirds of respondents had no specific long-term retirement savings goals. Of those who did have goals, 70 percent targeted accumulating less than $1 million. The majority took a conservative stance in their investment posture. Almost 47 percent park some of their money in a regular interest-bearing savings account. Once they reach retirement age, 28 percent stated that less than 5 percent of their retirement money will be in stocks or mutual funds while approximately 50 percent said they will have 20 percent or more of their retirement money in stocks or stock funds.

Even more interesting, individuals who own stocks or stock mutual funds expect average annual returns on their investments of 13 percent. Those with **none** of their retirement savings in equities expect returns of 10 percent. One wonders how they arrived at those expectations in light of historical returns.

Table 2-2 shows historic returns for various asset classes through 1995. For the purposes of this illustration, Treasury Bill rates are used to show money market performance.

Table 2-2
HISTORIC RETURNS

	26 Years	70 Years
U.S. Treasury Bills*	7.0%	3.7%
Long-Term Government Bonds**	9.7%	5.7%
Common Stocks***	11.8%	10.5%

* Constructed using the shortest-term bill having not less than one month to maturity. ** Constructed using an approximate 20-year maturity. *** Based on total return of the S & P Composite Index (S & P 500).

Source: *S.B.B.I. Yearbook*, 1996

As you can see from Table 2-2, common stocks outperformed both U.S. Treasury Bills (money market rates) and long-term government bonds and earned the only returns on the chart in excess of 10 percent during the two time frames. This fact is important to keep in mind as we analyze how to stay ahead of inflation and increase the purchasing power of your wealth.

The Twentieth Century findings suggest a nation of ultra conservative, passive investors hoping to outpace inflation. We need to find a way to light a fire under the average person before it is too late.

If you believe that money market rates will climb again and protect you from inflation let's put things into perspective. Since 1927, money market rates have exceeded 10 percent only during four years. On the other hand money market rates earned less than one percent in eighteen of those years. It doesn't take a brain surgeon to understand that investing at money market rates of return can put you deep in the hole with a negative real rate of return after taxes and inflation.

If your total tax burden approximates that of our typical client you would have suffered a negative real rate of return (after taxes and inflation) during both the past 26 and 70-year periods. In both cases, your real rate of return would have been around the negative .5 percent range despite earning average yields on Treasury Bills of 3.7 percent over the 70-year period and 7.0 percent over the 26-year time frame. See Table 2-3.

Table 2-3
REAL RATES OF RETURN

	26 Years	70 Years
Average Treasury Bill Yield	7.00%	3.70%
Less Taxes (28% rate)	-2.00%	-1.04%
Subtotal	5.00%	2.64%
Less Inflation	-5.60%	-3.10%
Real Rate of Return	-0.60%	-0.46%

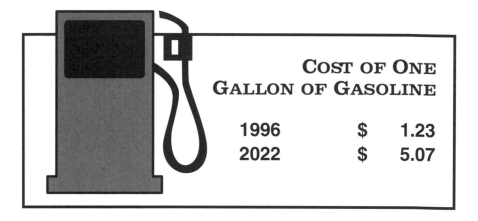

COST OF ONE
GALLON OF GASOLINE

1996	$	1.23
2022	$	5.07

"It's important to distinguish between certainty and safety. Certainty is having someone guarantee you the same number of dollars at some point in the future. Safety is the accretion of purchasing power after taxes and inflation, so you don't outlive your money."

—*Nick Murray*

While past performance is no guarantee of future results, Charts 2-6 and 2-7 compare the nominal and real returns of stock dividends and bond interest over a recent 25-year period.

STOCK DIVIDENDS INFLATION ADJUSTED

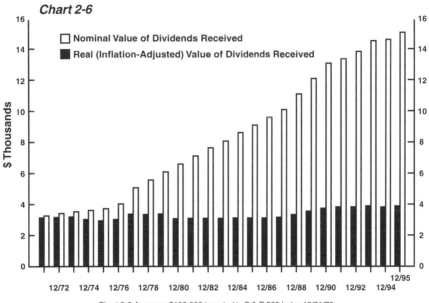

Chart 2-6

□ Nominal Value of Dividends Received
■ Real (Inflation-Adjusted) Value of Dividends Received

Chart 2-6 Assumes $100,000 invested in S & P 500 Index 12/31/70.

As you can see from the bar graphs in Chart 2-6, the growth of stock dividends has protected purchasing power by delivering a nearly four percent real (inflation-adjusted) rate of return. In contrast, the value of bond interest has been eroded, declining from over 6 percent in 1970 to less than 3 percent in real terms in 1995 as shown in Chart 2-7.

Taking the analysis one step further, Chart 2-8 and Chart 2-9 shows how effectively the original investment principal has been safeguarded against the ravages of inflation. Again, common stocks come through for investors with the real principal value of stock in 1995 exceeding its real value in 1970 by almost 70 percent as shown in Figure 2-8. On the other hand, the real value of the bond principal declined dramatically from $100,000 to about $30,000. Charts 2-6 through 2-9 were adapted from a study by T. Rowe Price and Associates.

Bond Interest Inflation Adjusted

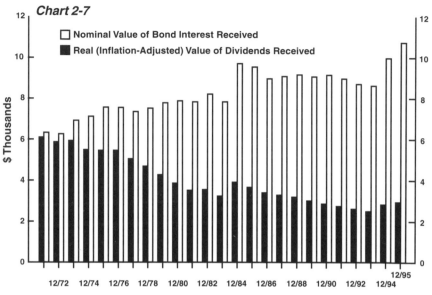

Chart 2-7

☐ Nominal Value of Bond Interest Received

■ Real (Inflation-Adjusted) Value of Dividends Received

Chart 2-7 Assumes $100,000 invested in Long-Term Government Bond Index on 12/31/70.

Stock Portfolio Value Inflation Adjusted

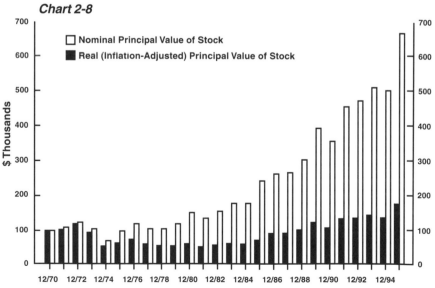

Chart 2-8

☐ Nominal Principal Value of Stock

■ Real (Inflation-Adjusted) Principal Value of Stock

Chart 2-8 Assumes $100,000 invested in S & P 500 Stock Index on 12/31/70 and dividends taken in cash.

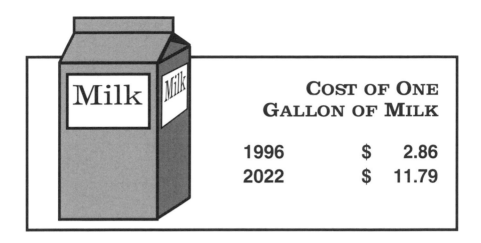

COST OF ONE
GALLON OF MILK

1996	**$ 2.86**
2022	**$ 11.79**

BOND PORTFOLIO VALUE INFLATION ADJUSTED

Chart 2-9

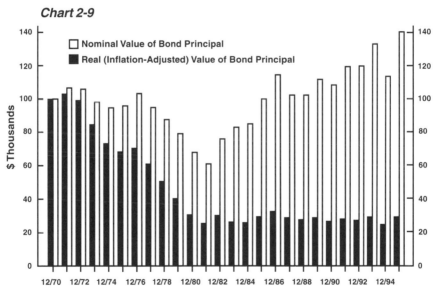

□ Nominal Value of Bond Principal
■ Real (Inflation-Adjusted) Value of Bond Principal

Chart 2-9 Assumes $100,000 invested in Long-Term Government Bond Index on 12/31/70 and interest taken in cash.

From the above analysis it is clear that Treasury Bills and other forms of fixed income investments have been losers after taking into account the impact of taxes and inflation. Common stocks, despite their more risky profile, have delivered the return needed to preserve purchasing power and increase wealth. This trend is expected to continue in the future. Equities are at the heart of a successful investing strategy designed to preserve value and create wealth. The challenge lies in reducing the risk of equity investments down to your sleeping level.

	COST OF NEW FORD	
1996	$	14,046
2022	$	57,918

"...My examination into nearly two centuries of financial data reveals...over the long run the returns on stocks are so stable that stocks are actually **safer** than either government bonds or Treasury Bills. The constancy of the long-term, after-inflation returns on stocks was truly astonishing, while the return on fixed income assets posed higher risks for the long-term investor."

— Jeremy J. Siegel Professor of Finance
The Wharton School, University of
Pennsylvania
Stocks for the Long Run, 1994

Siegel's study convinces me that stocks are the best asset class to use in an effective investment strategy. However, years of experience have shown that you cannot usually get clients to buy and hold common stocks through major market declines of 25 percent, 30 percent, 40 percent or more. Since bear markets are a fact of life, this poses a real dilemma. How can I keep investors committed to an equities-oriented investment strategy over the long haul in order to achieve their financial objectives? During my more than a quarter century in the investment business, I have found only one practical solution, reducing risk.

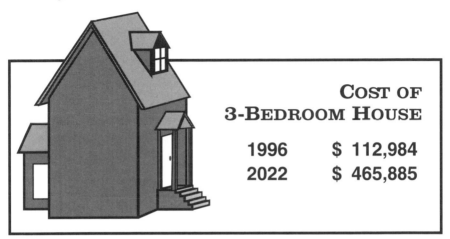

COST OF 3-BEDROOM HOUSE

1996	$ 112,984
2022	$ 465,885

REDUCING RISK

Reducing risk represents the key element in helping keep investors committed to stocks over the long haul in order to earn real returns that preserve portfolio value and accumulate wealth. I accomplish this by getting my clients to commit to a disciplined risk management strategy, whether we want to call it market timing, tactical asset allocation, dynamic asset allocation, or active asset allocation. For a more detailed description of these timing strategies and the differences between them, refer to the discussion in Chapter 3.

Simply put, these risk management or market timing strategies strive to smooth out the ride so you can sleep at night. This is accomplished by keeping client losses low enough during those inevitable bear markets, convincing investors to stay committed over the long-term to equities and, as a by-product, providing investors with a superior risk-adjusted return on their principal.

I am not a crapshooter or one who bets on long shots. I consider myself a very conservative investor. Like others, I would be content to invest entirely in fixed income assets for the rest of my life if someone could guarantee me that they would indeed cover my future living costs after factoring in inflation. Since no one can deliver on that guarantee, it's prudent to employ a strategy that reduces overall risk while delivering a real return over and above the rate of inflation.

I am convinced that market timing is destined to be the "investment phenomenon" of the 21st Century. It has the tools to save the boomers from bust. It represents a logical and workable solution to the real world problems of periodic bear markets, inflation and taxes. Forget the conventional wisdom of putting the bulk of your portfolio assets in fixed income assets that fail to keep pace with inflation. Don't sit back and watch taxes and inflation erode the value of your purchasing power. Market timing makes it possible to achieve real rates of return on equities that surpass inflation and preserve purchasing power. This strategy makes it possible to build wealth within a risk reduction framework. So, as the price of postage stamps rise to $1.00 or more and other living expenses follow suit, you can sleep comfortably at night secure in the knowledge that market timing is at work protecting your portfolio value, reducing risk and achieving attractive real rates of return on a risk-adjusted basis.

ASSESSING YOUR RISK TOLERANCE

In an efficient marketplace a trade-off exists between risk and reward. The higher the expected return, the greater the uncertainty (risk) of receiving that return. U.S. Treasury bills and bonds are considered among the safest investments because they are backed by the "full faith and credit" of the United States Government. Due to this safety factor, which guarantees that the principal will be returned, government securities pay lower yields.

Despite the virtual guarantee of principal return, government fixed income investments make poor investments for several reasons. Treasury investments, like other fixed income investments, are susceptible to price fluctuations in response to interest rate changes. The investor who needs his or her funds before maturity is at the mercy of the interest rate cycle and bond prices in the secondary market. Remember, the U.S. Government guarantee only applies to repaying the principal at maturity. Investors who dispose of these securities in the secondary market prior to maturity can incur a loss. Treasury bond investors learned this lesson firsthand during 1994.

Second, history shows that fixed income investments have failed to keep pace with the tax bite and inflation thereby causing the investor to lose purchasing power. Common stocks have beaten fixed income assets in terms of real rates of return and building wealth over the long-term.

Each person must decide for himself or for herself how much risk he/she is willing to assume to earn a given return and achieve his/her investment goals. As a general rule, potential returns from a given investment should compensate you for the level of risk undertaken. If the anticipated returns are not enough to compensate you adequately for the additional risks taken, you should not make the investment.

You cannot avoid risk in the world of investing. The greatest risk of all is the unwillingness to take a risk. Unless you take some risk, you have a 100 percent probability of accomplishing nothing and will be worse off than if you had accepted some reasonable level of risk. People investing in "so-called" safe fixed income investments run the risk of taxes and inflation eroding their wealth and purchasing power. For example, certificates of deposit have turned in negative real rates of return in three out of the last four decades.

I realize that money is a very emotional subject. Money symbolizes many of our needs and desires, encompassing a complex panorama of financial security, freedom, love, respect, power and happiness. It can also represent a source of stress and depression. Whether you feel richer or poorer can be influenced by moves in the financial markets. Investment profits can create feelings of elation and overconfidence while losses can trigger regret and depression. Every person must feel comfortable with the level of risk undertaken while investing in specific assets and strategies.

Given that background, I have found that one of the most important characteristics of successful investors lies in their ability to stick with their investment plan. Bear markets, investment setbacks and losses are part of the world of investing and should not cause a well-thought out investment plan to be hastily abandoned. Nor should a downturn in an investment category signal the need to pull out (this may be the opportune time to purchase quality at a discount).

RISK-ADJUSTED RETURNS

Structure your investments at a level that gives you peace of mind. That requires a proper matching of your risk tolerance with your investment goals. Understanding your risk tolerance comes down to understanding your attitude toward money and how it influences your life. This risk tolerance analysis should be a cornerstone of your investment strategy.

In addition, you must consider the level of risk assumed with specific investment options and analyze various investment alternatives on a risk-adjusted basis (See Chapter 6 under Risk Control). Only then can you make the proper investment decisions to achieve your financial goals.

MAJOR POINT SUMMARY

— Comparing returns without consideration of risk is flirting with disaster.

— Avoiding risk totally represents a losing proposition.

— Understanding the risk/return relationship is vital.

— Proper investment analysis takes into account the real rate of return after taxes and inflation.

— Fixed income assets have historically been losers on an inflation-adjusted basis.

— Common stocks have consistently outperformed other investment alternatives in terms of preserving purchasing power and building wealth.

— You must assess your own risk tolerance and investment goals.

— Proper analysis of investment alternatives includes comparison of returns on a risk-adjusted basis.

— Market timing has the potential to reduce risk and provide wealth building returns on a risk-adjusted basis.

— Market timing may be the "investment phenomenon" of the 21st Century.

"There is a tide in the affairs of men, which, taken at the flood, leads on to fortune; omitted, all the voyage of their life is bound in shallows and misery."

— Shakespeare

CHAPTER 3

Finding a Strategy That Works

THE FALLACY OF THE MOUNTAIN CHART

Climbing the investment mountain, like climbing Mount Everest, is fraught with danger. It is not an easy venture. First of all, savvy mountain climbers don't go straight up for fear of plummeting to disaster. The same holds true in the investment world. In both environments, you are likely to encounter some grizzly bears and other challenges along the way. The advice to simply buy and hold stocks and sit back while you accumulate a mountain of wealth simply does not hold up under close scrutiny.

Remember, nothing goes up in a straight line and nothing, especially the stock market, goes up forever. To paraphrase Sir John Templeton, founder of the Templeton family of funds, "There will continue to be bull markets followed by bear markets followed by subsequent bull markets but the long-term trend will continue to be higher and higher."

While the long-term trend may be successively higher, you will encounter periodic price pullbacks and even major down markets. They are a fact of life in the investment world. Just as the mountain climber retraces his or her steps to maneuver around a difficult obstacle or avoid a dangerous situation, the investor must learn how to deal with and avoid major market retracements that can prove devastating to your portfolio and your accumulation of wealth. That is precisely why this book is called *Lasting Wealth is a Matter of Timing*.

It is crucial to protect yourself against those inevitable down markets. There is an old saying that, "The only things certain in life are death and taxes." I would like to amend that truism to add the certainty of declining markets. You can be sure that declining markets and even brutal bear markets will continue to plague investors in the years to come. Despite all the hoopla by the financial press and so-called financial prophets or gurus, it is **not** different this time around! You must add the certainty of declining markets to the list of life's unpleasantries including death and taxes.

This is not a new idea. In the August 15, 1969 issue of the *Forbes* "Mutual Fund Survey," the editors issued the following warning, which holds just as true today:

> **"...don't listen to the salesman who tells you not to worry about down markets because the big trend is up. Maybe the big trend is up, but the intermediate downs aren't necessarily little ones. And sometimes people are forced to sell during the downs. Sure, their stocks will go up again, but somebody else will own them. For few, if any, humans is downside risk a matter of no concern."**

Attempting to build a mountain of wealth via the buy and hold strategy contains major risks. To illustrate, consider the results of the following buy and hold strategy calculated with historical data. In this example, we used the NYSE TR Index, which includes every NYSE stock equally weighted, as a proxy for the performance results of a typical stock portfolio. Assume you invested $100,000 in a buy and hold strategy from January 1, 1970 to December 31, 1995. Your investment would have delivered a net annual return of 14.7 percent and your $100,000 initial investment would have grown to over $3.5 million by the end of 1995 as shown in Chart 3-1.

PERFORMANCE SUMMARY

Chart 3-1	Net Annual Return	$100,000 Investment Value 12/31/95
Buy & Hold NYSE	14.7%	$3,516,094

Chart 3-1 NYSE= New York Stock Exchange Total Return Index
$100,000 invested 01/01/70

On the surface the accumulated $3.5 million mountain and net annual return approaching 15 percent looks attractive. However, as you climbed up the NYSE mountain, you were beaten back in excess of 53 percent during the bear market of April 14, 1972 through September 13, 1974. Similarly, if you were an investor in the high-flying Fidelity Magellan Fund during that same time frame, you would have had to survive a drop of over 58 percent before reaching the top of the mountain. The results are even more dramatic if you had invested in the Keystone S4 (small companies) Fund mountain. The bear would have devoured over 73 percent of your assets at the depth of the bear market. The critical question is...would you really have kept climbing to reach the top of the mountain? Or would you have opted to bail out to save what little remained of your portfolio assets? I doubt that you would have kept climbing! Most investors do not have the fortitude to continue to endure continuing pain with no hope of a turnaround in sight. They bail out and lock in their staggering losses.

> **"It's human nature to be influenced by the actions of the crowd, particularly in emotionally charged settings.... The crowd behaves the same way in every market cycle. Some trends last longer than others and some travel farther than others, but the**

psychological progression through each bull and bear market is always the same."

— Robert Prechter

For the naysayers who say that they will forgo the potentially higher returns of the above mutual funds and invest in a portfolio similar to the more conservative S & P 500, let's review its performance over the same period. Chart 3-2 illustrates the price action of the S & P 500 from January 1970 through December 1995. As you can see, the S & P 500 mountain does have a more gentle slope and has an 11.8% per year return versus 14.7% per year for the NYSE TR Index; but, you still experience a series of declines ranging from an 18 percent pullback to a more precipitous 48 percent bear market.

S & P 500 26-Year Performance

Chart 3-2

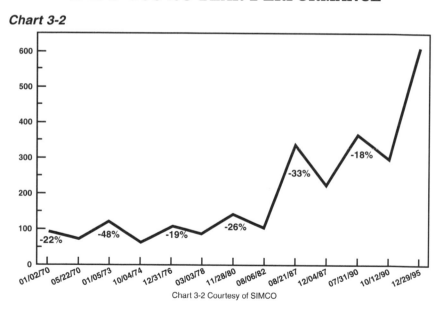

Chart 3-2 Courtesy of SIMCO

No investor in his or her right mind wants to buy high and sell low. However, in the real world of investing that scenario takes place far too often. As unlikely as it sounds, buying high and selling low is practiced by many investors despite their original intentions.

For example, an analysis of monthly mutual fund purchases and sales (net mutual fund flows) of United States stock funds versus the Lipper U.S. Stock Growth and Income Index from January 1987 through November 1995 by LBS Capital Management, Inc. in Clearwater, Florida found that many investors do in reality buy high. In other words, they purchase mutual funds when the market has already risen significantly. Likewise, on the sell side, investors tend to sell mutual funds AFTER major market declines when most of the damage has already occurred.

In the analysis, LBS chose the three points where mutual fund inflows were the greatest and the three points when mutual fund outflows were the greatest and overlaid these points on the Lipper Growth and Income Index trend line in Chart 3-3. The points of greatest inflows are represented by the dark boxes while the points of greatest outflows (or the greatest decline in inflows) are represented by the white circles.

As Chart 3-3 illustrates, major inflows occurred in December 1992, December 1993, and November 1995 after the market had achieved significant advances.

MAJOR MUTUAL FUNDS INFLOWS AND OUTFLOWS

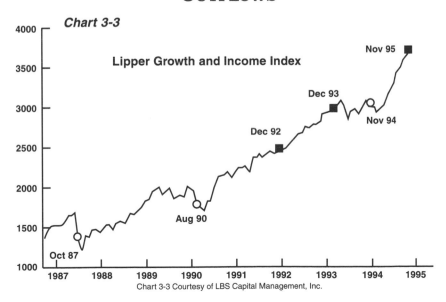

Chart 3-3 Courtesy of LBS Capital Management, Inc.

Major outflows occurred in October 1987 and August 1990 after major market declines. The third large outflow occurred in November 1994 after many mutual funds had experienced losses for the year and just before the bull market of 1995.

What is the reason for such irrational behavior? I believe that the answer lies in the human psyche. Crucial investment decisions are made at market turning points when human emotion interferes with proper investment judgment. As the investor watches a bear market decimate his or her investment portfolio and wealth declines by 20 percent, 30 percent, 40 percent, or more, the pain increases until his or her pain threshold is exceeded, triggering action to **stop the pain** by selling the shares and getting out of the market in an attempt to prevent the possibility of further losses.

However, this panic-driven action locks in investment losses, resulting in the investor having far less capital with which to re-enter the market at a later date. In addition, the memory of the pain suffered during the dramatic loss may actually prevent the investor from entering the market again or, at the very least, postpone the decision to reenter the market until after they are sure it is safe and have forgone major price rises in the meantime.

Too many investors wait until too late to gather up the courage to invest in the stock market and then turn right around and bail out when the market turns down. After suffering a loss, they are hard pressed to get back on that horse again and reenter the market. Their holding time in stocks is depicted on Chart 3-4 by the dotted line. I call these folks "emotional" asset allocators. This chart clearly illustrates the difference between "investment" results and "investor" results. These emotional investors invest too late during a market rise and bail out on the downside and subsequently miss the majority of the price rise after the market turns around.

Three recent separate studies by Dalbar Financial Services, Smith Barney, and Fidelity Investments have focused on the investment habits of stock market investors. All three studies reached similar conclusions, which confirm my own observations over the years, that a majority of investors lack the discipline to successfully hold a stock portfolio or equity mutual funds through the inevitable market ups and downs. Often these people are so busy with the challenges of daily life and their job or business that they don't have the time, much less the knowledge and experience, or proper data with which to make good investment decisions.

EMOTIONAL ASSET ALLOCATION

Chart 3-4

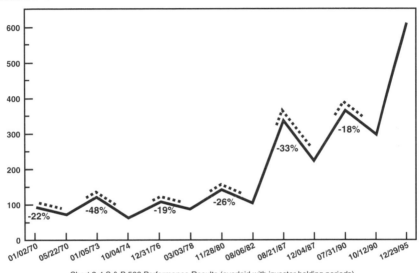

Chart 3-4 S & P 500 Performance Results (overlaid with investor holding periods).

Courtesy of SIMCO

Historically, stock market returns have been good enough to offset taxes and inflation, but all of the volatility exhibited by the stock market may prove to have **too much risk for many of you**. Stock averages cast the image of climbing the investment mountain and building wealth. However, it can be very illusory. It is very difficult for real people with real emotions to hold common stocks and equity mutual funds through major market declines.

> **"...The bulging files sum up a fascinating history, offering surprising evidence that the stock market has changed not a whit in the last century. Only its price history...There have been no significant changes in the market, as opposed to the marketplace...What all those stock tables and tales, books, and charts illustrate is an endless repetition of psychological patterns..."**
>
> *—John Dennis Brown*
> **101 Years on Wall Street**

Making money in the stock market is a lot like mountain climbing. From a distance it looks like a pretty straight path upward to the top...but a closer examination shows various levels (plateaus) and the need to backtrack periodically in order to find the safest route to the top. As shown in the "Debunking Buy and Hold Strategies" section in Chapter 1, and reiterated here, sitting on stocks while a bear market devastates the value of your portfolio and your wealth accumulation is not only catastrophic, it is foolhardy. This is doubly true if your current age does not realistically give you enough time to recoup your losses. Any buy and hold strategy requires two underlying principles to work. First of all, the investor must have the fortitude to buy and hold. Second, there must be enough time to weather the anticipated market declines.

If you were unfortunate enough to suffer a market decline as severe as occurred from August 30, 1929 to July 8 1932, it would take you twenty-five years just to get back to breakeven! Can you afford to take that kind of risk with your life's savings, your "serious" money?

As the studies show, most investors do not possess the emotional strength to hold on when others are panicking and selling after sharp price declines have decimated their portfolio. As mentioned earlier, buy and hold is a young person's game at best and may not be the best strategy for them either.

THE IDEAL INVESTMENT

So what is the answer? The "ideal investment" is one which earns enough return to offset the effects of inflation and taxes, and still allows you to sleep comfortably at night. The goal is to accumulate a nest egg generating a level of earnings you **cannot** outlive! This should be accomplished within a framework of risk reduction. Additionally, the ideal investment would provide liquidity, have tax-free or tax-deferred accumulation (see Chapter 8), and estate benefits. Historically, the investment closest to that ideal has been equities, but buy and hold investing in the stock market with its periodic price declines and bear markets may not let you sleep at night.

We believe a strategy that serves investors better is what we call market timing, a risk management strategy also known as tactical asset allocation, dynamic asset allocation, or active asset allocation. We will sort out all those terms later in this chapter. Our goal is 180 degrees different from emotional investing that gets investors into and out of investments at the wrong times. Through the disciplined use of time-tested econometric models, we as market timers attempt to be in a position to purchase stocks when the emotional investors are selling and sell stocks when the emotional investors are buying.

> **"To buy when others are despondently selling and to sell when others are avidly buying requires the greatest fortitude and pays the greatest rewards."**
>
> —*Sir John Templeton*

As you can see from the dotted lines on Chart 3-5, this strategy is not perfect. The dotted lines represent those periods of time when a professional market timer would expect to own stocks.

Our goal with this strategy is to capture 80 percent of major market advances and avoid 80 percent of major market declines. Appropriately applied, this ideal investment strategy works to prevent bear markets from devouring your portfolio and positions you early to capitalize on significant market advances.

If our strategy proves successful, the results will approximate the solid and dashed line in Chart 3-6. The solid portion of the line represents the time spent in the market while the dashed line represents the portion of the time spent in bonds and/or the money market.

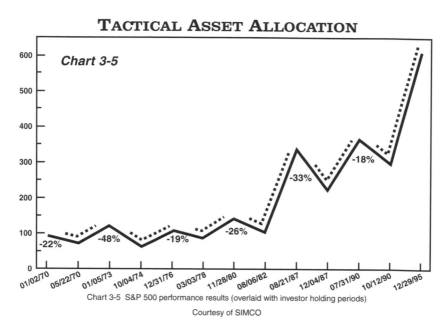

Chart 3-5 S&P 500 performance results (overlaid with investor holding periods)

Courtesy of SIMCO

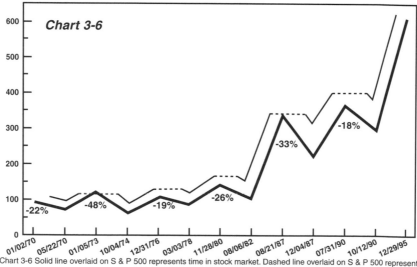

Chart 3-6 Solid line overlaid on S & P 500 represents time in stock market. Dashed line overlaid on S & P 500 represents time spent in bonds and/or money market.

Courtesy of SIMCO

There should be several evident conclusions from the presentation in this chart.

1. While risk will always remain a part of investing in the stock market and losses cannot be eliminated, market timing/tactical asset allocation tactics possess the potential to reduce risks down to levels acceptable by many investors.

2. An important by-product of market timing risk reduction strategies permits potential higher returns, especially on a risk-adjusted basis.

Let's look at the results from one market timing model in effect since 1970 versus a buy and hold New York Stock Exchange Index strategy (See Chart 3-7). An initial investment of $100,000 for the buy and hold strategy grew to $3.5 million yielding a compounded annual return of 14.7 percent. In comparison, the $100,000 invested under the Timing Model rose to $7.5 million after all expenses and

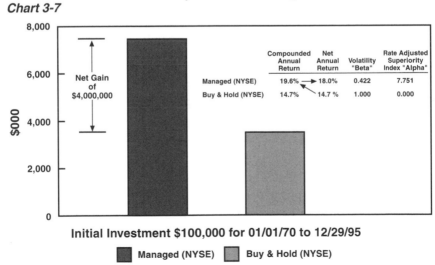

RESULTS OF ACTUAL SWITCHING SIGNALS
Generated by "The Timing Model"

Chart 3-7

	Compounded Annual Return	Net Annual Return	Volatility "Beta"	Rate Adjusted Superiority Index "Alpha"
Managed (NYSE)	19.6% →	18.0%	0.422	7.751
Buy & Hold (NYSE)	14.7%	14.7 %	1.000	0.000

Net Gain of $4,000,000

Initial Investment $100,000 for 01/01/70 to 12/29/95

■ Managed (NYSE)   ▨ Buy & Hold (NYSE)

See Appendix A for Disclosure Statement.
Chart 3-7 Courtesy of SIMCO

management fees for a compounded annual return of 18.0 percent. More importantly, the timing model outperformed the buy and hold strategy on a risk adjusted basis. Of course, past performance is no guarantee of future results.

THE REST OF THE STORY

One of the common criticisms of these risk management strategies (market timing/tactical asset allocation/dynamic asset allocation/active asset allocation) is the possibility of missing some of the gains in bull markets and not avoiding all the losses in bear markets. While the criticism has some validity, there is more to the story.

A review of the **big** quarterly buy and hold gains and losses (gains of more than 5 percent and losses exceeding 3 percent) compared with the results for the same quarters of risk management using the Timing Model sheds some interesting light.

In Chart 3-8, note that the risk management results averaged 2.8 percent less than the buy and hold strategy in the highly profitable quarters. That's to be expected. On the other hand, the risk management strategy results outperformed the buy and hold investment approach by an average 10.7 percent in the worst losing quarters.

COMPARISON OF "BUY-AND-HOLD" VS. "THE TIMING MODEL"
01-01-70 to 12-29-95
NYSE Index

Chart 3-8

# of Highly Profitable Quarters Buy-and-Hold	51
Average Profit per Highly Profitable Quarter Buy-and-Hold	12.1%
Average Same Quarter Profit with The Timing Model	9.3%
Advantage with Buy-and-Hold	2.8%
# of Very Unprofitable Quarters Buy-and-Hold	18
Average Loss per Very Unprofitable Quarter Buy-and-Hold	-12.4%
Average Same Quarter Results with The Timing Mode l	-1.7%
Advantage with The Timing Model	10.7 %

Chart 3-8 Adaptation of a study by Paul Merriman

Conclusion: Risk management market timing accomplishes its goal of reducing losses in the worst markets and nearly matching the big gain performances of buy and hold strategies in the best markets. Think of market timing risk management as insurance against disaster. It stands ready to protect your portfolio from disastrous price declines yet turns in respectable returns in strong upside markets, especially when you compare returns on a risk-adjusted basis.

> **"The question is NOT, can you make more money timing than "buy and hold?" The question IS, would you stay in the market "buy and hold" through thick and thin? Or is the volatility too much? If the volatility is too much, then if timing can reduce the volatility enough to keep you invested, it has provided a valuable service."**
>
> — *Mark Hulbert*

BETA BASICS

Up to now we have mentioned risk management and risk-adjusted returns. At this point, it is appropriate to discuss some "Beta Basics". Beta is a measure of volatility comparing the returns of an individual investment relative to the market return. Securities with a beta of 1.0 are equal in volatility to that of the overall market. Stocks with betas greater than 1.0 possess more volatility risk than the market while stocks with betas less than 1.0 have less volatility risk than the market.

On average, potential returns from a particular investment should compensate you for the level of risk undertaken. If they do not properly compensate you for the higher level of risk, you should not make the investment. It is as logical as that.

However, how do you determine the correct measurement of risk and return? How does an investor evaluate investments and their corresponding level of risk?

Fortunately, Modern Portfolio Theory provides a conceptual starting point in the Capital Asset Pricing Model. The model shows the relationship between risk and return. T-Bills are used as a proxy for a risk-free return, while the S & P 500 approximates the market return. Traditionally, investment professionals have calculated risk using beta and/or standard deviation. In reality, both measure volatility, calculating how much a particular investment moves in comparison with a standard or benchmark.

Beta, for example, measures an investment's tendency to exaggerate or underestimate the market's mood swings. It measures volatility relative to a stock market index. Standard deviation simply measures volatility within the investment itself. The lower the beta or standard deviation, the lower the risk profile of the investment.

In the Capital Asset Pricing Model, 3-month T-Bills have a beta of 0, while the S & P 500 beta stands at 1.0. See Chart 3-9. Ideally, an investor should select investments which fall in the left hand side of the chart, above the expected return line. In other

Capital Asset Pricing Model
ANOTHER WAY TO SHOW RISK VS. RETURN
January 1, 1970 to December 29, 1995

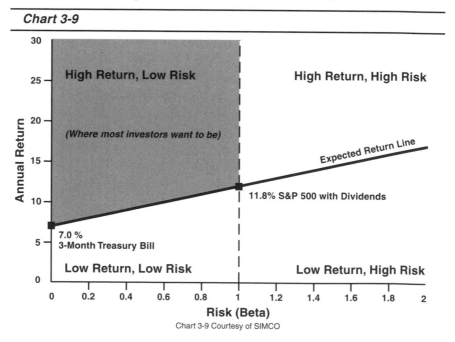

Chart 3-9 Courtesy of SIMCO

words, you should seek out investments in the shaded high return/ low risk sector of the chart.

In order to determine where your investments fall within the Capital Asset Pricing Model, first select a specific time period and plot the annual rate of return for the 3-month T-Bill (beta=0) and the S & P 500 (beta=1) for that period. A straight line connecting those two points and extending beyond is the "Expected Return Line."

In Chart 3-9, the expected return line runs from a return of 7.0 percent for T-Bills through 11.8 percent for the S & P 500. Next, locate the annual return rate and beta for your prospective investment for the same time period on the graph. To obtain the respective betas for specific investments, you can consult such rating services as *Morningstar* and *Value Line*. Are your investments in the high return/low risk area of the graph or is your risk posture higher than anticipated? Looking at returns without adjusting for risk is like flying a kite without the string. It may fly high, but you'll never get it back.

As you can see from the Continental Airlines billboard below, **"Timing is Everything."**

Photo Courtesy of SIMCO

> **"Timing may not be everything in life, but when it comes to success, it is difficult to think of another single factor that makes or breaks more peoples lives."**
>
> — *Denis Waitley*
> Timing Is Everything

When you are in the timing business, as I am, you tend to notice other companies and other industries who also recognize the importance of timing. In recent months, advertisements for airlines (Continental), automobiles (Honda), long-distance service (AT&T), and even a local nursing home (St. Regis) emphatically state that **"Timing Is Everything!"** The July 18, 1996 *Wall Street Journal* carried an interesting article on the rising popularity of chronotherapy, the process of timing medicines to the body's clock.

Does it make sense to you that timing would be so critical in all these industries, but not in the stock market? I don't think so! I believe that Denis Waitley is right on target with his assessment of the importance of timing in virtually every facet of life.

DEFINING ASSET ALLOCATION

Up to now we have used terms for various risk management strategies such as market timing, tactical asset allocation, dynamic asset allocation, and active asset allocation somewhat interchangeably. However, there are some subtle and a few significant differences you should know. With that in mind, we present the following asset allocation definitions for your review:

ACTIVE ASSET ALLOCATION

— An investment allocation strategy involving continued monitoring and rebalancing of the portfolio among multiple asset classifications, usually accomplished in increments. See also dynamic asset allocation.

ASSET ALLOCATION

— Investment strategy of reducing risk and increasing return potential by investing in a variety of asset types (example:

60% stocks, 30% bonds, 10% cash). Changes in allocations are made very infrequently thus this tactic is also called strategic or passive asset allocation.

DYNAMIC ASSET ALLOCATION

— An asset allocation strategy involving continuous monitoring and rebalancing of the portfolio among multiple asset classifications based on an analysis of the current reward/ risk ratio in each class as well as changes in investor circumstances. Rebalancing is usually accomplished in increments. See also active asset allocation.

MARKET TIMING

— The strategy of measuring the direction of a market or market index and moving funds in or out of the market based on those measurements. Classic market timing usually involves 100 percent moves between stocks and cash. A disciplined strategy for reducing the risks of stock market investing. See also tactical asset allocation.

RISK MANAGEMENT

— An investment strategy designed to reduce the exposure to market risk when the probability of loss is high. See also active, dynamic, and tactical asset allocation and market timing.

STRATEGIC ASSET ALLOCATION

— An investment strategy similar to passive asset allocation. It uses principles of Modern Portfolio Theory and the Efficient Frontier to set dedicated allocation percentages or targets. Rebalancing back to the target is accomplished periodically to adjust for differences in performance (usually $\pm 5\%$ or more).

TACTICAL ASSET ALLOCATION

— A market timing investment strategy that can utilize more than just the two classical asset classes (stocks and cash). However, the same principles of market measurement and risk control, in response to changing economic and market conditions, are employed. The risk tolerance of the investor is assumed to remain constant.

> **"Poppy petals fall softly...quietly...calmly, when they are ready."**
>
> — *Etsujin*
> **Haiku Harvest**

MANAGING RISK

As indicated above, there are a variety of risk management strategies. They differ primarily in frequency and percentages of rebalancing, and in the number of asset classifications utilized. However, the overall objective remains the same: to keep investors committed to equity investing over the long haul, but with a lower risk posture.

Table 3-1 gives you a quick overview of the various risk management strategies and their attributes.

RISK MANAGEMENT STRATEGIES
Table 3-1

Strategy	Employs Market Model	Frequency of Exhanges	Exchange Increments	Asset Classes Employed	Approx. Range-Stock Allocation
Classic Mkt Tmg[#]	yes	usually active	all or none	stock/cash	0-100%
Tac Asset Alloc[#]	yes	as necessary	large	more than two	0-100%*
Dyn Asset Alloc	yes	as necessary	usually small	multiple	0-100%*
Act Asset Alloc	yes	as necessary	usually small	multiple	0-100%
Str Asset Alloc	no[1]	periodic rebalancing	very small	multiple	10-60%*
Asset Alloc (pass)	no[1]	very infrequent	very small	multiple	10-60%

* Within this % you could experience sector rotation
[#] Sometimes also called fund timing, fund conversion, fund switching
[1] A manager not employing a market model is not usually a member of SAAFTI

Steve Shellans, editor of the *MoniResearch Newsletter* in Portland, Oregon has followed market timing for sixteen years and tracks over 60 market timers in his newsletter. He classifies market timing along a continuum. On one end are the pure or classic market timers who move 100 percent of the portfolio into some asset class such as stocks. At a sell signal, these timers move 100 percent into bonds or cash such as a money market account. According to Shellans, "These are the quintessential market timers."

On the other end of the timing spectrum are the dynamic asset allocators who invest in a variety of asset classes and shift money around from one asset class to another. The goal is to transform a portfolio's asset mix from more risky assets to safer asset classes in order to deliver the portfolio's expected return within the acceptable risk parameters. As the market changes, the investment manager adapts the portfolio mix. Due to the technical difficulties involved in dynamic asset allocation, its primary users are professional investors on behalf of their clients.

Tactical asset allocation attempts to improve portfolio returns through periodic revision of the portfolio asset mix. The tactical asset allocation manager uses securities (funds) selection and market timing approaches to achieve this. Sector rotation such as moving from industrial to financial services stocks, and market timing are traditional tactical asset allocation techniques.

PREVENTING CALAMITY

Some skeptics point out that most timing data is only from 1970 or 1980 and question whether or not market timing will work if we ever have the misfortune to suffer another period like 1929-32, i.e. the Great Depression. No one can predict the future, but through the magic of computer simulation, I have been able to test my timing model back to 1927 and the results are extremely encouraging. I'll give you a detailed printout and performance summary in Chapter 4, but here is the bottom line. $100,000 invested in 1927 would have grown to over $22.4 billion at the end of 1995 for a net annual return of 19.6 percent. In contrast, buy and hold strategies for the NYSE Total Return Index and S & P 500 Total Return Index would have only grown to $510.5 million or a net annual return of 13.2 percent and $95.2 million or 10.5 percent, respectively.

A balanced buy and hold mixture of 60 percent NYSE Total Return Index and 40 percent T-Bills would have fared even worse with a value of $68.3 million and net annual return of 9.9 percent. More importantly, it appears that you could have avoided most of the losses of the depression, which were almost 85 percent in 1929-32, and preserved your capital to invest at the bargain basement prices of the early 1930s. God forbid that we ever have another financial crisis like that, but it gives me great comfort to know that we have a plan that would have helped us survive a debacle of that scope. Of course, it is possible that future conditions will not be like any of the periods we have studied. And, even if they are similar, we realize that past performance is in no way a guarantee of future results. But I study the past carefully, because I believe that anyone who ignores the past is doomed to repeat it!

MAJOR POINT SUMMARY

— Climbing the investment mountain is not as easy as it looks.

— You have to take protective actions against market pullbacks.

— It's rare that you can get real people to buy and hold common stocks through major market declines.

— The real question: Are you going to practice "emotional" market timing or "disciplined" market timing?

— "Investor" returns are often less than "investment" returns.

— Financial success requires accumulating a financial nest egg that will generate an income stream you cannot outlive.

— The ideal investment earns enough return to offset taxes and inflation — and still allows you to sleep at night.

— Risk will remain a part of investing.

— Risk reduction strategies work.

— The goal of market timing is to avoid 80% of bear market losses and capture 80% of bull market gains.

— It's important to understand how to compare investments using the Capital Asset Pricing Model.

— Timing is critical in many industries, including the investment business

— There are a variety of risk management techniques. Market timing and tactical asset allocation are close cousins. So are dynamic asset allocation and active asset allocation, as are strategic asset allocation and passive asset allocation.

> **"In selecting the soundest financial invest-
> ments, the question of when to buy is far more
> important than what to buy."**
>
> *— Roger Babson*

CHAPTER 4
Market Timing Works

ASSET ALLOCATION REVISITED

Taking a closer look at asset allocation sets the stage for a review of market timing. As we saw in Chapter 3, asset allocation is an investment strategy aimed at reducing risk and enhancing investment return by investing in a variety of asset types with infrequent changes in the allocation mix.

The theory behind asset allocation lies in attempting to invest in a sufficiently diversified asset universe with an optimal mix to achieve the desired return or some increment above it, with reduced risk. A number of studies have shown that 90 percent of a portfolio's return can be traced to the classes of investments held, with less than 10 percent of the return attributable to the individual securities in the portfolio. Infrequent rebalancing realigns the portfolio to counter market drift. Rebalancing helps eliminate the risk of the portfolio becoming too concentrated in any one asset class and exposing the portfolio to sharp value declines due to a change in the economic climate.

A major benefit of asset allocation is that it removes the emotional aspect from investment decision making, allowing investors to make a long-term commitment to a specific investment strategy. Another major benefit of employing asset allocation is the ability to diversify your assets to guard against poor performance in one asset category from devastating your portfolio. As one asset class in the portfolio under performs due to changing economic and market conditions, other classes negatively correlated with that asset class compensate for that declining performance with rising returns. For example, during inflationary times, total returns on fixed income investments such as long-term government bonds typically decline while total returns on hard assets such as precious metals increase.

Therefore, it is crucial that the optimum mix include asset classes that move in opposite directions to each other. Correlation coefficients are calculated for each class. Combinations of asset classes with low or negative correlations help to reduce risk. Once the acceptable level of risk is determined, the optimum combination of asset classes is created to provide the greatest level of return possible without exceeding the predetermined level of acceptable risk.

While the classic asset allocation strategy reduces risk, it also reduces potential return compared to the top performance of the individual investment classes in the portfolio. In order to maintain a reduced risk posture plus enhance portfolio returns, investment managers have turned to dynamic asset management.

GETTING DYNAMIC

The dynamic asset allocation strategy involves continuous monitoring and rebalancing of the portfolio among multiple asset allocations. While the rebalancing under classic passive (or strategic) asset allocation returns the portfolio to predetermined asset mix ranges, dynamic asset allocation analyzes the reward/risk ratio for each class and adjusts the portfolio mix in an attempt to select or weight investment classes with the greatest potential for superior returns in the current economic environment. Thus the allocation of assets takes on a dynamic nature...changing in response to market conditions and anticipated opportunities for investment gain. The rebalancing usually takes place in increments.

Economic realities make dynamic asset allocation a more realistic strategy. First of all, financial markets tend to move in cycles. It only makes good economic sense to try to capitalize on the upside potential of asset classes poised to outperform less vibrant or declining asset classes via a shift in weighting within the portfolio mix.

Second, investing in the right sector of the market at the right time can produce superior investment returns. It is not uncommon for top performing sectors to turn in annual returns of 50 percent or more. While the downside potential of some market sectors makes investing in these areas potentially dangerous in a fixed or static asset allocation strategy, dynamic asset allocation takes advantage of the unique opportunity to move in and out of these sectors as economic conditions dictate. As a result, investment returns can significantly outpace the overall market and fixed asset allocation strategies.

Third, participating in superior returns within established risk parameters means that the dynamic asset allocator does not have to be right 100 percent of the time. Dynamic asset allocation can reduce risk without unduly diminishing returns.

Fourth, bear markets are a fact of financial markets and investing. If implemented properly, dynamic asset allocation should reduce exposure to declining markets and a devastating bear attack on portfolio value. The more capital investors lose on the downside, the longer it takes to recapture their losses. Likewise, the more money lost, the less available to capitalize on opportunities when the market moves higher. A review of bear markets shows that investors spent 76 percent of their time suffering through bear markets and trying to recoup their losses to get back to breakeven. Less than a fourth of their time was actually spent increasing the value of their original investment. See Chart 4-1 for a recap of the impact of various bear markets since September 1929.

S&P 500 Index Bear Market Study
September 1929 through September 1996

Chart 4-1 Bear Market	Duration	% Decline	Time Needed To Breakeven
Sept. '29 — June '32	33 months	86.7	25.2 years
July '33 — Mar. '35	20 months	33.9	2.3 years
Mar. '37 — Mar. '38	12 months	54.5	8.8 years
Nov. '38 — Apr. '42	41 months	45.8	6.4 years
May '46 — Mar. '48	22 months	28.1	4.1 years
Aug. '56 — Oct. '57	14 months	21.6	2.1 years
Dec. '61 — June '62	6 months	28.0	1.8 years
Feb. '66 — Oct. '66	8 months	22.2	1.4 years
Nov. '68 — May '70	18 months	36.1	3.3 years
Jan. '73 — Oct. '74	21 months	48.2	7.6 years
Nov. '80 — Aug. '82	21 months	27.1	2.1 years
Aug. '87 — Dec. '87	4 months	33.5	1.9 years
July '90 — Oct. '90	3 months	19.9	0.6 years

Chart 4-1 Courtesy of Fabian Investor Resource

Of course, no investment system is perfect. The success of dynamic asset allocation rests on the ability of the investment professional to properly identify those asset classes poised to deliver the highest returns in each market phase. Remember, you don't have to be right 100 percent of the time. The key is to be right enough times over a full market cycle to deliver superior returns on a risk- adjusted basis. If you achieve this, you will outpace the impact of inflation and taxes and achieve real investment growth to add to your retirement nest egg.

Tapping Technology

Without a doubt, we live in a technological age. Many facets of dynamic asset allocation and market timing would not exist without the state-of-the-art computers, software, and on-line databases available today. Savvy investment managers have at their fingertips powerful analysis tools for studying the market and developing complex proprietary dynamic asset allocation and timing models. Using models backtested against historical data, investment managers have created criteria and models which indicate which asset class or classes are positioned to outperform other asset classes given the current market environment.

> **"Starting with the basic signal, we will add new features, building on the model progressively. At each stage of development, we test for curve- fitting. What finally emerges is a profitable stock market timing model that is also robust."**
>
> — *Nelson Freeburg*
> **Formula Research**

Assuming a working knowledge of the market and economic cycles, investment advisors can track a range of indicators to determine a number of factors such as actions or data which signal a fundamental change in the economic climate, what people are doing in the market, and the relative attractiveness of specific asset classes. Armed with this information, the investment manager develops an asset allocation strategy which apportions monies among the portfolio's different asset classes/funds based on return probabilities and portfolio risk parameters.

Fixed asset allocation keeps you locked into asset classes which are exhibiting signs of decline or which are unlikely to show much return in the near-term. The use of technology opens up new horizons for detecting market moves and the expected relative returns from specific asset classes in the current or anticipated environment. The adept money manager can move in and out of investments to take advantage of superior return opportunities and sidestep devastating bear market moves.

A private research study by Barra/Micropal released in William Donoghue's August 1993 *Moneyletter*, found that Peter Lynch's success during his years at the helm of Fidelity's Magellan Fund was grounded in the fund's asset allocation. When biotechnology stocks were on the upswing, those stocks were the most heavily represented in the Magellan portfolio. When blue chips outpaced the market as a whole, blue chip stocks dominated the portfolio.

Dynamic asset allocation delivers the following distinct investment advantages:

— Diversification among a number of asset classes reduces risk and increases the potential that an investor will be invested in the top performing asset classes when they are making their upside moves.

— Changing the weights or allocation ratios allows an investor to take greater advantage of top performing segments of the market.

— Adjusting the allocation in response to market trends means the likelihood of less loss when the value of an asset class tumbles.

— Adopting a disciplined dynamic asset allocation strategy eliminates the emotional factor that can trigger poor investment decisions.

"The stock market has a history of moving to irrational extremes because, on a short-term basis, stock prices are often more a reflection of fear, greed, or other psychological factors than of business and monetary fundamentals."

— Joseph L. Oppenheimer

There are as many potential ways to track the market as there are investment managers. For example, fundamental forecasting models attempt to project the market's overall direction in the next period by identifying specific data series or combinations of series that lead the market. Trend following models, on the other hand, calculate moving averages and attempt to ferret out buy and sell signals as prices and moving averages cross or you have crossings between moving averages of different time intervals. Overextended models seek to discriminate between normal and extreme behavior signalling overbought or oversold situations.

Dynamic asset allocation strategies do not always outperform the broad market. However, as a general rule, they do reduce losses during down markets, preserving portfolio value and safeguarding assets to be reinvested during upside moves. Overall, they are designed to outperform buy and hold strategies on a risk-adjusted basis and often outperform buy and hold strategies on a total return basis.

To clear up any confusion over passive and dynamic asset allocation consider the following distinctions. Some people confuse a buy and hold strategy with passive asset allocation. The buy and hold investor purchases securities and hangs on to them for the long haul despite changes in market conditions. The passive asset allocation investor periodically rebalances the portfolio because market action causes it to stray from predetermined targets or ranges for asset classes. Asset classes experiencing strong market performance become overweighted relative to their target, and portfolio maintenance requires bringing them back in line with the original targets, for example; 60% stocks, 30% bonds, and 10% cash.

"You do have to know what time of market it is. Markets go in cycles like all the other rhythms of life."

— *Adam Smith*
The Money Game

Think of it this way. When an investment manager periodically rebalances back to the target, that is considered passive asset allocation. Adding a new dimension, dynamic asset allocation adjusts the portfolio mix in reaction to changes in market conditions. If the investment manager evaluates current economic conditions and chooses to depart from the strategic mix in order to take advantage of market opportunities, that's dynamic asset allocation. The investment manager is attempting to adjust the portfolio mix based on relative undervaluations and overvaluations in order to capitalize on opportunities as market dynamics change over time.

MARKET TIMING

"Timing–Reaching its highest effectiveness at just the right moment."

— Webster's Dictionary

Market timing consists of measuring the direction of a market or market index and moving funds in or out of the market based on those measurements. Classic market timing usually involves 100 percent moves between stock and cash. The market timing strategy of using other asset classes in addition to stock and cash to take advantage of market changes is called tactical asset allocation. The goal of all market timing strategies is to reduce risk and deliver higher returns on a risk-adjusted basis.

You want to manage risk instead of avoiding it by hiding your assets in savings accounts, money market accounts, certificates of deposit, and T-Bills as Connie Conservative did. As we saw in Chapter 1, Connie's strategy failed to keep up with the ravages of inflation and taxes.

Through the use of a time-tested econometric model, I try to be in position to purchase stocks when the emotional sellers are selling and dispose of stocks when the emotional buyers are buying.

As I have said earlier, the goal of market timing is to capture 80 percent of major market advances and avoid 80 percent of major market declines. If successful, you can participate in the bulk of stock price rises and avoid being devastated by major bear markets.

"Look for people with a solid system and (the) discipline to stick with their indicators."

— Robert Farrell
Merrill, Lynch, Pierce, Fenner, & Smith

An example will clearly illustrate the benefit of market timing if we are successful in achieving our 80/80 goals. The Market Cycle Report in Chart 4-2 uses the NYSE TR Index, an unmanaged index of all stocks trading on the New York Stock Exchange, as the index for calculating returns and the different performance results of a buy and hold strategy versus risk management market timing. It should be noted that you cannot invest directly in the NYSE TR Index.

In determination of the Market Cycle Report, I used a beginning date of January 2, 1970 and ending date of December 29, 1995. For the purpose of this report, a cycle is defined as a market drop of 20 percent or more and a market rise of 25 percent or more.

MARKET CYCLE REPORT
January 2, 1970 Thru December 29, 1995

| Chart 4-2 | | | Buy and Hold | Risk Management Goal Avoid 80% |
Date	Top	Bottom	Change	Capture 80%
01/02/70	17.538			
07/30/70		12.009	-31.55%	-6.31%
04/14/72	20.847		+73.59%	+58.87%
09/13/74		9.655	-53.69%	-10.74%
02/08/80	36.912		+282.31%	+225.85%
03/28/80		29.457	-20.20%	-4.04%
08/21/87	187.262		+535.71%	+428.57%
12/04/87		129.896	-30.63%	-6.13%
10/06/89	223.919		+72.38%	+57.90%
10/12/90		174.879	-21.90%	-4.38%
12/29/95	612.609		+250.30%	+200.24%

Chart 4-2 Courtesy of SIMCO

Translating the above information into a summary bar chart, gives us the Summary Report in Chart 4-3. The Summary Report assumes an initial investment of $100,000.

While this hypothetical analysis using past performance cannot guarantee investment success in the future, there is a preponderance of evidence that risk reduction market timing strategies can and do work in the real investment world, as we have already shown in this book. For example, note how close the results in Chart 3-7 are to the 80/80 goal portrayed in Chart 4-3.

SUMMARY REPORT

Chart 4-3

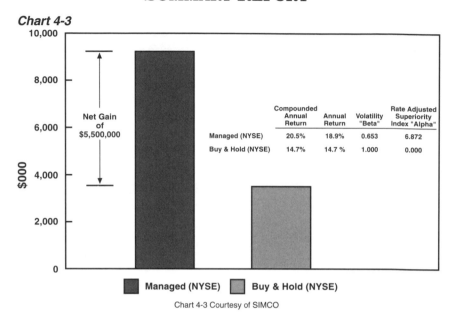

	Compounded Annual Return	Annual Return	Volatility "Beta"	Rate Adjusted Superiority Index "Alpha"
Managed (NYSE)	20.5%	18.9%	0.653	6.872
Buy & Hold (NYSE)	14.7%	14.7 %	1.000	0.000

Net Gain of $5,500,000

■ Managed (NYSE)   ▨ Buy & Hold (NYSE)

Chart 4-3 Courtesy of SIMCO

In Chapter 3, I also referred to a 70-year test of one timing model in use today. Chart 4-4, which starts on Page 82, shows how an initial investment of $100,000 in 1927 grows to over $22 billion by the end of 1995 despite The Great Depression, several subsequent recessions, and stock market corrections. Keep in mind that results using this model in the future may be materially different from those inferred from a computer simulation of past history. While this chart covers the period from 1927 through 1995, it is possible that future conditions will not be similar to any of the periods studied. Past performance is no guarantee of future results for any type of investment strategy.

As you can see from the chart, the portfolio was 100 percent in money market funds or cash during the worst part of the Stock Market Crash beginning in early 1929, thereby missing the debacle that devastated or completely wiped out portfolios which stayed fully invested. On the upside, the fund was fully invested in stocks in early-to-mid 1933 when the market advanced over 200 percent. The model preserved the portfolio's capital in 1929 so it could participate in the upward market surge later on. A buy and hold strategy would have either been wiped out or have had its portfolio value severely deteriorated so that it had far less capital on which to make investment gains during the subsequent stock market rebound. This pattern is repeated throughout the seven decades, resulting in a portfolio value of $22.4 billion at the end of 1995.

Review of the Performance Summary also points out some interesting facts. The risk management model solidly outperformed various buy and hold strategies. While the market timing approach grew to over $22 billion for a 19.6 percent net annual return, the NYSE buy and hold strategy delivered a net annual return of 13.2 percent for a portfolio value of $510.5 million at the end of 1995. The S & P 500 (with dividends invested) buy and hold and 60 percent NYSE/40 percent T-bill buy and hold strategies fared even worse with portfolio values of $95.2 million and $65.3 million, respectively, at the end of December 1995.

> **"There is no Holy Grail or single indicator that can always forecast the market...and there never will be. However, by developing and following several time-proven indicators, a market analyst can answer a number of questions with surprising accuracy."**
>
> *— James B. Stack*
> *Investech Research*

It is obvious from the above analysis that market timing does work and can deliver solid investment returns in a reduced risk environment. To be sure, no one can accurately time the market 100 percent of the time, however, remember that our goal is to capture 80 percent of major stock market advances and avoid 80 percent of major stock market declines.

TIMING MODEL

Chart 4-4	04/08/27 to 12/29/95			
— For the Period —				**Money**
Beginning	**Ending**	**Stocks**	**Bonds**	**Market**
04/08/27	05/20/27	0%	0%	100%
05/20/27	07/01/27	100%	0%	0%
07/01/27	10/07/27	100%	0%	0%
10/07/27	12/16/27	100%	0%	0%
12/16/27	01/06/28	0%	0%	100%
01/06/28	03/23/28	0%	0%	100%
03/23/28	04/06/28	100%	0%	0%
04/06/28	06/15/28	100%	0%	0%
06/15/28	07/06/28	0%	0%	100%
07/06/28	07/27/28	0%	0%	100%
07/27/28	10/05/28	100%	0%	0%
10/05/28	01/04/29	100%	0%	0%
01/04/29	02/01/29	100%	0%	0%
02/01/29	04/05/29	0%	0%	100%
04/05/29	07/05/29	0%	0%	100%
07/05/29	10/04/29	0%	0%	100%
10/04/29	01/03/30	0%	0%	100%
01/03/30	04/04/30	0%	0%	100%
04/04/30	07/04/30	0%	0%	100%
07/04/30	10/03/30	0%	0%	100%
10/03/30	01/02/31	0%	0%	100%
01/02/31	04/03/31	0%	0%	100%
04/03/31	07/03/31	0%	0%	100%
07/03/31	10/02/31	0%	0%	100%
10/02/31	01/01/32	0%	0%	100%
01/01/32	04/01/32	0%	0%	100%
04/01/32	07/01/32	0%	0%	100%
07/01/32	10/07/32	0%	0%	100%
10/07/32	11/04/32	0%	0%	100%
11/04/32	11/25/32	100%	0%	0%
11/25/32	12/02/32	0%	0%	100%
12/02/32	01/06/33	100%	0%	0%
01/06/33	02/03/33	100%	0%	0%
02/03/33	02/10/33	0%	0%	100%
02/10/33	04/07/33	100%	0%	0%
04/07/33	07/07/33	100%	0%	0%
07/07/33	07/21/33	100%	0%	0%
07/21/33	08/04/33	0%	0%	100%
08/04/33	09/08/33	100%	0%	0%
09/08/33	09/29/33	0%	0%	100%

Net Change for Period	Net Change Last Exchange	Quarterly Return	Yearly Return	Year	$100,000 Inv. Now Worth
0.2%	0.2%				
0.0%		0.2%			
8.7%		8.7%			
5.8%	15.0%				
0.2%		6.0%	15.5%	1927	115,465
0.6%	0.8%				
3.2%		3.8%			
4.3%	7.6%				
0.3%		4.6%			
0.3%	0.6%				
10.0%		10.3%			
14.4%		14.4%	35.0%	1928	155,920
2.8%	29.4%				
0.7%		3.5%			
1.3%		1.3%			
1.1%		1.1%			
1.2%		1.2%	5.2%	1929	163,968
0.8%		0.8%			
0.8%		0.8%			
0.5%		0.5%			
0.4%		0.4%	0.5%	1930	164,768
0.3%		0.3%			
0.3%		0.3%			
0.1%		0.1%			
0.4%		0.4%	−0.9%	1931	163,280
0.6%		0.6%			
0.2%		0.2%			
0.1%		0.1%			
0.0%	9.2%				
−3.2%	−3.2%				
0.0%	0.0%				
7.1%		3.7%	2.5%	1932	167,414
−8.3%	−1.8%				
0.0%	0.0%				
−1.7%		−9.9%			
210.5%		210.5%			
−23.2%	134.4%				
0.0%	0.0%				
3.4%	3.4%				
0.0%	0.0%				

TIMING MODEL (Cont.)
04/08/27 to 12/29/95

— For the Period —		Stocks	Bonds	Money Market
Beginning	**Ending**			
09/29/33	10/06/33	100%	0%	0%
10/06/33	11/10/33	100%	0%	0%
11/10/33	11/17/33	0%	0%	100%
11/17/33	01/05/34	100%	0%	0%
01/05/34	03/16/34	100%	0%	0%
03/16/34	04/06/34	0%	0%	100%
04/06/34	05/04/34	100%	0%	0%
05/04/34	06/01/34	0%	0%	100%
06/01/34	07/06/34	100%	0%	0%
07/06/34	08/03/34	100%	0%	0%
08/03/34	10/05/34	0%	0%	100%
10/05/34	01/04/35	0%	0%	100%
01/04/35	04/05/35	0%	0%	100%
04/05/35	07/05/35	0%	0%	100%
07/05/35	10/04/35	100%	0%	0%
10/04/35	10/11/35	0%	0%	100%
10/11/35	01/03/36	100%	0%	0%
01/03/36	04/03/36	100%	0%	0%
04/03/36	04/24/36	100%	0%	0%
04/24/36	06/19/36	0%	0%	100%
06/19/36	07/03/36	100%	0%	0%
07/03/36	08/28/36	100%	0%	0%
08/28/36	10/02/36	0%	0%	100%
10/02/36	10/09/36	0%	0%	100%
10/09/36	01/01/37	100%	0%	0%
01/01/37	03/05/37	100%	0%	0%
03/05/37	04/02/37	0%	0%	100%
04/02/37	07/02/37	0%	0%	100%
07/02/37	10/01/37	0%	0%	100%
10/01/37	01/07/38	0%	0%	100%
01/07/38	04/01/38	0%	0%	100%
04/01/38	05/13/38	100%	0%	0%
05/13/38	07/01/38	0%	0%	100%
07/01/38	08/19/38	100%	0%	0%
08/19/38	09/09/38	0%	0%	100%
09/09/38	10/07/38	100%	0%	0%
10/07/38	12/02/38	100%	0%	0%
12/02/38	12/09/38	0%	0%	100%
12/09/38	01/06/39	100%	0%	0%
01/06/39	02/03/39	100%	0%	0%

Net Change for Period	Net Change Last Exchange	Quarterly Return	Yearly Return	Year	$100,000 Inv. Now Worth
6.0%		−15.8%			
−7.1%	−1.5%				
0.0%	0.0%				
−3.7%		−10.5%	106.9%	1933	346,338
36.4%	31.4%				
0.0%	0.0%	36.4%			
−7.0%	−7.0%				
0.0%	0.0%				
6.6%		−0.9%			
−16.1%	−10.6%				
0.0%		−16.1%			
0.0%		0.0%	11.4%	1934	385,929
0.0%		0.0%			
0.0%	0.0%	0.0%			
15.6%	15.6%	15.6%			
0.0%	0.0%				
31.1%		31.1%	48.9%	1935	574,595
25.3%		25.3%			
−9.5%	48.7%				
0.0%	0.0%				
−0.7%		−10.1%			
11.1%	10.3%				
0.0%		11.1%			
0.0%	0.0%				
10.5%		10.5%	36.1%	1936	782,249
17.2%	29.5%				
0.0%		17.2%			
0.1%		0.1%			
0.1%		0.1%			
0.0%		0.0%	15.8%	1937	905,739
0.0%	0.2%	0.0%			
20.3%	20.3%				
0.0%	0.0%	20.3%			
5.7%	5.7%				
0.0%	0.0%				
6.8%		12.9%			
0.0%	6.8%				
0.0%	0.0%				
4.1%		4.1%	39.5%	1938	1,263,829
−6.5%	−2.7%				

TIMING MODEL (Cont.)
04/08/27 to 12/29/95

— For the Period — Beginning	Ending	Stocks	Bonds	Money Market
02/03/39	03/17/39	0%	0%	100%
03/17/39	04/07/39	100%	0%	0%
04/07/39	04/14/39	100%	0%	0%
04/14/39	04/21/39	0%	0%	100%
04/21/39	07/07/39	100%	0%	0%
07/07/39	08/18/39	100%	0%	0%
08/18/39	09/08/39	0%	0%	100%
09/08/39	10/06/39	100%	0%	0%
10/06/39	01/05/40	100%	0%	0%
01/05/40	01/19/40	100%	0%	0%
01/19/40	01/26/40	0%	0%	100%
01/26/40	04/05/40	100%	0%	0%
04/05/40	04/19/40	100%	0%	0%
04/19/40	07/05/40	0%	0%	100%
07/05/40	10/04/40	0%	0%	100%
10/04/40	01/03/41	0%	0%	100%
01/03/41	04/04/41	0%	0%	100%
04/04/41	07/04/41	0%	0%	100%
07/04/41	10/03/41	0%	0%	100%
10/03/41	01/02/42	0%	0%	100%
01/02/42	04/03/42	0%	0%	100%
04/03/42	07/03/42	0%	0%	100%
07/03/42	08/21/42	0%	0%	100%
08/21/42	10/02/42	100%	0%	0%
10/02/42	01/01/43	100%	0%	0%
01/01/43	04/02/43	100%	0%	0%
04/02/43	06/18/43	100%	0%	0%
06/18/43	07/02/43	0%	0%	100%
07/02/43	08/06/43	100%	0%	0%
08/06/43	08/13/43	0%	0%	100%
08/13/43	10/01/43	100%	0%	0%
10/01/43	01/07/44	100%	0%	0%
01/07/44	03/03/44	100%	0%	0%
03/03/44	04/07/44	0%	0%	100%
04/07/44	07/07/44	0%	0%	100%
07/07/44	10/06/44	0%	0%	100%
10/06/44	01/05/45	0%	0%	100%
01/05/45	04/06/45	100%	0%	0%
04/06/45	04/13/45	0%	0%	100%
04/13/45	07/06/45	100%	0%	0%

Net Change for Period	Net Change Last Exchange	Quarterly Return	Yearly Return	Year	$100,000 Inv. Now Worth
0.0%	0.0%				
−17.8%		−23.1%			
0.9%	−17.1%				
0.0%	0.0%				
2.7%		3.6%			
0.9%	3.6%				
0.0%	0.0%				
7.0%		8.0%			
−2.6%		−2.6%	−17.4%	1939	1,044,150
−5.4%	−1.4%				
0.0%	0.0%				
8.3%		2.5%			
−4.5%	3.4%				
0.0%		−4.5%			
0.0%		0.0%			
0.0%		0.0%	−3.5%	1940	1,007,823
0.0%		0.0%			
0.0%		0.0%			
0.0%		0.0%			
0.0%		0.0%	−1.4%	1941	994,056
0.0%		0.0%			
0.1%		0.1%			
0.0%	0.1%				
7.7%		7.7%			
9.4%		9.4%	16.4%	1942	1,156,741
45.3%		45.3%			
7.7%	84.4%				
0.0%	0.0%	7.7%			
−7.7%	−7.7%				
0.0%	0.0%				
2.2%		−5.7%			
2.7%		2.7%	50.0%	1943	1,734,599
2.8%	7.9%				
0.0%		2.8%			
0.1%		0.1%			
0.1%		0.1%			
0.1%	0.3%	0.1%	2.0%	1944	1,769,294
5.5%	5.5%	5.5%			
0.0%	0.0%				
10.5%		10.5%			

TIMING MODEL (Cont.)
04/08/27 to 12/29/95

— For the Period —		Stocks	Bonds	Money Market
Beginning	Ending			
07/06/45	07/20/45	100%	0%	0%
07/20/45	08/31/45	0%	0%	100%
08/31/45	10/05/45	100%	0%	0%
10/05/45	01/04/46	100%	0%	0%
01/04/46	03/01/46	100%	0%	0%
03/01/46	03/08/46	0%	0%	100%
03/08/46	04/05/46	100%	0%	0%
04/05/46	06/28/46	100%	0%	0%
06/28/46	07/05/46	0%	0%	100%
07/05/46	09/27/46	100%	0%	0%
09/27/46	10/04/46	0%	0%	100%
10/04/46	01/03/47	0%	0%	100%
01/03/47	04/04/47	0%	0%	100%
04/04/47	07/04/47	0%	0%	100%
07/04/47	10/03/47	0%	0%	100%
10/03/47	12/26/47	0%	0%	100%
12/26/47	01/02/48	100%	0%	0%
01/02/48	04/02/48	100%	0%	0%
04/02/48	07/02/48	100%	0%	0%
07/02/48	07/16/48	100%	0%	0%
07/16/48	08/06/48	0%	0%	100%
08/06/48	10/01/48	100%	0%	0%
10/01/48	11/19/48	100%	0%	0%
11/19/48	12/03/48	0%	0%	100%
12/03/48	01/07/49	100%	0%	0%
01/07/49	04/01/49	100%	0%	0%
04/01/49	07/01/49	100%	0%	0%
07/01/49	10/07/49	100%	0%	0%
10/07/49	01/06/50	100%	0%	0%
01/06/50	04/07/50	100%	0%	0%
04/07/50	06/16/50	100%	0%	0%
06/16/50	07/07/50	0%	0%	100%
07/07/50	08/25/50	0%	0%	100%
08/25/50	10/06/50	100%	0%	0%
10/06/50	01/05/51	100%	0%	0%
01/05/51	03/23/51	100%	0%	0%
03/23/51	03/30/51	0%	0%	100%
03/30/51	04/06/51	100%	0%	0%
04/06/51	05/18/51	100%	0%	0%
05/18/51	06/08/51	0%	0%	100%

Net Change for Period	Net Change Last Exchange	Quarterly Return	Yearly Return	Year	$100,000 Inv. Now Worth
−2.5%	7.7%				
0.1%	0.1%				
8.7%		6.1%			
15.5%		15.5%	41.4%	1945	2,501,736
3.1%	29.4%				
0.0%	0.0%				
6.4%		9.7%			
2.7%	9.3%				
0.0%	0.0%	2.7%			
−22.5%	−22.5%				
0.0%		−22.5%			
0.1%		0.1%	−13.5%	1946	2,165,211
0.1%		0.1%			
0.1%		0.1%			
0.1%		0.1%			
0.2%	0.6%				
2.0%		2.2%	1.5%	1947	2,197,233
1.5%		1.5%			
12.1%		12.1%			
−2.8%	12.8%				
0.1%	0.1%				
−4.5%		−7.1%			
−3.3%	−7.7%				
0.0%	0.0%				
2.0%		−1.4%	3.3%	1948	2,268,668
−0.4%		−0.4%			
−7.0%		−7.0%			
15.1%		15.1%			
11.6%		11.6%	17.8%	1949	2,672,732
8.2%		8.2%			
4.0%	36.6%				
0.1%		4.1%			
0.2%	0.3%				
8.0%		8.2%			
11.4%		11.4%	34.6%	1950	3,596,295
3.8%	24.9%				
0.1%	0.1%				
0.8%		4.7%			
−0.4%	0.4%				
0.1%	0.1%				

TIMING MODEL (Cont.)
04/08/27 to 12/29/95

— For the Period —		Stocks	Bonds	Money Market
Beginning	Ending			
06/08/51	07/06/51	100%	0%	0%
07/06/51	10/05/51	100%	0%	0%
10/05/51	10/19/51	100%	0%	0%
10/19/51	11/30/51	0%	0%	100%
11/30/51	01/04/52	100%	0%	0%
01/04/52	02/15/52	100%	0%	0%
02/15/52	04/04/52	0%	0%	100%
04/04/52	07/04/52	0%	0%	100%
07/04/52	10/03/52	0%	0%	100%
10/03/52	01/02/53	0%	0%	100%
01/02/53	04/03/53	0%	0%	100%
04/03/53	07/03/53	0%	0%	100%
07/03/53	10/02/53	100%	0%	0%
10/02/53	01/01/54	100%	0%	0%
01/01/54	04/02/54	100%	0%	0%
04/02/54	07/02/54	100%	0%	0%
07/02/54	10/01/54	100%	0%	0%
10/01/54	10/15/54	100%	0%	0%
10/15/54	10/29/54	0%	0%	100%
10/29/54	01/07/55	100%	0%	0%
01/07/55	04/01/55	100%	0%	0%
04/01/55	05/13/55	100%	0%	0%
05/13/55	05/27/55	0%	0%	100%
05/27/55	07/01/55	100%	0%	0%
07/01/55	10/07/55	100%	0%	0%
10/07/55	01/06/56	0%	0%	100%
01/06/56	03/09/56	0%	0%	100%
03/09/56	04/06/56	100%	0%	0%
04/06/56	05/11/56	100%	0%	0%
05/11/56	07/06/56	0%	0%	100%
07/06/56	08/24/56	100%	0%	0%
08/24/56	10/05/56	0%	0%	100%
10/05/56	11/23/56	100%	0%	0%
11/23/56	01/04/57	0%	0%	100%
01/04/57	04/05/57	0%	0%	100%
04/05/57	06/21/57	100%	0%	0%
06/21/57	07/05/57	0%	0%	100%
07/05/57	10/04/57	0%	0%	100%
10/04/57	12/27/57	0%	0%	100%
12/27/57	01/03/58	100%	0%	0%

Net Change for Period	Net Change Last Exchange	Quarterly Return	Yearly Return	Year	$100,000 Inv. Now Worth
−1.4%		−1.7%			
12.6%		12.6%			
−2.0%	8.8%				
0.3%	0.3%				
2.4%		0.7%	15.7%	1951	4,160,002
0.2%	2.6%				
0.2%		0.4%			
0.4%		0.4%			
0.5%		0.5%			
0.4%		0.4%	0.8%	1952	4,194,872
0.5%		0.5%			
0.5%	2.5%	0.5%			
−4.4%		−4.4%			
3.4%		3.4%	−1.0%	1953	4,152,218
12.6%		12.6%			
8.3%		8.3%			
8.9%		8.9%			
−1.0%	30.0%				
0.1%	0.1%				
16.5%		15.5%	52.1%	1954	6,314,552
8.8%		8.8%			
0.5%	27.4%				
0.1%	0.1%				
3.7%		4.3%			
−2.3%	1.3%	−2.3%			
0.5%		0.5%	10.6%	1955	6,985,493
0.4%	0.9%				
3.9%		4.3%			
−2.4%	1.4%				
0.4%	0.4%	−2.0%			
1.2%	1.2%				
0.3%	0.3%	1.5%			
0.1%	0.1%				
0.4%		0.5%	3.5%	1956	7,230,979
0.7%	1.1%	0.7%			
3.5%	3.5%				
0.2%		3.7%			
0.8%		0.8%			
0.8%	1.8%				
3.8%		4.6%	9.4%	1957	7,907,121

TIMING MODEL (Cont.)
04/08/27 to 12/29/95

— For the Period —				Money
Beginning	Ending	Stocks	Bonds	Market
01/03/58	04/04/58	100%	0%	0%
04/04/58	07/04/58	100%	0%	0%
07/04/58	10/03/58	100%	0%	0%
10/03/58	01/02/59	100%	0%	0%
01/02/59	04/03/59	100%	0%	0%
04/03/59	06/05/59	100%	0%	0%
06/05/59	06/12/59	0%	0%	100%
06/12/59	07/03/59	100%	0%	0%
07/03/59	09/04/59	100%	0%	0%
09/04/59	10/02/59	0%	0%	100%
10/02/59	12/04/59	0%	0%	100%
12/04/59	01/01/60	100%	0%	0%
01/01/60	01/15/60	100%	0%	0%
01/15/60	04/01/60	0%	0%	100%
04/01/60	04/29/60	0%	0%	100%
04/29/60	07/01/60	100%	0%	0%
07/01/60	07/15/60	100%	0%	0%
07/15/60	07/29/60	0%	0%	100%
07/29/60	10/07/60	100%	0%	0%
10/07/60	01/06/61	100%	0%	0%
01/06/61	04/07/61	100%	0%	0%
04/07/61	06/23/61	100%	0%	0%
06/23/61	06/30/61	0%	0%	100%
06/30/61	07/07/61	100%	0%	0%
07/07/61	10/06/61	100%	0%	0%
10/06/61	12/22/61	100%	0%	0%
12/22/61	12/29/61	0%	0%	100%
12/29/61	01/05/62	100%	0%	0%
01/05/62	03/30/62	100%	0%	0%
03/30/62	04/06/62	0%	0%	100%
04/06/62	06/29/62	0%	0%	100%
06/29/62	07/06/62	100%	0%	0%
07/06/62	09/07/62	100%	0%	0%
09/07/62	10/05/62	0%	0%	100%
10/05/62	12/21/62	0%	0%	100%
12/21/62	01/04/63	100%	0%	0%
01/04/63	04/05/63	100%	0%	0%
04/05/63	07/05/63	100%	0%	0%
07/05/63	08/02/63	100%	0%	0%
08/02/63	08/09/63	0%	0%	100%

Net Change for Period	Net Change Last Exchange	Quarterly Return	Yearly Return	Year	$100,000 Inv. Now Worth
7.2%		7.2%			
13.2%		13.2%			
14.4%		14.4%			
12.0%		12.0%	54.5%	1958	12,214,307
8.8%		8.8%			
0.4%	76.3%				
0.0%	0.0%				
3.8%		4.2%			
−1.6%	2.1%				
0.3%		−1.3%			
0.6%	0.9%				
1.6%		2.2%	13.7%	1959	13,891,320
−1.1%	0.5%				
1.0%		−0.1%			
0.2%	1.2%				
4.8%		5.0%			
−0.8%	4.0%				
0.1%	0.1%				
−2.4%		−3.1%			
7.3%		7.3%	8.5%	1960	15,068,546
20.2%		20.2%			
0.6%	26.6%				
0.2%	0.2%				
1.1%		1.9%			
1.0%		1.0%			
2.5%	4.7%				
0.2%	0.2%				
−2.0%		0.7%	23.9%	1961	18,670,792
2.2%	0.2%				
0.0%		2.2%			
0.7%	0.7%				
2.8%		3.5%			
4.6%	7.5%				
0.2%		4.8%			
0.5%	0.7%				
2.9%		3.4%	14.1%	1962	21,306,951
9.2%		9.2%			
4.5%		4.5%			
−2.5%	14.5%				
0.0%	0.0%				

TIMING MODEL (Cont.)
04/08/27 to 12/29/95

— For the Period —		Stocks	Bonds	Money Market
Beginning	**Ending**			
08/09/63	09/27/63	100%	0%	0%
09/27/63	10/04/63	0%	0%	100%
10/04/63	01/03/64	100%	0%	0%
01/03/64	04/03/64	100%	0%	0%
04/03/64	04/24/64	100%	0%	0%
04/24/64	05/01/64	0%	0%	100%
05/01/64	07/03/64	100%	0%	0%
07/03/64	08/07/64	100%	0%	0%
08/07/64	08/28/64	0%	0%	100%
08/28/64	10/02/64	100%	0%	0%
10/02/64	01/01/65	100%	0%	0%
01/01/65	04/02/65	100%	0%	0%
04/02/65	06/04/65	100%	0%	0%
06/04/65	06/11/65	0%	0%	100%
06/11/65	07/02/65	100%	0%	0%
07/02/65	07/30/65	0%	0%	100%
07/30/65	10/01/65	100%	0%	0%
10/01/65	11/26/65	100%	0%	0%
11/26/65	01/07/66	0%	0%	100%
01/07/66	03/18/66	0%	0%	100%
03/18/66	03/25/66	100%	0%	0%
03/25/66	04/01/66	0%	0%	100%
04/01/66	04/29/66	0%	0%	100%
04/29/66	06/03/66	100%	0%	0%
06/03/66	07/01/66	0%	0%	100%
07/01/66	10/07/66	0%	0%	100%
10/07/66	11/04/66	0%	0%	100%
11/04/66	01/06/67	100%	0%	0%
01/06/67	04/07/67	100%	0%	0%
04/07/67	07/07/67	100%	0%	0%
07/07/67	09/01/67	100%	0%	0%
09/01/67	09/15/67	0%	0%	100%
09/15/67	10/06/67	100%	0%	0%
10/06/67	10/20/67	100%	0%	0%
10/20/67	11/24/67	0%	0%	100%
11/24/67	01/05/68	100%	0%	0%
01/05/68	02/02/68	100%	0%	0%
02/02/68	03/22/68	0%	0%	100%
03/22/68	04/05/68	100%	0%	0%
04/05/68	07/05/68	100%	0%	0%

Net Change for Period	Net Change Last Exchange	Quarterly Return	Yearly Return	Year	$100,000 Inv. Now Worth
2.2%	2.2%				
0.0%	0.0%	−0.4%			
0.5%		0.5%	13.8%	1963	24,238,879
8.9%		8.9%			
−1.0%	8.4%				
0.0%	0.0%				
3.1%		2.1%			
0.2%	3.3%				
0.3%	0.3%				
3.2%		3.7%			
1.3%		1.3%	16.3%	1964	28,184,103
8.9%		8.9%			
0.5%	14.4%				
0.0%	0.0%				
−1.3%	−1.3%	−0.8%			
0.3%	0.3%				
7.3%		7.6%			
6.3%	14.1%				
0.3%		6.6%	23.4%	1965	34,789,528
0.7%	1.0%				
1.5%	1.5%				
0.0%		2.2%			
0.3%	0.3%				
−6.9%	−6.9%				
0.4%		−6.2%			
1.2%		1.2%			
0.4%	2.0%				
7.3%		7.7%	4.0%	1966	36,197,443
15.8%		15.8%			
8.6%		8.6%			
4.8%	41.4%				
0.0%	0.0%				
1.5%		6.4%			
−2.7%	−1.2%				
0.8%	0.8%				
6.6%		4.6%	39.3%	1967	50,434,299
−1.1%	5.4%				
0.4%	0.4%				
5.0%		4.3%			
17.3%		17.3%			

Timing Model (Cont.)
04/08/27 to 12/29/95

— For the Period —		Stocks	Bonds	Money Market
Beginning	Ending			
07/05/68	07/26/68	100%	0%	0%
07/26/68	09/13/68	0%	0%	100%
09/13/68	10/04/68	100%	0%	0%
10/04/68	11/01/68	100%	0%	0%
11/01/68	01/03/69	0%	0%	100%
01/03/69	04/04/69	0%	0%	100%
04/04/69	06/20/69	100%	0%	0%
06/20/69	07/04/69	0%	0%	100%
07/04/69	10/03/69	0%	0%	100%
10/03/69	01/02/70	0%	0%	100%
01/02/70	04/03/70	0%	0%	100%
04/03/70	07/03/70	0%	0%	100%
07/03/70	07/10/70	0%	0%	100%
07/10/70	10/02/70	100%	0%	0%
10/02/70	10/23/70	100%	0%	0%
10/23/70	10/30/70	0%	0%	100%
10/30/70	01/01/71	100%	0%	0%
01/01/71	04/02/71	100%	0%	0%
04/02/71	06/11/71	100%	0%	0%
06/11/71	06/18/71	0%	100%	0%
06/18/71	07/02/71	100%	0%	0%
07/02/71	09/24/71	100%	0%	0%
09/24/71	10/01/71	0%	100%	0%
10/01/71	10/29/71	0%	100%	0%
10/29/71	01/07/72	100%	0%	0%
01/07/72	03/31/72	100%	0%	0%
03/31/72	04/07/72	0%	100%	0%
04/07/72	04/21/72	0%	100%	0%
04/21/72	07/07/72	0%	0%	100%
07/07/72	07/21/72	0%	0%	100%
07/21/72	10/06/72	100%	0%	0%
10/06/72	10/13/72	100%	0%	0%
10/13/72	01/05/73	0%	0%	100%
01/05/73	04/06/73	0%	0%	100%
04/06/73	07/06/73	0%	0%	100%
07/06/73	10/05/73	0%	0%	100%
10/05/73	01/04/74	0%	0%	100%
01/04/74	04/05/74	0%	0%	100%
04/05/74	07/05/74	0%	0%	100%
07/05/74	10/04/74	0%	0%	100%

Net Change for Period	Net Change Last Exchange	Quarterly Return	Yearly Return	Year	$100,000 Inv. Now Worth
−3.3%	19.1%				
0.4%	0.4%				
3.7%		0.7%			
0.1%	3.8%				
0.9%		1.0%	23.9%	1968	62,493,537
1.5%	2.4%	1.5%			
−8.4%	−8.4%				
0.5%		−7.9%			
1.7%		1.7%			
1.8%		1.8%	−3.6%	1969	60,236,958
1.8%		1.8%			
1.6%		1.6%			
0.0%	7.6%				
23.7%		23.7%			
−4.1%	18.6%				
0.5%	0.5%				
12.7%		8.6%	38.5%	1970	83,416,203
19.1%		19.1%			
−1.0%	32.9%				
0.0%	0.0%				
0.9%		−0.1%			
−1.2%	−0.3%				
0.0%		−1.2%			
1.7%	1.7%				
11.2%		13.1%	32.5%	1971	110,512,266
5.4%	17.2%				
0.0%		5.4%			
0.0%					
0.9%		0.9%			
0.0%	0.9%				
−1.7%		−1.7%			
−1.2%	−2.9%				
1.1%		−0.1%	4.1%	1972	115,017,231
1.3%		1.3%			
1.5%		1.5%			
2.0%		2.0%			
1.9%		1.9%	6.5%	1973	122,511,141
1.8%		1.8%			
2.1%		2.1%			
2.1%		2.1%			

TIMING MODEL (Cont.)
04/08/27 to 12/29/95

| — For the Period — | | Stocks | Bonds | Money Market |
Beginning	Ending			
10/04/74	11/08/74	0%	0%	100%
11/08/74	12/13/74	0%	100%	0%
12/13/74	01/03/75	100%	0%	0%
01/03/75	04/04/75	100%	0%	0%
04/04/75	07/04/75	100%	0%	0%
07/04/75	08/01/75	100%	0%	0%
08/01/75	08/22/75	0%	100%	0%
08/22/75	09/19/75	0%	0%	100%
09/19/75	10/03/75	100%	0%	0%
10/03/75	01/02/76	100%	0%	0%
01/02/76	04/02/76	100%	0%	0%
04/02/76	04/30/76	100%	0%	0%
04/30/76	05/07/76	0%	100%	0%
05/07/76	07/02/76	100%	0%	0%
07/02/76	08/20/76	100%	0%	0%
08/20/76	08/27/76	0%	75%	25%
08/27/76	10/01/76	100%	0%	0%
10/01/76	01/07/77	100%	0%	0%
01/07/77	02/25/77	100%	0%	0%
02/25/77	03/18/77	0%	50%	50%
03/18/77	04/01/77	100%	0%	0%
04/01/77	05/06/77	100%	0%	0%
05/06/77	07/01/77	0%	50%	50%
07/01/77	10/07/77	0%	50%	50%
10/07/77	11/04/77	0%	50%	50%
11/04/77	01/06/78	0%	0%	100%
01/06/78	03/03/78	0%	0%	100%
03/03/78	04/07/78	100%	0%	0%
04/07/78	06/23/78	100%	0%	0%
06/23/78	07/07/78	0%	0%	100%
07/07/78	08/04/78	0%	0%	100%
08/04/78	09/29/78	100%	0%	0%
09/29/78	10/06/78	0%	0%	100%
10/06/78	11/03/78	0%	0%	100%
11/03/78	01/05/79	100%	0%	0%
01/05/79	03/02/79	100%	0%	0%
03/02/79	03/30/79	0%	0%	100%
03/30/79	04/06/79	100%	0%	0%
04/06/79	05/11/79	100%	0%	0%
05/11/79	06/15/79	0%	0%	100%

Net Change for Period	Net Change Last Exchange	Quarterly Return	Yearly Return	Year	$100,000 Inv. Now Worth
0.5%					
3.0%	18.7%				
6.6%		10.3%	16.7%	1974	142,991,392
29.8%		29.8%			
20.1%		20.1%			
−4.6%	58.5%				
0.0%					
0.5%	0.5%				
−0.9%		−5.0%			
8.8%		8.8%	60.6%	1975	229,702,388
25.8%		25.8%			
−0.9%	34.4%				
0.0%	0.0%				
3.2%		2.3%			
−0.6%	2.6%				
1.7%	1.7%				
3.3%		4.4%			
11.6%		11.6%	49.5%	1976	343,333,406
−1.9%	13.1%				
0.0%	0.0%				
−1.7%		−3.6%			
2.8%	1.1%				
1.9%		4.8%			
1.1%		1.1%			
−0.3%					
1.0%		0.7%	2.5%	1977	351,984,773
1.0%	4.8%				
6.5%		7.6%			
8.9%	16.0%				
0.5%		9.4%			
0.6%	1.1%				
3.2%	3.2%				
0.0%		3.8%			
0.7%	0.7%				
4.7%		5.4%	28.5%	1978	452,169,168
0.0%	4.7%				
0.8%	0.8%				
1.4%		2.2%			
−4.0%	−2.7%				
0.8%	0.8%				

TIMING MODEL (Cont.)
04/08/27 to 12/29/95

| — For the Period — | | | | Money |
Beginning	Ending	Stocks	Bonds	Market
06/15/79	07/06/79	100%	0%	0%
07/06/79	10/05/79	100%	0%	0%
10/05/79	10/12/79	100%	0%	0%
10/12/79	11/09/79	0%	0%	100%
11/09/79	01/04/80	100%	0%	0%
01/04/80	02/22/80	100%	0%	0%
02/22/80	04/04/80	0%	0%	100%
04/04/80	04/25/80	0%	0%	100%
04/25/80	07/04/80	100%	0%	0%
07/04/80	10/03/80	100%	0%	0%
10/03/80	10/31/80	100%	0%	0%
10/31/80	11/14/80	0%	0%	100%
11/14/80	12/12/80	100%	0%	0%
12/12/80	01/02/81	0%	0%	100%
01/02/81	04/03/81	0%	0%	100%
04/03/81	07/03/81	0%	0%	100%
07/03/81	10/02/81	0%	0%	100%
10/02/81	12/25/81	100%	0%	0%
12/25/81	01/01/82	0%	0%	100%
01/01/82	03/05/82	0%	0%	100%
03/05/82	03/12/82	0%	100%	0%
03/12/82	04/02/82	100%	0%	0%
04/02/82	07/02/82	100%	0%	0%
07/02/82	07/09/82	100%	0%	0%
07/09/82	07/16/82	0%	0%	100%
07/16/82	10/01/82	100%	0%	0%
10/01/82	01/07/83	100%	0%	0%
01/07/83	04/01/83	100%	0%	0%
04/01/83	07/01/83	100%	0%	0%
07/01/83	07/15/83	100%	0%	0%
07/15/83	09/09/83	0%	0%	100%
09/09/83	10/07/83	100%	0%	0%
10/07/83	01/06/84	100%	0%	0%
01/06/84	01/27/84	100%	0%	0%
01/27/84	04/06/84	0%	0%	100%
04/06/84	04/13/84	0%	0%	100%
04/13/84	07/06/84	100%	0%	0%
07/06/84	10/05/84	100%	0%	0%
10/05/84	01/04/85	100%	0%	0%
01/04/85	03/15/85	100%	0%	0%

Net Change for Period	Net Change Last Exchange	Quarterly Return	Yearly Return	Year	$100,000 Inv. Now Worth
2.0%		−1.3%			
7.6%		7.6%			
−7.7%	1.3%				
0.9%	0.9%				
10.0%		2.4%	10.9%	1979	501,293,777
4.8%	15.3%				
2.1%		7.0%			
1.3%	3.4%				
18.7%		20.2%			
13.8%		13.8%			
−0.8%	34.0%				
0.0%	0.0%				
−5.3%	−5.3%				
1.3%		−4.8%	38.9%	1980	696,345,334
3.4%		3.4%			
3.6%		3.6%			
3.8%	12.6%	3.8%			
7.3%	7.3%				
0.0%		7.3%	18.9%	1981	828,281,158
1.7%					
0.0%	1.7%				
6.2%		8.0%			
−2.2%		−2.2%			
0.4%	4.3%				
0.0%	0.0%				
13.9%		14.4%			
27.1%		27.1%	53.1%	1982	1,267,784,816
11.7%		11.7%			
15.7%		15.7%			
−2.2%	83.0%				
1.5%	1.5%				
2.1%		1.4%			
1.8%		1.8%	32.9%	1983	1,685,377,099
−1.8%	2.1%				
1.4%		−0.4%			
0.0%	1.4%				
−3.2%		−3.2%			
8.4%		8.4%			
2.8%		2.8%	7.1%	1984	1,804,810,430
11.7%	20.5%				

TIMING MODEL (Cont.)
04/08/27 to 12/29/95

| — For the Period — | | | | Money |
Beginning	Ending	Stocks	Bonds	Market
03/15/85	04/05/85	0%	100%	0%
04/05/85	04/26/85	0%	100%	0%
04/26/85	07/05/85	100%	0%	0%
07/05/85	08/09/85	100%	0%	0%
08/09/85	09/27/85	0%	100%	0%
09/27/85	10/04/85	100%	0%	0%
10/04/85	01/03/86	100%	0%	0%
01/03/86	04/04/86	100%	0%	0%
04/04/86	07/04/86	100%	0%	0%
07/04/86	10/03/86	100%	0%	0%
10/03/86	10/10/86	0%	100%	0%
10/10/86	12/19/86	100%	0%	0%
12/19/86	12/26/86	0%	100%	0%
12/26/86	01/02/87	100%	0%	0%
01/02/87	04/03/87	100%	0%	0%
04/03/87	04/17/87	100%	0%	0%
04/17/87	06/05/87	0%	0%	100%
06/05/87	07/03/87	100%	0%	0%
07/03/87	08/28/87	100%	0%	0%
08/28/87	10/02/87	0%	0%	100%
10/02/87	12/04/87	0%	0%	100%
12/04/87	12/11/87	0%	100%	0%
12/11/87	01/01/88	100%	0%	0%
01/01/88	04/01/88	100%	0%	0%
04/01/88	05/13/88	100%	0%	0%
05/13/88	06/03/88	0%	0%	100%
06/03/88	07/01/88	100%	0%	0%
07/01/88	08/19/88	100%	0%	0%
08/19/88	08/26/88	0%	0%	100%
08/26/88	10/07/88	100%	0%	0%
10/07/88	01/06/89	100%	0%	0%
01/06/89	04/07/89	100%	0%	0%
04/07/89	07/07/89	100%	0%	0%
07/07/89	09/15/89	100%	0%	0%
09/15/89	09/29/89	0%	75%	25%
09/29/89	10/06/89	100%	0%	0%
10/06/89	01/05/90	100%	0%	0%
01/05/90	04/06/90	100%	0%	0%
04/06/90	07/06/90	100%	0%	0%
07/06/90	07/27/90	100%	0%	0%

Net Change for Period	Net Change Last Exchange	Quarterly Return	Yearly Return	Year	$100,000 Inv. Now Worth
3.1%		15.2%			
2.4%	5.6%				
7.3%		9.9%			
0.1%	7.4%				
2.4%	2.4%				
0.8%		3.3%			
14.7%		14.7%	49.5%	1985	2,698,303,995
12.8%		12.8%			
6.1%		6.1%			
−4.3%	32.4%	−4.3%			
0.0%	0.0%				
3.4%	3.4%				
−0.2%	−0.2%				
0.6%		3.8%	18.5%	1986	3,198,658,645
19.7%		19.7%			
−3.2%	16.6%				
0.8%	0.8%				
2.9%		0.4%			
6.2%	9.3%				
0.4%		6.6%			
1.0%					
0.0%	1.4%				
6.3%		7.4%	37.2%	1987	4,387,517,262
16.3%		16.3%			
−0.1%	23.5%				
0.5%	0.5%				
4.3%		4.7%			
−2.8%	1.4%				
0.6%	0.6%				
4.5%		2.2%			
1.7%		1.7%	26.2%	1988	5,536,171,617
7.0%		7.0%			
9.1%		9.1%			
4.7%	29.9%				
0.3%	0.3%				
1.1%		6.2%			
−2.4%		−2.4%	20.6%	1989	6,676,683,901
−3.8%		−3.8%			
3.4%		3.4%			
−1.2%	−3.0%				

·

TIMING MODEL (Cont.)
04/08/27 to 12/29/95

— For the Period —		Stocks	Bonds	Money Market
Beginning	Ending			
07/27/90	10/05/90	0%	0%	100%
10/05/90	10/12/90	0%	0%	100%
10/12/90	01/04/91	100%	0%	0%
01/04/91	01/11/91	100%	0%	0%
01/11/91	01/18/91	0%	100%	0%
01/18/91	04/05/91	100%	0%	0%
04/05/91	06/28/91	100%	0%	0%
06/28/91	07/05/91	0%	75%	25%
07/05/91	10/04/91	100%	0%	0%
10/04/91	11/22/91	100%	0%	0%
11/22/91	11/29/91	0%	75%	25%
11/29/91	01/03/92	100%	0%	0%
01/03/92	04/03/92	100%	0%	0%
04/03/92	04/10/92	0%	75%	25%
04/10/92	07/03/92	100%	0%	0%
07/03/92	10/02/92	100%	0%	0%
10/02/92	01/01/93	100%	0%	0%
01/01/93	03/05/93	100%	0%	0%
03/05/93	03/19/93	0%	100%	0%
03/19/93	04/02/93	100%	0%	0%
04/02/93	07/02/93	100%	0%	0%
07/02/93	09/24/93	100%	0%	0%
09/24/93	10/01/93	0%	75%	25%
10/01/93	12/03/93	0%	75%	25%
12/03/93	12/10/93	0%	25%	75%
12/10/93	01/07/94	100%	0%	0%
01/07/94	02/04/94	100%	0%	0%
02/04/94	02/25/94	0%	25%	75%
02/25/94	04/01/94	0%	0%	100%
04/01/94	07/01/94	0%	0%	100%
07/01/94	10/07/94	0%	0%	100%
10/07/94	12/16/94	0%	0%	100%
12/16/94	01/06/95	100%	0%	0%
01/06/95	04/07/95	100%	0%	0%
04/07/95	07/07/95	100%	0%	0%
07/07/95	10/06/95	100%	0%	0%
10/06/95	11/03/95	100%	0%	0%
11/03/95	12/01/95	0%	50%	50%
12/01/95	12/29/95	100%	0%	0%

An illustration using NYSE as stock fund, GBTP as bond fund,
BILL as money market fund, and SPTR as market index, and after all fees.

Net Change for Period	Net Change Last Exchange	Quarterly Return	Yearly Return	Year	$100,000 Inv. Now Worth
1.3%		0.1%			
0.0%	1.3%				
10.1%		10.1%	9.3%	1990	7,296,328,706
−2.1%	7.8%				
0.0%	0.0%				
31.1%		28.3%			
1.2%	32.7%				
0.0%	0.0%	1.2%			
6.6%		6.6%			
−0.4%	6.2%				
0.7%	0.7%				
10.5%		10.8%	53.0%	1991	11,162,811,862
7.2%	18.5%	7.2%			
0.0%	0.0%				
1.6%		1.6%			
2.2%		2.2%			
11.4%		11.4%	23.6%	1992	13,800,459,265
7.8%	24.7%				
0.0%	0.0%				
−0.5%		7.3%			
4.3%		4.3%			
5.1%	9.1%				
0.0%		5.1%			
−1.1%					
0.0%	−1.1%				
3.1%		2.0%	19.5%	1993	16,495,784,457
1.8%	5.0%				
−1.0%					
0.3%		1.1%			
0.9%		0.9%			
1.1%		1.1%			
0.7%	2.0%				
2.1%		2.8%	5.7%	1994	17,436,130,072
7.6%		7.6%			
10.9%		10.9%			
4.5%		4.5%			
−0.5%	26.7%				
1.3%	1.3%				
2.6%	2.6%	3.4%	28.7%	1995	22,434,271,785

Legend: NYSE = NYSE Total Return Index GBTP = Ltd Gvt Bds BILL = U.S. Treasury Bills
SPTR = S&P 500 Total Return Index

PERFORMANCE SUMMARY

	Compounded Annual Return	Net Annual Return	$100,000 Inv. Now Worth	Volatility 'Beta'	Risk Adjusted Superiority Index 'Alpha'
MANAGED (NYSE)	20.5%	19.6%	22,434,271,785	0.462	12.758
Buy and Hold (NYSE)		13.2%	510,507,500	1.115	1.918
Buy and Hold (SPTR)		10.5%	95,245,929	1.000	0.000
Buy and Hold (60% NYSE/40% BILL)		9.9%	65,293,369	0.670	1.64

	Net Returns for Past			STD Deviation	Sharpe Ratio
	1 Yr	5 Yrs	10 Yrs		
MANAGED (NYSE)	30.2%	23.9%	22.1%	14.14%	1.12
Buy and Hold (NYSE)	31.9%	26.4%	17.8%	21.80%	0.44
Buy and Hold (SPTR)	37.8%	16.7%	15.0%	17.78%	0.38
Buy and Hold (60% NYSE/40% BILL)	21.5%	19.5%	14.2%	13.08%	0.67

	R2 Coefficient	Average # of Exchanges/Yr	High/Low	Percentage of Time In Stock
MANAGED (NYSE)	0.337	3.288	9/1	59.967%
Buy and Hold (NYSE)	0.827	0.000	N/A	100.000%
Buy and Hold (SPTR)	0.999	0.000	N/A	100.000%
Buy and Hold (60% NYSE/40% BILL)	0.829	0.000	N/A	100.000%

	Avg Length of Time in Stock (wks)	High/Low
MANAGED (NYSE)	19.907	80/1
Buy and Hold (NYSE)	N/A	N/A
Buy and Hold (SPTR)	N/A	N/A
Buy and Hold (60% NYSE/40% BILL)	N/A	N/A

Trade Statistics	# Stock Trades	%	Total Return On Stock Trades	Ave Return Per Stock Trade	Ratio Of Ave Win % to Ave Loss %
Winning Trades	89	81.7%	1537.6%	17.28%	
Losing Trades	20	18.3%	−115.2%	−5.76%	
Total Trades	109	100.0%			3.00:1

	# Bond/MM Trades	%	Total Return On Bond/MM Trades	Ave Return Per Bond/MM Trade	Ratio of Ave Win % To Ave Loss %
Winning Trades	107	98.2%	110.3%	1.03%	
Losing Trades	2	1.8%	−1.3%	−0.65%	
Total Trades	109	100.0%			1.58:1

See Appendix B for Disclosure Statement

Chart 4-4 Courtesy of SIMCO

> **"It has become popular, especially in academic circles, to believe that no one can consistently outperform the averages. Nothing could be farther from the truth."**
>
> — *Norman G. Fosback*
> **Market Logic**

> **"It's ironic that people question market timing, but accept stock picking. If you believe that someone can pick stocks and beat the market, why can't they time the market? In the long run, it's easier to time the market than to pick stocks!"**
>
> — *Marty Zweig, PhD.*

In a September 1994 interview in *Investment Advisor,* Zweig summed up his investment approach this way, "I'm not a stock picker... Rather my focus is determining how much exposure one should have in the markets...We're paid to protect capital in down markets. So, if we under perform in up markets, I would hope that the bulk of our clientele would be satisfied with that. Obviously, there's some who wouldn't be. I'm not saying I'm trying to lag the markets during bullish periods. In fact, sometimes we're fully invested and there have been up markets that we've beaten.

Based on models I've developed and tested over the years, I determine how much risk is in the stock market. The more risk I see, the more the fund moves into cash. We can be 100 percent invested in stocks or 100 percent in cash or any mix in between."

Zweig went on to discuss the coming market environment. "That said, we're in a decade in which the defensive style of investing— which is what I favor—will be more valuable. After all, who needs a defensive manager if it's an '80s type environment and markets are going up, up, up? But if we have a severe bear market or several modest bear markets in the years ahead, the defensive style we practice will become more valuable.

Market timing works for me, although I realize a lot of people question it. If you want to be fully invested all the time because you think, in the long run, you can make more money...fine, go ahead. To do that, you've got to be willing to take the pain of living through severe bear markets. I can't because I can't tolerate losing money."

Zweig hit it right on the head. I couldn't have said it any better myself.

CLOSET MARKET TIMERS

While Zweig boldly professes to be a market timer, there are a number of well known investment professionals who claim not to be market timers. No matter what they call themselves, I contend that their actions make them out to be 'closet' market timers. Many stock market gurus expound buy and hold strategies but close analysis reveals they practice market timing. Analysis of the actions of legendary investors reveals that their strategies often rely on the basic principles of market timing and that market timing does indeed work.

At one time or another, Warren E. Buffet, Peter Lynch, John C. Bogle, and other investing heroes of the day have urged ordinary investors not to attempt to time the market, stating that timing doesn't work. But do their own investment philosophies match their words?

Not really. Fidelity says buy and hold yet they invented sector funds which encourage timing. A recent Fidelity Brokerage Services, Inc. advertisement proclaims "The right idea at the right time...for 50 years." Yet they say they don't believe in timing.

It is interesting to note that Warren Buffet, often quoted as the ultimate buy and hold investor, decided in 1969 that the market as a whole was overpriced and opted to sell. In his book, *Warren Buffet, The Good Guy of Wall Street*, author Andrew Kilpatrick quotes a letter from Buffet to his partners stating that the investing environment was becoming more negative and frustrating. When Buffet liquidated the Buffet Partnership in 1969 (after ringing up a 29.5 percent annual compounded return versus 7.4 percent for the Dow Jones Industrial Average), Buffet offered to help former partners make "bond" investments.

Buffet's concern about market conditions and his timing in exiting the market kept the partnership from suffering the slow market decline that culminated in the bear market of 1973-74. In the midst of the 1973-74 bear market, Buffet returned to equity investments, stating that there were just too many good bargains to pass up. Unlike buy and hold investors, he had no losses to recoup. His capital was intact due to his excellent sense of timing.

Buffet has acclaimed *The Intelligent Investor* by Benjamin Graham "by far the best book about investing ever written." Included in Graham's classic investment book are such statements describing market timing strategies as:

> **"According to tradition, the sound reason for increasing the percentage in common stocks would be the appearance of the 'bargain price' levels created in a protracted bear market. Conversely, sound procedure would call for reducing the common stock component below 50 percent when, in the judgement of the investor, the market has become dangerously high."**

Malcolm S. Forbes Jr. picked up on Buffet's timing tendencies. Author Kirkpatrick quoted Forbes as saying, "We know Buffet as a value investor but I think he's a market timer, too...We interviewed him (for *Forbes* magazine) in 1969 when he was a virtual unknown and he said the market was too high and that he was selling everything. We said, gosh, he sure called that one right. We interviewed him again in 1974 when the market had declined two-thirds in value in real terms, after inflation. He said it was a time to buy and that he felt like a sex-starved man in a harem."

In Peter Lynch's investment book, *Beating the Market*, check out Peter's Principle #8. It's the only exception to the general rule that owning stocks is better than owning bonds as expressed by Lynch. Principle #8 is provided below.

> **"When yields on long-term government bonds exceed the dividend yield on the S & P 500 by 6 percent or more, sell your stocks and buy bonds."**

Lynch goes on to explain that "I didn't buy bonds for defensive purposes because I was afraid of stocks... I bought them because the yields exceeded the returns one could normally expect to get from stocks." Another piece of timing advice from Lynch is, "Buy shares when the stock price is at or below the earnings line and not when the price line diverges into the danger zone, well above the earnings line."

In his book, Lynch also offered advice that fits well with a seasonal timing strategy. "In the late fall...annual tax selling drives the prices of smaller issues to pathetic lows...you could make a nice living buying stocks from the low list in November and December during the tax-selling period and holding them through January, when prices always seem to rebound."

Timing also played a role in Lynch's strategy with Magellan Fund. "I divided the Magellan portfolio into two parts: the small growth and cyclical stocks and the conservative stocks. When the market heads lower, I sell the conservative stocks and add to the others. When the market picks up, I sell some of the winners from the growth stocks and cyclical stocks and add to the conservative stocks...For brief periods at Magellan, I had 10 percent of the fund invested in utilites. Usually this happened when interest rates were declining and the economy was in a sputter. In other words, I treated the utilities as interest-rate cyclicals and tried to *time* my entrances and my exits accordingly."

Other evidence of Lynch's closet market timer status is his statement in *Worth* magazine that, "On average every two years the market has a 10 percent decline. Every six years: 25 percent."

The following statement is attributed to John C. Bogle in his book, *Bogle on Mutual Funds, New Perspectives for the Intelligent Investor.* Bogle is chairman of the Vanguard Group of Investment Companies.

> **"...there is another approach, one that does not assure success but offers the prospect of extra returns at the margin, perhaps with less exposure to market risk. It is called tactical asset allocation...One type of tactical allocation strategy involves changing the stock/bond ratio based on the relative outlooks for the respective financial markets."**

Bogle hedges his statement by recommending placing severe restrictions on the extent of allocation changes, specifically varying by no more than 15 percentage points on either side. Thus, a portfolio would never have less than 35 percent nor more than 65 percent in stocks.

Even John Templeton, the dean of mutual fund investing and master value hunter, employs market timing. In July 1993 Templeton urged investors to switch more into stocks and trim holdings of bonds. Later that year, Templeton shed his holdings in the Templeton Emerging Market Fund. When asked why he had not yet reinvested the money, Templeton replied," There just didn't seem to be any hurry." In my book, that's market timing.

Paul C. Cabot, one of the founding fathers of the mutual fund industry, rounds out our list of prominent closet market timers. Cabot managed the State Street Investment Trust Fund during the Roaring Twenties, through the Stock Market Crash beginning in 1929, and through World War II. Cabot's fund survived a number of stock market crashes and earned an annual rate in excess of 13 percent from 1929 through 1948.

"As early as February 1928 we felt it wasn't safe to assume that the past four years of good returns would continue. Therefore, we did some selling ahead of time and turned into buyers when stocks became cheap (in the 1930s)," said Cabot.

State Street reduced its investment margin (leverage) in 1928 and 1929 and was 5 percent in cash by December 1929, moving to a 62 percent cash position by 1932. It didn't move back into equities until April 1933.

Cabot continually advised investors to use common sense and stick to fundamentals. He advocated avoiding market timing and using dollar cost averaging in their mutual fund investments. Cabot may have advised against market timing but he practiced it at the most critical time in his career, 1929-1933.

All of these men are considered legendary investors, investors who have proven their ability to outperform the markets. In addition, they approach the market with a level of information, knowledge, and intelligence that few investors can hope to match. Plus, each of them possess a strategy that they follow to determine not only when to buy, but when to sell. After all, buy and hold investing only makes sense when the reason you bought an investment still holds true today. As each of these investors have proved, selling at the right time is as important as buying at the right time.

Donald L. Cassidy, an analyst with Lipper Analytical Services, Inc. and a *cum laude* graduate of the Wharton School of Finance and Commerce at the University of Pennsylvania, covers this point well in his book, *It's Not What Stocks You Buy, It's When You Sell That Counts.* Like Cassidy, my goal is to help investors identify trouble early to cut losses before all that's left is false hope and a devastated portfolio.

> **"It's my belief that every money manager, whether he or she professes to be or not, is a market timer. It's just that some managers' cycles are longer than others. Warren Buffet's cycle may be an extraordinary 20 years while Rich Paul's may be 20 days. Everyone else probably falls somewhere in between."**
>
> — *John K. Sosnowy*

Market timing is a disciplined approach for reducing risk of stock market investing. While the average investor may not be able to use market timing due to the onset of emotional versus rational asset allocation, market timing can work in the hands of a disciplined professional, whether it be a Warren Buffet or a member of SAAFTI that you hire to manage your personal investments. Don't let the confusion over the definition of market timing or the naysayers, who have not been able to figure out how to use it properly, discourage you from evaluating its contributions to achieving solid risk-adjusted returns. You can sit back with a buy and hold strategy and watch the bear market chew up your portfolio or employ market timing to reduce risk and conserve your portfolio assets for investment when the market turns around.

MAJOR POINT SUMMARY

— Asset allocation reduces risk, but some asset allocation strategies can reduce return, too!

— Simple passive asset allocation will not save you from financial disaster during a bear market.

— Changing economic realities call for dynamic asset allocation.

— Technology provides the tools to employ market timing.

— Market timing can deliver higher risk-adjusted returns.

— Some market timing models have been tested as far back as 70 years.

— The coming bear market will make believers out of investors.

— Look at the actions, not words, of "closet" market timers.

— I believe that every successful investor is a market timer — it's just that some have longer exchange cycles than others.

— Give market timing a fair assessment, it could mean your financial future.

"Market timing is often oversold as a panacea that solves all investor problems. It isn't, but it helps to solve the problem of market volatility better than any other system I know..."

— *Paul Merriman*
Investing for a Lifetime

CHAPTER 5
Market Timing Does Not Have to be Perfect

BEATING THE BEAR

A recent University of Michigan study on the effect of daily and monthly market swings on a portfolio's performance came up with an interesting statistic on market timing. Based on monthly data..."the perfect timer would have turned a $1 investment in January 1926 into $690 million in December 1993. In comparison, a $1 investment in the market index would have grown to $637.30 while $1 invested in Treasury bills would have grown to $9.20."

Why the dramatic difference in portfolio returns? It comes down to the mathematics of gains and losses. It is far easier to lose money in the markets than it is to make money. In order to make up a 25 percent loss, it takes a 33 percent gain. Likewise, a 50 percent loss requires a 100 percent gain to get back to breakeven.

The University of Michigan study also looked at the impact of missing the best and worst months of the market between January 1926 and 1993. It comes as no surprise that the study concluded that missing the best months of the market dramatically reduced investment returns. On the other hand, missing the worst months delivered dramatically improved portfolio returns. Missing both the worst and best months resulted in returns outperforming a buy and hold investment strategy. This is extremely important because arguments against market timing typically focus on the impact of missing the best periods of the market while overlooking the results of missing both the best and worst periods.

It is true that some of the market's best performance comes on the heels of a down market. For example, the highest monthly return for large company stocks over the past twenty-five years occurred in 1974, after seven consecutive down months. The S & P 500 surged 16.57 percent over a one month period before turning around and dropping for another two months. Market timing critics claimed that market timing would have missed that large gain. The real point is would it have really mattered if the market timing strategy also resulted in missing nine months of dropping stock prices?

A close look at the numbers illustrates that investors would have been far better off missing the nine down months and the one up month than employing a buy and hold strategy that participated in both the market's ups and downs. Over that 10-month period in 1974, large company stocks declined 43.72 percent. It would have taken a 78 percent gain to recoup the capital lost during the negative nine months, far outweighing the benefit of participating in the best month (+16.57 percent) for large company stocks over the twenty-five year period.

One of the most advanced researchers today is Ned Davis of Ned Davis Research, Inc. in Venice, Florida. He calculated that if you had missed the ten best days of the stock market from 1980 to 1989, based on the S & P 500, your return would have declined from 17.6 percent to 12.7 percent. However, if you had missed the ten worst days, your compounded annual return would have increased to 26.6 percent. Missing both the best and worst days, generated a 21.1 percent return, outperforming the buy and hold results by 20 percent. Refer to Chart 5-1.

The most logical result is that you would miss both the worst and best days because the worst days and the best days often occur very close together during very volatile market periods. For example, in

1987 the worst day took place on October 19th with a downside move of 508 points or 22.6 percent. This was followed by the best day on October 21st with an upside rebound of 187 points or 10.1 percent. In all probability, if you missed one, you missed the other.

S&P AVERAGE ANNUAL RETURN (1980-1989): 17.6%

Chart 5-1

The buy-and-hold argument

If you missed the *best*	Your average annual return fell to
10 days	12.7 %
20 days	9.6%
30 days	6.9%
40 days	4.4%

What if you missed the bad days?

If you just managed to miss the *worst*	Your average annual return soared to
10 days	26.6 %
20 days	30.5%
30 days	33.8%
40 days	36.9%

And if you missed both?

If you missed both the *worst* and the *best*	Your average annual return was
10 days	21.1 %
20 days	21.4%
30 days	21.4%
40 days	21.3%

Chart 5-1 Courtesy of Ned Davis Research, Inc.

In order to be a successful risk management investment strategy, market timing does not have to be perfect. Despite belief to the contrary, market timing does not target getting in and out of the market at the absolute bottoms and tops. It does, however, strive to get an investor's funds out of the market before a major bear market devastates the portfolio. Market timing's first and foremost priority is the preservation of capital.

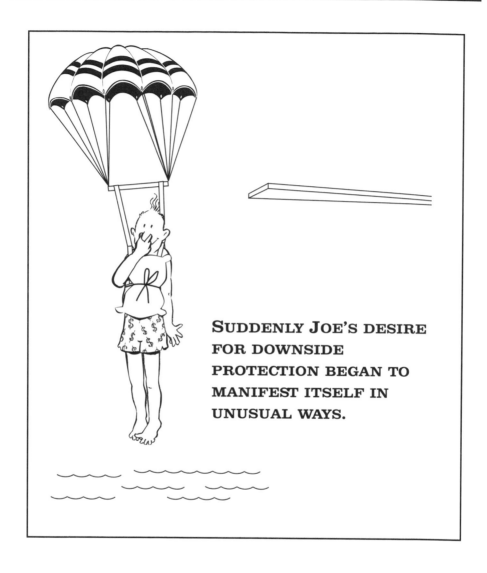

SUDDENLY JOE'S DESIRE FOR DOWNSIDE PROTECTION BEGAN TO MANIFEST ITSELF IN UNUSUAL WAYS.

To be sure, there is no such thing as a perfect market timing (or any other investment) strategy. However, the University of Michigan study dramatically illustrates the value of missing the worst days of the market. With a nearly $689 million margin for error over the 68-year period, market timing does not have to be perfect to produce superior risk-adjusted returns over a full market cycle of both bull and bear market moves.

By exiting the market before the onset of the major portion of the bear market, this strategy conserves capital for those subsequent bull market periods and positions an investor to participate in the bulk of the upside swing with a majority of his or her investment funds intact. As shown in Chart 5-2, this creates the winning combination of lower risk and greater growth.

> **"When times are tough, particularly like in the 1970s, market timing or asset allocation reduces risk and can create a huge (positive) difference in relative performance."**
>
> — *David Rights, President*
> *RTE Asset Management*

LOWER RISK AND GREATER GROWTH

Chart 5-2

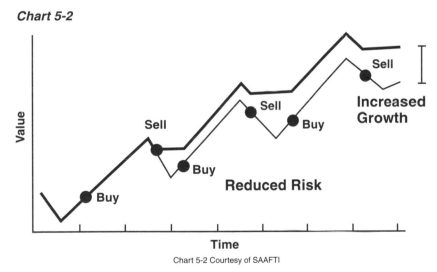

Chart 5-2 Courtesy of SAAFTI

The key is to avoid bear markets that can devastate a portfolio. Market timing has demonstrated its ability to accomplish this goal over the long-term and deliver higher risk-adjusted investment returns.

As you saw in the bear market study, Chart 4-1, in the previous chapter, bear markets represent a permanent part of financial markets and stock market investing. On average, a bear market has reared its ugly head about every five years since 1929. The average duration of a bear market lasts approximately seventeen months. Equally important, it takes an average three and one half years to make up the loss suffered during a bear market.

Some simple calculations point out a major flaw in the buy and hold strategy. Using the above statistics, you can see that an investor can suffer through seventeen months of a down market and take another forty-two months to recover from the bear market loss. That adds up to fifty-seven months, almost in time to participate in the next bear market. Why allow bear markets to eat up your hard earned investment gains and spend the majority of your time recouping losses suffered during a bear market? It simply does not make good economic sense. Yet that is exactly what buy and hold proponents suggest you do.

AVOIDING CATASTROPHE

Ironically, some critics have used the University of Michigan study to attack market timing. It is interesting to note that many of those deriding market timing are investment management firms managing equity, bond, and balanced portfolios with a definite interest in keeping investors in the market.

In response to articles critical of market timing in the wake of the University of Michigan study, SAAFTI analyzed three simplistic market timing strategies developed by Dan Traub of Tandem Financial Services, Inc. Traub studied a 21 1/2 year period and identified when the strategies missed the best and worst days, and then compared the results with a S & P 500 buy and hold strategy. Refer to Chart 5-3 for the results of this analysis.

As you can see, all three of the market timing strategies outperformed the S & P 500 buy and hold strategy despite not doing very well at participating in the best weeks of the market. This is because all three market timing strategies missed the majority of the fifteen worst weeks of the market, thus avoiding catastrophe.

Please note the 'Maximum Drawdown' percentage in Chart 5-3 for each of the market timing strategies as compared to that for a buy

THREE MARKET TIMING STRATEGIES

Chart 5-3

	S&P 500 Buy & Hold	Fundamental Strategy	Over-Extended	Trend-Following
Missing the best weeks				
No. missed of the BEST 5	0	2	4	4
No. missed of the BEST 10	0	4	7	7
No. missed of the BEST 15	0	5	9	10
Missing the worst weeks				
No. missed of the WORST 5	0	4	4	5
No. missed of the WORST 10	0	7	8	8
No. missed of the WORST 15	0	11	11	10
Compound Average				
Annual Return	6.8%	9.8%	9.6%	7.4%
Total Return	335.2%	716.8%	686.9%	397.0%
% of Time Invested	100.0%	56.3%	68.8%	67.9%
Maximum Drawdown	47.0%	18.0%	14.0%	11.0%
Total Number of Complete Buy/Sell Transactions Over 21.5 Years	0	22	15	10

Chart 5-3 Courtesy of Tandem Financial Services, Inc.

and hold strategy. I have found that drawdown is probably the easiest measure of risk for the average investor to understand. Maximum drawdown is simply the largest overall downtrend in your account value that has occurred over a defined period of time. In this study, the three market timing strategies have maximum drawdowns from 62 percent to 77 percent **less** than the drawdown for the buy and hold strategy. In other words, not only was the return for buy and hold less, but you also had to suffer through a 47 percent portfolio loss without bailing out of stocks to achieve that 6.8 percent per year return. With the three timing strategies, the substantially lower drawdowns make it easier to stick with your commitment to stocks, and as a result, you ended up with higher returns, too!

The power of the bear to decimate investment portfolios is clearly illustrated from historical examples. Chart 5-4 shows the impact of the two worst bear market declines of the 20th Century, using the New York Stock Exchange Total Return Index (NYSE) as the basis for a buy and hold strategy.

PORTFOLIO PERFORMANCE

Chart 5-4

Year	Buy and Hold Stocks (NYSE)
1929	-33.2%
1930	-34.3%
1931	-47.9%
1973	-26.9%
1974	-28.7%

Chart 5-4 Courtesy of SIMCO

You may be thinking, "That happened a long time ago. It's different now and it won't happen again." Keep that thought in mind as you look at Chart 5-5 and see the devastation that took place in the Japanese stock market in the early nineties.

The $42,560 ($68,854 - $26,294) drawdown from the high at the end of 1989 to late 1992 represents a 62 percent overall decline. If this was your account, the loss would push you backward approximately six years to 1985. As a result, your compounded return declined substantially from a high near 21 percent to less than 8 percent. Can this happen again and can it happen to the United States stock markets? You bet it can. You had better be prepared with appropriate risk management investment strategies like market timing.

As you can see, losses can deliver a double whammy: they eat up your capital and they eat up the time you have to earn investment gains and build your financial nest egg. Chart 5-6 illustrates the amount of gains needed to recover from various stock market declines.

TOKYO STOCK EXCHANGE INDEX

Chart 5-5

Year	Total Return*	Account Value	Compound Return
11/12/79		$10,000	
1979	0.47%	$10,047	3.67%
1980	8.98%	$10,949	8.36%
1981	16.88%	$12,797	12.28%
1982	5.68%	$13,524	10.13%
1983	24.77%	$16,874	13.51%
1984	25.83%	$21,233	15.81%
1985	15.81%	$24,590	15.81%
1986	49.15%	$36,676	19.99%
1987	11.48%	$40,886	18.91%
1988	37.08%	$56,047	20.78%
1989 Hi Pt	**22.85%**	**$68,854 Hi Pt**	**20.98% Hi Pt**
1990	-39.34%	$41,767	13.71%
1991	-0.48%	$41,566	12.46%
8/19/92	-36.26%	**$26,294 Low Pt**	**7.93% Low Pt**
1992	-22.86%	$32,064	9.38%
1993	+10.86%	$35,546	9.48%

*Total Return information obtained from Chase Global Data and Research
Chart 5-5 Courtesy of SIMCO

MATHEMATICS OF DECLINES AND ADVANCES

Chart 5-6

Decline Amount	Advance Required to Breakeven
25%	33%
33%	50%
50%	100%
75%	300%
90%	900%

Chart 5-6 Courtesy of SIMCO

None of us has an infinite amount of time for our money to be working toward our investment goals. The larger the loss, the longer the time eaten up unproductively just recouping your capital. Remember, it took twenty-five years for the S&P 500 Index to recover from its 1929-32 loss.

Just one bear market could deliver a substantial negative blow to your investment returns. Look at the hypothetical results of suffering through a mild and a major bear market as illustrated in Chart 5-7. Just one bad year can cut a gain of nearly $160,000 almost in half while a major bear market could slash investment earnings by nearly three quarters to $41,476. Could you afford to have your financial nest egg shrink by those amounts, especially if you are approaching retirement?

THE TOLL OF EXPERIENCING ONE BEAR MARKET

Chart 5-7

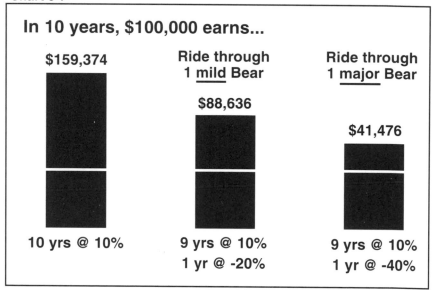

Chart 5-7 Adaptation of a chart by InvesTech Research

Consider the following. Assume you start with an investment of $100,000 and earn 10 percent each year for three consecutive years, and then lost 10 percent in the fourth year, what investment return would you have to achieve in order to have a 10 percent per year compounded annual return over the five year period? See Chart 5-8.

RISK PROTECTION IMPORTANCE

Chart 5-8

Year	Return	$100,000 Now Worth
1	+10%	$110,000
2	+10%	$121,000
3	+10%	$133,100
4	-10%	$119.790
5	?	$161,051

Chart 5-8 Courtesy of SIMCO

You may be surprised to discover that you will need to earn a whopping return of 34.4 percent in year five to regain your 10 percent annual compounded annual return. The major point of these examples is to drill home the crucial fact that risk protection is much more important than capturing the last dollar of return by staying in the market.

All of this clearly shows why risk management market timing is the key to financial performance. The mathematics of investing tells us that losses cost more than gains help us. That's why careful risk management plays such an important role in prudent investment management.

"In a black-and-white, two choices only world, I'd be classified as a market timer...My results, I believe, come not because I've invented some market timing system that lets me call tops and bottoms but because my system lets me control risk by increasing the cash portion of my portfolio when I think the market has become too dicey."

— *James B. Stack*
Worth, *October 1994*

As stated earlier, the goal of market timing rests in capturing 80 percent of the bull market move and avoiding 80 percent of the bear market debacle. While market timing may trail buy and hold strategies during sustained bull market periods such as experienced recently, the day of reckoning is coming when the bear's return will devastate buy and hold portfolios. Market timing clients benefit from a lower risk posture, attractive risk-adjusted investment returns, and far superior portfolio returns (in comparison to buy and hold strategies) during bear markets.

A study by Caldwell & Orkin found that missing the worst days even during a prolonged bull market can deliver substantially higher returns for investors. According to the study, a fully invested strategy from January 1983 through November 1994 would have provided investors with an average annual return of 15.3 percent. In comparison, a market timing strategy that successfully avoided the ten worst days in the market would have returned an average 25.9 percent per year. The return comparisons are even more dramatic if the market timing strategy proved adept at missing the twenty (30.6 percent) and forty (38.9 percent) worst days in the market.

MARKET TIMING DOES NOT HAVE TO BE PERFECT

The perfect market timing strategy would capture all of the market advances and avoid all of the market declines. Obviously, no investment manager and no investment strategy is perfect. Using some hypothetical examples to illustrate the point, imperfect market timing systems can safeguard your portfolio from devastating losses and deliver superior long-term investment returns, especially on a risk-adjusted basis. Chart 5-9 assumes each strategy starting with an original investment of $100,000.

The perfect market timing system would have grown the $100,000 investment to $286,000 versus a market return valuation of $120,806. My goal is to time the market to allow my clients to miss 80 percent of the market declines and participate in 80 percent of the market advances. If successful, this strategy would deliver a portfolio value of $207,791 compared with only $120,806 for the buy and hold strategy. Even if accurate only 50 percent of the time, market timing would still outperform a buy and hold strategy with a portfolio value of $122,585 versus $120,806. Only when the accuracy of market tim-

PORTFOLIO PERFORMANCE COMPARISONS

Chart 5-9

Market Return Example	Perfect!	Avoid 80% Of Losses Get 80% Of Gains	Avoid 60% Of Losses Get 60% Of Gains	Avoid 50% Of Losses Get 50% Of Gains	Avoid 40% Of Losses Get 40% Of Gains	Avoid 20% Of Losses Get 20% Of Gains	Avoid 0% Of Losses Get 0% Of Gains
+10%	+10%	+8.0%	+6.0%	+5.0%	+4.0%	+2.0%	0%
-20%	0	-4.0%	-8.0%	-10.0%	-12.0%	-16.0%	-20%
+30%	+30%	+24.0%	+18.0%	+15.0%	+12.0%	+6.0%	0%
-12%	0	-2.4%	-4.8%	-6.0%	-7.2%	-9.6%	-12%
+100%	+100%	+80.0%	+60.0%	+50.0%	+40.0%	+20.0%	0
-40%	0	-8.0%	-16.0%	-20.0%	-24.0%	-32.0%	-40%
$120,806	$286,000	$207,791	$147,236	$122,585	$101,210	$66,995	$42,240

Chart 5-9 Courtesy of SIMCO

ing falls below 50 percent does the market outperform market timing. If your investment advisor is right less than half of the time, it's time to seek out another advisor, no matter what approach he or she uses. Over the years, I have not always achieved that 80/80 goal myself, but when I have not, I have been close enough to believe it is reasonable and within reach of the better professional market timers.

Avoiding the risk management advantages of market timing in the face of a bear market is like jumping out of an airplane with only half a parachute. Wouldn't a whole parachute be smarter? If you are bearish enough to move 50 percent of your portfolio out of the market, wouldn't 100 percent be better? Yes indeed!

While the stock market has historically outperformed other investment categories over the long-term, you can still lose a lot of money in the stock market. Inertia and emotional investment decisions short-circuit many well-intentioned investment plans, resulting in inferior performance and even devastated portfolios. Employing a disciplined risk management strategy such as market timing is one way to avoid incurring large portfolio losses during a bear market and preserving your capital to better participate in the eventual market upturn.

As reported in the June 1995 issue of *Research*, Mark Hulbert, publisher of *The Hulbert Financial Digest*, which ranks the performance of market timing newsletters, stated that, "The real question is how you measure the success of market timing." If you just consider the ability of market timers to deliver superior returns, the answer is: They don't consistently deliver superior returns. "On the other hand, market timers can and do deliver comparative and superior returns with a reduction in investment risk," he continues.

"In my opinion, a market timer delivering a performance that under performs the market by 10 percent with a 40 percent reduction in risk is still a winning combination. If you ask a market timer to beat the market while reducing risk, you are not only likely to be disappointed, you also will overlook some timers who genuinely can add value," says Hulbert.

Market timing tactics in newsletters are one thing but putting the investment strategy to work in the real world takes it to a whole new dimension. That is why Jerry Wagner (president of Flexible Plan Investments, Ltd.), Steve Shellans (editor of *MoniResearch Newsletter* and president of MoniResearch Corporation), and Richard Paul (President of Potomac Fund Management, Inc.) put market timing to the test to determine whether or not it delivered superior risk-adjusted returns. The study was prepared under the auspices of SAAFTI and appeared in the Summer 1992 issue of *The Journal of Portfolio Management* under the title, "Market Timing Works Where it Matters Most...in the Real World."

This study represented the first empirical evidence on market timing applying the measurement tools of modern portfolio theory to the performance of a sample of real world market timers. In other words, the results of market timing investment managers actually implementing timing strategies using no-load mutual funds for their clients.

MoniResearch used the S & P 500 with dividends reinvested as a surrogate for no-load mutual funds during buy signals. Following sell signals, it assumed that investments are made in a medium yielding twenty-five basis points over the ninety-one-day T-bill rate (a proxy for the money fund). The study covered the period from October 1, 1985 through September 30, 1990 and included the results of twenty-five market timers, with an average managed portfolio of $120 million, tracked by MoniResearch. Round-trip market timing transactions averaged three per year with a high of fourteen.

Comparisons were made to a buy and hold investment in the S & P 500 with dividends reinvested and in three-month T-bills. Study results were evaluated according to the returns factors, variability of returns, and risk-adjusted return.

Analysis of month-to-month performance reveals that returns generated by timers show exceptional performance in declining as compared to advancing markets. In declining market months, the average timer outperformed the S & P 500 91 percent of the time while bettering the index only 8 percent of the time in rising markets. Overall, the greater savings during declining months contributed to the average timer slightly outperforming the market averages for the entire period under study.

The average annual compounded return on investment earned by market timers ranged from 13.1 percent to 14.94 percent, depending on whether maximum or minimum fees were charged. That compares with an average annual return of 14.85 percent for the S & P 500, 11.18 percent for long-term U.S. government bonds, and 6.4 percent for T-bills. Individual timer returns on investment ranged from 22.31 percent to a low of 8.71 percent, with minimum fees. Twelve of the twenty-five market timers were able to outperform the market averages. See Chart 5-10.

The relatively close performance of market timers and the market averages brings up the question: Why employ a market timing strategy if the returns are so close? The answer lies in the reduced risk posture of the market timing strategy. While you may have to forgo a minimal amount of return during advancing markets, your downside protection will more than compensate you on a risk-adjusted basis. It is important to note that 92 percent of the timers outperformed the market averages in the October 1987 crash and 96 percent of the timers outperformed the market averages during the declines of January 1990 and August 1990. Only a fool would chose a higher risk alternative among investments offering similar long-term returns. Yet that is exactly what many investors do when they employ a buy and hold strategy.

MARKET TIMER SURVEY

Chart 5-10

Portfolio	Annual ROI	Alpha	Beta	Standard Deviation
S&P	14.85%	0.00%	1.00	5.42%
T-bills	6.40	0.00	0.00	0.00
Long-Term Govt Bds	11.18	3.13	0.20	3.32
60% Stks — 40% Bds	13.29	1.16	0.68	3.89
57% Stks — 43% T-bills	11.07	-0.16	0.57	3.10
Firm 20	21.98%	12.62%	0.35	2.65%
Firm 18	22.31	12.47	0.41	4.46
Firm 14	21.86	11.26	0.50	3.80
Firm 16	18.82	9.34	0.36	3.12
Firm 11	17.33	8.65	0.27	2.79
Firm 5	18.61	8.24	0.47	3.44
Firm 17	18.54	8.19	0.47	3.71
Firm 3	17.27	7.57	0.39	3.38
Firm 19	15.80	7.24	0.26	2.77
Firm 24	16.83	6.62	0.45	3.22
Firm 7	14.70	5.84	0.29	2.82
Firm 4	15.82	5.58	0.45	3.37
Firm 10	16.64	4.66	0.66	4.13
Firm 9	13.37	4.26	0.32	2.96
Firm 21	13.20	3.80	0.36	2.90
Firm 13	12.36	3.33	0.31	2.92
Firm 27	12.92	2.97	0.42	3.28
Firm 22	12.57	2.60	0.42	3.16
Firm 8	10.22	1.21	0.31	3.11
Firm 23	11.39	0.73	0.50	3.92
Firm 26	10.95	-0.08	0.55	3.03
Firm 25	9.00	-0.67	0.39	3.30
Firm 6	13.18	-0.70	0.89	5.01
Firm 15	8.71	-0.98	0.39	2.75
Firm 12	9.14	-1.43	0.49	3.73
Average Timer	14.94	4.93	0.43	3.35

— Minimum Fees (0.5%)

Chart 5-10 Courtesy of SAAFTI

Equally important, you can not determine when the bear market will decimate your portfolio with a buy and hold strategy. If it occurs just prior or during retirement, your financial nest egg could be wiped out, leaving you in dire financial straits during your golden years.

That's where successful risk management investment strategies earn their keep. Reviewing the returns of the market timer sample you will find an average monthly standard deviation of 3.35 with a range of 2.65 to 5.01. That compares favorably with a standard deviation of 5.42 percent for the S & P 500 and a standard deviation of 3.89 percent for a balanced portfolio of 60 percent stocks and 40 percent bonds. Every market timer in the survey achieved a lower standard deviation than that of the S & P 500!

Next, look at the variability of the market timers returns in comparison with the market as a whole. Compared to the S & P 500's beta of 1.00, the timers averaged just 0.43 for the entire five-year study period. This translates to a 57 percent reduction in volatility from the market index and a 37 percent reduction from the balanced portfolio. This lower beta occurred because the average market timer spent approximately 43 percent of the five-year period in relatively riskless T-bills and only 57 percent of the time in the volatile stock market.

Now, using alpha, you can compare portfolio performances on a risk- adjusted basis. Alpha is the average premium achieved over an unmanaged portfolio of T-bills and the S & P 500 adjusted by market risk (as measured by beta). This calculation highlights the value added by market timing strategies. On an alpha basis, the timers compared very well with other types of portfolios. They outperform the alphas of the bond and balanced portfolios.

Overall, market timing results in this study appear superior to those provided by a buy and hold strategy on a variety of measures. More importantly, risk has been substantially reduced. However, as you can see from Chart 5-10 there is considerable variation in the performance of timers. Your challenge then is to find the best timer for your individual situation. I will give you some suggestions to help you in your search in Chapters 6 and 9.

Now that we have set the stage for why you should consider market timing as your risk management investment strategy, Part 2 will build on this foundation and show you how to achieve superior risk-adjusted returns and secure your financial future.

MAJOR POINT SUMMARY

— It is far easier to lose money in the market than to make it.

— Valid market timing comparisons must include missing both the best and the worst periods.

— It takes a larger percentage gain to recoup from a given percentage loss.

— Market timing does not have to be perfect to be valid.

— A 22-year study shows market timing strategies offer lower drawdowns and higher returns.

— Avoiding the catastrophic bear market is crucial to investment success.

— Losses deliver a double whammy: lost capital and lost time.

— Risk-adjusted returns tell the real story of market timing.

PART II

Securing your Financial Future

> "It should be self-evident that investors who frequently change their philosophy or style are losers in general. But it is surprising how many do!"
>
> — *David Hammer*
> Dynamic Asset Allocation

CHAPTER 6
Keys to Investment Success

KEYS TO SUCCESS

After more than twenty-seven years in the investment business, I offer the following keys to investment success in the 21st century. Listing them is the easy part, following them is crucial.

1. Use a Purely Objective System

2. Require Disciplined Implementation

3. Be Patient—Give Your System Time to Work

PERFECTING THE SYSTEM

There is no 'one best way' to time the market. Each market timer develops his or her own proprietary model based on educational and financial background, personal experience, investment convictions, and available computer and database capabilities. While the techniques may differ, the underlying objective remains the same. Market timers seek to deliver competitive returns within a framework of reduced investment risk.

As we discussed in Chapter 3, one manager may move in and out of the market 100 percent while others may make incremental shifts in asset classes as economic and financial market factors change over time. Some market timers place more emphasis on fundamental and/or monetary factors while giving less weight to technical indicators. The reverse may be true for others timing the market. Steve Shellans of MoniResearch Corporation classifies timing strategies into six basic types of models: trend-following, fundamental-forecasting, overextended, cyclical, pattern recognition, and artificial intelligence or expert systems.

Performance results of market timers differ across the board and at various periods of the market cycle. Some timers may be more adept at exiting the market at the onset of a bear market but remain behind the pack in reentering the market when the signals appear right. Along the same lines, different managers use different mixes of asset classes to achieve their investment objectives.

The major point is to find the investment manager whose investment style and strategies match your investment goals. Remember, market timers will likely trail the results of buy and hold investment managers during periods of steadily rising stock prices. However, and this is critical, market timers should produce superior returns on a risk-adjusted basis over the long-term.

Since crunching the numbers represents a big part of creating an efficient trading model, it is not surprising that an informal survey of the most successful members of SAAFTI discovered that a majority possessed engineering or mathematical backgrounds. As an engineer you are taught to work with numbers and come up with logical conclusions based on the numerical results.

My own background and experience follows this trend. I am a member of The MENSA Society and hold a Bachelor of Science in Mathematics and a Master of Science in Industrial Engineering. After graduate school, I worked for Union Carbide Corporation as an engineer. Ironically, my first exposure to investing came with an investment club started by several of us engineers. Little did I know then that I would later launch an investment management business based on a proprietary model and became the founder of SAAFTI.

Of course, that came after I worked for several investment firms and continued my academic study of the stock market.

Early on in my research, I came to one major conclusion that sparked my interest and belief in market timing. I became convinced that approximately 60 percent to 70 percent of why any stock went up or down had to do with the overall direction of the stock market and not what the company's or the industry group's prospects were. That's when I started to develop a market model that led me to what I refer to today as a market timing or tactical asset allocation program, in order to optimize investment results with lower risk.

This was long before people talked much about asset allocation and market timing, and if they did, they didn't use those terms. At the time 'switching' or 'switch timing', as it was called then, was considered a radical investment idea. The go-go markets of the late nineteen sixties and early nineteen seventies found little interest in reducing risk by investors enjoying the benefits of a rising market. Not until the bear markets of 1973 and 1974 did people start to sit up and take notice. The appearance of devastated portfolios validated for me and my clients that the concept had true merit. That was almost a quarter of a century ago and since then my belief in market timing has only been strengthened.

The current run of the bull market and the aging of the baby boomers gave birth to this book. Boomers who employ a strict buy and hold investment strategy are severely putting their retirement nest eggs at risk. Market timing can help baby boomers and others from going bust.

My market timing risk management model is based on a set of proprietary indicators and calculations, which I first originated in 1970. This system employs a combination of fundamental, monetary, and technical indicators. It is a quantitative, fact-based model with trend following safeguards, researched all the way back to 1927. More than a quarter century of results have proven its usefulness in timing the market and safeguarding client financial assets while delivering a superior risk-adjusted return. The results of the Sammy Savvy character in Chapter 1 demonstrate how this model has performed over the years, as does Chart 3-7 in Chapter 3.

You can develop the best model in the world and the best fund selection in the world; but unless the client understands the risk-return relationship, you are beating your head against the wall. In the final analysis, you need to assess whether you made a good return, taking into account the level of risk undertaken. It is paramount that the client understands this concept.

I track three types of indicator groups: fundamental indicators such as price/earnings ratios, dividend yield, and the number of stocks below book value; monetary indicators such as M1, M2, institutional cash postions, and moving averages of fed funds rates; and market psychology or technical indicators (sentiment and momentum) such as advisor sentiment, market breadth, margin activity, specialist action, and insider trading. My psychological indicators carry more weight in the market timing model than do the fundamental or monetary indicators.

To effect movement in and out of the market I typically use a widely diversified, aggressive portfolio of mutual funds and/or variable annuities. As a proxy for the market in my analysis, I use the New York Stock Exchange Total Return Index (NYSE TR). It is very important that the index chosen be a good proxy for the portfolio in order to effectively time the market. If the market timing model is not matched with the proper index, it's a waste of time and, more than likely, results in a waste of investment money.

To recap, the major components of a disciplined risk management investment system combine two subsystems:

1. A market timing model that generates 'Buy' and 'Sell' signals for the broad U.S. stock market.

2. A growth fund selection system that picks the best funds when a 'Buy' signal is generated.

Chart 6-1 illustrates the flow of the market timing model. The relationship with the client works through a limited power of attorney in order to be able to respond in time to market moves. Selection of funds for the portfolio takes into account exchange privileges, liquidity, and low-cost diversification. The portfolio may include a variety of fairly aggressive growth funds and/or tax-deferred annuities.

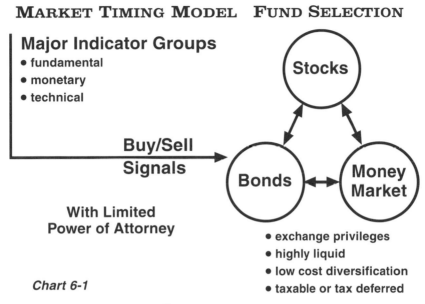

MARKET TIMING MODEL   FUND SELECTION

Major Indicator Groups
- fundamental
- monetary
- technical

Buy/Sell Signals

With Limited Power of Attorney

Stocks

Bonds

Money Market

- exchange privileges
- highly liquid
- low cost diversification
- taxable or tax deferred

Chart 6-1

Chart 6-1 Courtesy of SIMCO

Some investors are of the notion that if you have the choice be-tween no-load and load funds, you should always pick no-load. My advice is to keep an open mind, and to look at fund results net of all costs, expenses, and loads. When you do that, the results may sur-prise you. For example, using a proprietary selection program I developed, I tested the performance of fifty of my favorite stock funds using my timing model during the most recent market cycle that be-gan October 12, 1990.

Out of the fifty funds, eighteen were no-load, seventeen were front load, and fifteen were back load. Of the ten that performed the best (first quartile); three were no-load, two were front load, and five were back load. The bottom line is that no single type of fund organization has a corner on the top managers. Your preconceptions about any type of fund could cost you money. For a precise definition of the types of funds refer to the Glossary.

There's also another point to consider. Since the average holding period for an investor in no-load funds is less than for front or back load funds, it may also be good personal discipline for many investors to use back end load funds, especially considering half of the top ten funds in the above analysis fell into that category anyway. Regardless of which type of fund you prefer, or decide to use, ask for and examine a prospectus carefully before you invest.

As I mentioned earlier, the proprietary econometric model I developed and use in my market timing model includes fundamental, monetary, and technical indicators. A partial listing of indicators and

TIMING MODEL INDICATORS

Chart 6-2

* Adj. Institutional Cash	* Negative Volume Index
* Bond Investment Indicator	* NYSE Total Return Index
* Changes in Reserve Requirements	* NIKKEI Index
* CRB Futures Index	* % Stocks Below Book Value
* Daily Advances and Declines	* Price/Earnings Ratios
* Discount Rate	* Prime Interest Rate
* Dow Dividend Growth	* Producer Price Index
* Dow Dividend Yield	* Put/Call Statistics
* Dow Jones Industrials	* Relative Strength Analysis
* Dow Jones Transports	* Risk/Reward Ratios
* Dow Jones 20 Bond Average	* Short Range Oscillator
* Earnings Growth	* Specialist Shorts
* Exponential Moving Averages	^ Speculative Group Activity
* Federal Funds Yields	* Standard and Poors '500'
* Insider Trading	* S&P Long Term Risk Index
* Margin Debt	* Trading Volume
* Money Market Yields	* Treasury Bond Futures
* Money Supply Figures	* U.S. Dollar
* Mutual Funds and Annuity Prices	* Valuation Indicator

input data is included in Chart 6-2. Ongoing research helps keep the models current in today's rapidly changing markets.

Optimum market forecasting requires not only the use of multiple indicators versus a single "magic" indicator, but also knowledge of the market correlation factor for each indicator as well as the proper weighting of each factor given the time horizon being forecast. Because my econometric model is designed to capture the major

Intermediate Term Forecast
Approximate Weighting of the Major Indicator Groups
Chart 6-3

Momentum 10%
Sentiment 45%
Monetary 25%
Fundamentals 20%

intermediate trends in the market, I have found that the optimal weighting of the four major indicator groups to be as shown in Chart 6-3.

The market timing system must be set down formally or it runs the risk of not being objective and letting emotions take over the investment decision making process. That leads us to discipline.

DISCIPLINE, DISCIPLINE, DISCIPLINE

Mark Hulbert says, "The difference between managers is more *discipline* than methodology." In other words, the very best investment managers never second guess their system, and the most successful clients never second guess their investment manager.

Successful investing requires a disciplined approach that demands that emotions be kept out of the decision making process. You must follow every signal and not second guess the market or your indicators.

Discipline means sticking to your guns. Market timing systems are developed to achieve a variety of purposes and with a variety of different timing features. Therefore, different timing models require different reactions to market and economic indicators based on the model's purposes and the particular market timer's interpretations of those indicators.

You can't worry about what other people are doing, you must stick to your proprietary market timing model after you are thoroughly convinced that it accurately portrays the market and properly signals market changes. You then use that information to change your asset allocation and/or enter or exit the market. Second guessing other market timers can only lead to disaster since you don't know what indicators they are using, the relative weighting of the indicators, and how the market timer uses the information and signals. That's like trying to drive to Washington, D.C. from Cameron, Texas using a map of Europe. While the map may be accurate and useful for someone else, it won't get you where you want to go.

INVESTMENT MANAGEMENT PHILOSOPHIES

With that in mind, it is time to look at the different types of investment managers. Typically, an investment manager will use one of three different investment philosophies which tend to vary primarily in the frequency and degree of changes of investment in different asset classes. The traditional investment manager bases the investment decision on a combination of the client's attributes such as age, financial resources, and acceptable risk posture. He or she would then construct a long-term investment strategy advising, for example, 65 percent of the investor's capital in stocks, 30 percent in bonds, and 5 percent in cash. A periodic review may or may not result in a change of the investment mix. As the investor ages, the portfolio mix may be adjusted to a more conservative stance. This is the strategic or passive asset allocator we discussed in Chapter 3.

On the other extreme, you find the pure or classic market timer. Here, the investment manager changes positions in asset classifications frequently, sometimes on a daily basis. A number of market timers go from 0 percent stocks to 100 percent stocks overnight. It's usually an all or nothing move.

Finally, you get to the risk manager or tactical asset allocator which I consider myself to be. Here, you could be 100 percent in stocks, completely out of stocks, or anywhere in between at any given point in time. The frequency of portfolio adjustments would be far lower than for the pure market timer because we target intermediate-term market moves. By intermediate, I mean moving in or out of a position for six months or a year at a time versus daily or weekly moves made by the purists. My goal is to catch the major upside market moves and to avoid the major downtrends. It's a middle of the road approach. I don't try to catch short-term market moves and don't let investment assets sit for a long time, subject to the ravages of a bear market. Most dynamic asset allocators would also place themselves in this category, but they would typically utilize more different asset classes and move in smaller increments than the tactical allocator.

I did not have any preconceived notion about the optimum length of time to be in or out of the market when I set out to develop my risk management model. I tried all sorts of cycle lengths to determine the optimum approach in generating superior returns within certain risk parameters. A lot of fine tuning has culminated in the market timing model I use successfully today. This model usually triggers around two or three round trips a year, and in many years, I don't even make that many moves.

I believe that overtrading can be as risky as employing a strict buy and hold strategy. Incurring less round trip frequency keeps you from getting whipsawed in the market. Whipsaws cost you return as well as precious time to recover.

Of course, the intermediate-term investment approach impacts which indicators you use and how you weight them. Refer back to Chart 6-3. For example, most short-term market timing models don't use fundamental indicators at all. On the other hand, an economic forecasting model with a five-year time horizon may employ fundamentals comprising as much as 50 percent of the model weighting. In my case, fundamental indicators account for approximately 20 percent of the weighting in my model. I use them to help determine the current value of the market, to measure the degree that the market is fairly valued, undervalued, or overvalued at any given point in time.

After determining value, I look at what can fuel the stock market in terms of monetary indicators. How much money is out there and where it is likely to go. To be sure, the unprecedented inflow of capital into mutual funds in the late nineteen eighties and early nineteen nineties helped fuel the dramatic stock market rise. The question now is "where is it likely to go from here?" That's why I am following and interpreting information on institutional cash positions, level of interest rates, and other monetary indicators.

The final and largest piece of the puzzle lies in the market psychology or technical indicators. Unless something motivates investors to invest their money today in stocks they believe have good value, stocks are not going to rise.

Consider this analogy. The stock market is like the Indianapolis 500. You need a combination of three things to enter the race and win: a solid chassis and engine (fundamental indicators), proper fuel (monetary indicators), and someone to turn on the engine (market psychology indicators). When all three are in sync, it's time to enter the race. If not, caution is in order. If the engine blows up, the car runs out of fuel, or someone shuts down the power, it's time to enter the pits and regroup.

Of course, it's a bit more complicated than I have described, but this gives you the basics. After all, you don't have to know how a car runs internally to take advantage of using it to get where you are going. The same holds true for market timing. You don't have to understand the intricacies of how it works to benefit from superior risk-adjusted returns, gain protection from bear markets, and achieve your investment goals.

"Timing is the key."

> — *J.M. Hurst*
> **The Profit Magic of Stock**
> **Transaction Timing**

RISK CONTROL

The major thrust behind market timing lies in earning superior investment returns, taking into account the level of risk incurred to achieve that profit. Without a doubt, the risk factor is as important as the profitability. Too many investors are concerned about earning a certain level of return without even considering risk. That mindset can only lead to tragedy as evidenced by the savings and loan debacle we discussed in Chapter 2, when investors chased high interest rates in jumbo CDs without looking at the underlying financial stability of the financial institutions issuing the certificates of deposit. The illusion of higher returns melted into significant losses for many investors.

Risk and return go hand in hand, don't ever forget that. The only way you will get a higher return is in compensation for the higher risk level of the investment. That is the premier economic rule that you avoid to the detriment of your financial well-being. This relationship between risk and return, however, does not mean that you avoid investing in higher yielding investments or those offering the possibilities of higher returns. It does mean that you recognize the amount of risk taken, assess the probability of negatively impacting your investment return, and take safeguards to limit that risk.

Too many people are at one extreme or the other in relation to risk. They either take on too much and risk losing their principal or they take too little risk and end up with an investment return that does not keep pace with inflation and the tax bite.

In Chapter 3, under 'Beta Basics', I gave you an overview of the Capital Asset Pricing Model. A review of those concepts is illustrated in the Risk-Adjusted Performance Graph in Chart 6-4.

RISK ADJUSTED PERFORMANCE GRAPH

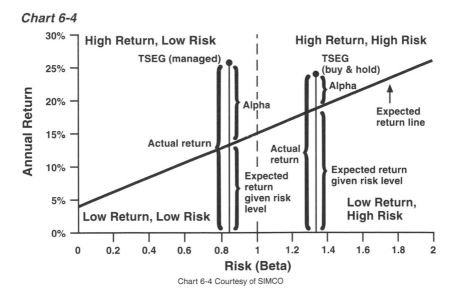

Chart 6-4 Courtesy of SIMCO

This graph is a great tool to show potential investors what a reasonable return would be in the context of acceptable risk parameters. It also points out where their existing investments fit. It gives them a clear picture of how much risk they are taking on for the amount of return received or anticipated. Very often, they are in for a real shock. Without realizing it, investors find themselves in the high risk category with too many of their investment holdings.

Sure, their return looks attractive in absolute numbers; but when compared with other investments on a risk-adjusted basis, it looks far less favorable or even unfavorable. Once investors understand the risk/return relationship and how much risk they are taking on to earn a certain level of return they can begin to make the proper investment decisions relative to their desired risk level. They need to find that balance between too much risk and not enough risk.

I work hard at helping investors discover the proper balance for their financial situations and risk tolerance. It is a very important part of the investment management process. As an individual investor, you must assess your own risk threshold. Using the risk adjusted performance graph in Chart 6-4, you can compare the returns of your investment with the returns of your market index such as the S & P 500 or the New York Stock Exchange Total Return Index.

The x-axis of the graph represents the risk (beta) while the y-axis represents the annual return. The market index used for comparison would have a beta of 1. For a low-return, risk-free investment, you can use the return of a T-bill or a money market fund. Connect the line from the risk-free money market return (4% in this example) through the return of the market index at a beta of 1. That is the expected return line.

Using a least squares regression calculation you can measure the fund's excess return over T-Bills compared with the excess return over the benchmark index, such as the S & P 500. That gives you your beta for the performance of the fund. Next, check out where the return of your fund based on its beta falls in relation to its expected return. If you are successfully managing or timing the fund, you should see a return higher than the expected return but with lower beta or risk than the market index. As you can see, the farther the actual return is above the expected return line, the greater the risk-adjusted return or alpha.

With over twenty years of data on many mutual funds in the computer, I can select all the funds that I follow which fall into the risk parameters set by the client (such as maximum allowable drawdown). Their performance within that group can be calculated using my timing model and then ranked by risk-adjusted return.

There are a number of reasons for using mutual funds versus individual securities to achieve market timing objectives. They help create a diversified portfolio (reducing risk) at reasonable costs, feature professional investment management, and are extremely liquid. And with more mutual funds than stocks on the New York Stock Exchange from which to choose, why would I want to reinvent the wheel? I leave the sector and stock picking to the fund manager and concentrate my efforts on correctly calling the primary trend of the market, which is 60 percent to 70 percent of the ballgame anyway.

Years ago, I was taught the 60-20-20 Rule. It states that 60 percent of the reason why a stock you buy today goes up is simply because the market as a whole is rising and not because you are a great stock picker. Another 20 percent of the reason of why a stock rises is simply because it is in a hot group and not because you are a great stock picker. Only 20 percent of a stock's price rise stems from your stock picking ability. Some experts say that due to the increased influence of tactical asset allocators and sector rotation programs, the rule should be changed to 65-25-10.

Whichever percentages best reflect reality today, the conclusion remains the same: You can put the highest probabilities of success in your favor when you concentrate your energies where they do the most good, i.e. in identifying and putting your portfolio in sync with the primary trend of the market. Even if you are a perfect stock picker or fund picker, you have only put 10 percent to 40 percent of the probabilities of success in your favor. That means your risk exposure, especially to the ravages of a full-fledged bear market, can be way too high for comfort.

"This suggests that investors should spend more time evaluating the overall market...than evaluating the fundamentals of the individual stock (or fund)."

— *Thomas J. Dorsey*
Point and Figure Charting

To put the probabilities in our favor, I employ the following risk control procedures.

1. Not taking market risk much of the time.

2. Employing econometric model signals and stop-loss trigger points.

3. Diversifying portfolios.

PATIENCE, PATIENCE, PATIENCE

Like so many things in life, there is no right way or wrong way to invest all of the time. Investing styles represent a matter of personality and personal risk tolerance and goals. What works for one person may not be appropriate for another. But no matter what investment approach you decide to use, or whether you plan to develop and follow your own set of indicators or hire a professional money manager, one thing remains true. You will need to exercise a great deal of patience. I advise giving your investment approach at least one complete market cycle to work. That usually covers five years at the minimum, ten years would be even better.

"After spending many years in Wall Street and making and losing millions of dollars I want to tell you this: It was never my thinking that made the big money for me. It was always my sitting. Got that? My sitting tight! It is not a trick to all be right on the market. You always find lots of early bulls in bull markets and early bears in bear markets...Men who can both be right and sit tight are uncommon. I found it one of the hardest things to learn. That is

why so many men in Wall Street, who are not at all in the sucker class...nevertheless lose money. The market does not beat them. They beat themselves because though they have brains, they cannot sit tight."

— Jesse Livermore, famous stock speculator
Reminiscences of a Stock Operator

Time is an essential factor in the success of any investment strategy because there is no such thing as an infallible investment. With any investment strategy, including market timing, you are going to have your share of winners and losers. The critical thing is to develop an investment approach based on good, sound reasoning and to allow it enough time to work so that the winners outnumber the losers.

Changing horses in midstream often results in drowning. Likewise, changing course, moving on to a new investment approach, or switching investment managers every time you suffer a loss will extract a heavy toll on your portfolio performance in terms of fees and transaction costs, as well as, lost benefits from the learning curve. Instead of abandoning your investment approach too early, use the time to continually refine and fine tune it.

In order for market timing to outperform the market, you have to experience periods of down markets. It is during these times, when the investor is able to move out of the market in advance of the major decline and move back into the market with his or her capital intact, that timing delivers its greatest reward.

Before you adopt an investment approach or consider changing it, ask yourself the following series of questions:

1. Does the investment approach make sense to you? Do you understand how it should work and believe in the underlying principles (not the intricacies or all the details) of the approach?

2. Are the reasons you first decided to follow the investment approach still valid? While you want to give the approach enough

time to work, do not be blindsided by dramatically changing economic and market conditions which make the premises, upon which your original strategy is based, useless.

3. Do you trust the investment manager's (or your own) ability to implement the program? Has the manager been in business long enough for his approach to be time-tested over a variety of different economic scenarios?

4. What is the worst possible scenario or outcome from the investment approach? Can you live with that outcome?

In the investing world, there's always the temptation to jump to the latest hot trend, the widely hailed hot pick. The problem with this approach is that the 'hot' fund or idea has probably already made its major move. Following the crowd can be much like being one of the last people in a pyramid scheme. Remember the word 'hot' means there's a good likelihood that you can get burned.

Many financial publications and investment subscription services place their emphasis on highlighting last year's winners. That's not where to find next year's winners. It has been proven that last year's top performers are seldom the following year's winners.

Being successful frequently means looking for opportunities away from the maddening crowd and sticking with those investments until the reason you first found them attractive materializes or until it is clear the investment plan is never going to come to fruition. Otherwise, if everything is performing as it was designed, then stay the course.

INVESTMENT PERFORMANCE

Chart 6-5

Year	Return	Ending Value
1	-8.1%	$ 91,941
2	+20.6%	110,842
3	+5.0%	116,385
4	-26.9%	85,129
5	-28.7%	60,677

Chart 6-5 Courtesy of SIMCO

Here's an exercise to see if you possess staying power. Assume you received $100,000 to invest in a growth stock portfolio and you achieved the results in Chart 6-5 for the first five years.

The market is showing a definite downside drift and the world around you appears to have gone to heck in a handbasket over the past five years. From my experience, almost no one would 'hang in there' for the long haul if the first five years were like this. Most investors would 'swear off the stock market' and flee to CDs, bonds, or the money market until they felt comfortable with venturing back into the stock market. That would probably not be until the stock market has gone back up for another five or ten years or even longer. But, if you were that rare investor with a 'cast iron stomach' who opted to stay in the market, you would be a very happy camper indeed!

As shown in Chart 6-6, the market rebounded strongly in year 6, returning in excess of 51 percent and continued upward in an almost uninterrupted fashion over the next twenty years. Unfortunately, the figures in Chart 6-6 are mythical 'buy and hope' performance numbers very seldom realized by the average investor in the real world, because he or she bails out somewhere along the line. Almost all investors jump ship either in years 1, 4, or 5. While the buy and hold ending value of $3.5 million that we first saw in Chart 3-1 looks great on paper, it is virtually useless in real life.

THEORETICAL BUY AND HOPE PERFORMANCE

Chart 6-6

Year	Return	Ending Value
6	51.5%	$ 91,901
7	46.3	134,497
8	5.3	141,581
9	18.2	167,287
10	16.5	194,847
11	32.6	258,278
12	6.3	274,450
13	40.7	386,029
14	32.9	512,950
15	-0.8	508,899
16	36.7	695,709

Year	Return	Ending Value
17	19.3	830,294
18	-2.3	811,224
19	27.0	1,030,140
20	21.7	1,253,505
21	-11.9	1,104,436
22	56.3	1,726,179
23	23.3	2,127,835
24	27.6	2,715,507
25	-0.9	2,691,303
26	30.7	3,516,094

Chart 6-6 Courtesy of SIMCO

If, on the other hand, you had hired a professional market timer during that first five years, and he or she had accomplished the goal of avoiding 80 percent of bear market losses and capturing only 80 percent of bull market gains for you, look at the difference it makes in your results. While the 'buy and hope' investors were losing almost 40 percent of their capital, you were a little better than 6 percent ahead of your original investment and have beaten the buy and hold investor by a mile (+75.3%). See Chart 6-7.

If these were your results for the first five years, you probably would not be ecstatic, but you would probably give the investment a little more time, wouldn't you? If you did, you would be thrilled because, as you saw earlier in Chart 6-6, the stock market was in a bullish trend for the next twenty years.

This kind of market environment is where risk management market timing pays off big. It has historically been proven to smooth out the bumpy equity ride and eliminate the major brunt of bear markets,

INVESTMENT PERFORMANCE

Chart 6-7

Year	Return		Ending Value	
		-1.6%		*$98,400*
1	~~-8.1%~~	*+16.5%*	$ ~~91,941~~	*114,636*
2	~~+20.6%~~	*+4.0%*	~~110,842~~	*119,221*
3	~~+5.0%~~	*-5.4%*	~~116,385~~	*112,783*
4	~~-26.9%~~	*-5.7%*	~~85,129~~	*106,355*
5	~~-28.7%~~		~~60,677~~	

Chart 6-7 Courtesy of SIMCO

allowing the investor to stay committed to equities over the long-term and as a by-product earn superior risk-adjusted returns.

In fact, my timing model would have grown $100,000 to $169,942 during these same five years versus $106,355 for the advisor who accomplished our goal of avoiding 80% of losses and capturing 80% of gains. At the same time, the buy-and-hold investor ended up with only $60,677. As you can see, using forward-looking indicators can help ferret out the investments and market opportunities so you **can** participate in next year's winners.

Market timing is still a relatively new investment phenomenon. As such, it draws its share of detractors. For those who say market timing will never work, let them ponder these other famous prophesies from the past.

"Radio has no future."

"X-rays will prove to be a hoax."

"Heavier-than-air flying machines are impossible."

> — *William Thomson, Lord Kelvin*
> *English scientist (1824-1907)*

"Who the hell wants to hear actors talk?"

> — *Harry M. Warner*
> *Founder, Warner Bros. Studio*
> *(1927)*

"Rail travel at high speeds is not possible because passengers, unable to breathe, would die of asphyxia."

> — *Dionysius Lardner*
> *English scientist (1793-1859)*

"While theoretically and technically television may be feasible, commercially and financially I consider it an impossibility..."

> — *Lee DeForest*
> *American inventor (1873-1961)*

"Quite often, when someone says something won't work, what they really mean is, 'I can't make it work!'"

— John K. Sosnowy
SAAFTI Conference, May 1996

MAJOR POINT SUMMARY

— Investment success requires an objective system.

— Two main components...A timing model and a fund selection system.

— Market timing utilizes objective indicators to generate signals.

— Mutual funds deliver diversification and professional management.

— Mutual funds should be evaluated net of all fees, loads and deferred charges.

— Disciplined implementation of model signals is a must.

— Overtrading is as risky as buy and hold strategies.

— Intermediate-term models make sense.

— A successful model requires various indicators in sync.

— Risk control is paramount.

— Comparison of returns on a risk-adjusted basis is crucial.

— Employing risk control procedures is crucial to investment success.

— Patience is a virtue. Market timing must be evaluated over at least a complete market cycle.

— History often proves naysayers wrong.

— When someone says timing won't work, what they usually mean is, "I can't make it work."

"When the longer term, which has been all but ignored by random walk theorists, is viewed in the light of market forecasting indicators, it becomes clear that the market does not follow a random pattern, and that superior profits await investors willing to follow the guidance of those indicators!"

— Norman G. Fosback
Market Logic

CHAPTER 7

Making Money In Down Markets

SAY GOODBYE TO THE BULL MARKET

The days of the current roaring bull market are numbered. You can quote me on that. Sooner or later, the big bullish upward wave in stock prices will end and come crashing down. We quoted value hunter extraordinare Sir John Templeton earlier as saying, "There will always be bull markets followed by bear markets followed by bull markets followed by bear markets but the long term trend is up."

That is the exact foundation of which market timing is built. Capture most of the bull market advance while avoiding the bulk of the bear market downthrust. Every day that passes brings us closer to the next stock market debacle! Remember, nothing goes up forever. You can add that truism to the certainty of death and taxes.

Too many investors invest their financial resources as if the stock market will climb higher and higher, uninterrupted, forever. Compounding this problem is the misconception by many investors on the size of market declines. This misconception was clearly pointed out in an informal audience survey by Peter J. Eliades, editor and publisher of *StockMarket Cycles* at a recent investment conference. Eliades asked investors what they believed the average maximum Dow Jones Industrial Average decline has been within each calendar year since 1901.

The responses ranged from between 4 percent and 8 percent. Here's where reality hits home, **hard**. In the real world, the average maximum Dow closing price decline within a calendar year since 1901 came in at 16.9 percent, more than twice to over four times the typical investor's perception. The worst decline, not surprisingly, took place during the Great Depression, and resulted in a stunning 62 percent stock market decline in 1931. The mildest maximum decline took place in recent history, in 1995, with a 3.3 percent downward move in stock prices as measured by the Dow Jones Industrial Average.

While some people may call these statistics interesting but not relevant to the future, Eliades takes exception, and I wholeheartedly concur. These misconceptions prop up the complacency defining today's investors and the current high stock market level. With the Dow Jones Industrial Average having risen thousands of points over the past few years, it is hard to get investors to take downside moves and the potential of a major bear market seriously. The common attitude is, "Let the good times roll."

Far be it from me to spoil the party but it is important that investors recognize the dangers that lie ahead. Everybody has taken the Dow rise of several thousand points in stride but, as Eliades points out, try telling someone that if the Dow Jones Industrial Average declined 1,000 points, it would be an *average* price decline comparable to the declines of the preceding ninety-five years of this century.

The periodic market dips in the unprecedented market advance of recent years has reinforced another investor trait which may come back to haunt investors during a full fledged bear market. The 1987 crash taught investors an interesting behavior pattern...that it is prudent to always buy the dip in stock market prices in anticipation of the rebound. I understand that Templeton profited greatly as one of the heaviest buyers during this period. As a mutual fund with an unlimited life, Templeton has the luxury of waiting until stock prices rebound from perceived undervalued situations. As a mortal human, you may not have the emotional strength nor enough time to recoup losses before you need your money for college expenses, a new home, or retirement.

While investors who did buy the dip in 1987 have been handsomely rewarded for their courage and conviction to purchase stocks during that downward price move, that may not be the case if the dip turns into a rip roaring long-term bear. Unless investor attitudes change dramatically, I predict that buying the dip, in the hope of a price rebound, will be the downfall of many baby boomers and disastrous to their retirement years. That is what I hope to prevent by writing this book.

Jim Gipson, manager of the Clipper Fund, captures the essence of today's dangerous market psychology as follows:

"Some professional hunters favor a lazy way to bag a lion. They leave fresh meat at the same spot each day and then blow a high-pitched whistle which lions can hear at great distance. Eventually the lions come to associate the whistle with dinner time. On the last day the professional hunter brings his client and then blows his whistle. The old lion comes expecting food but gets a bullet instead. What works for old lions in Africa probably will work for Young Lions on Wall Street, too. For years the stock market has only gone up with occasional small dips. Young Lions, who have no experience with any other kind of market, have been conditioned to buy on dips in anticipation of a coming rise in stock prices. Some day that conditioning, which has been helpful to date, will be fatal in the face of a long bear market which goes through the traditional four stages: 1.My stock is down a little. I'll buy more before it goes back up; 2. It's down even more, what a bargain! I'll spend my last cash reserves; 3. It can't go any lower. I'll hang on until I break even; 4. I can't stand it. Get me out now!"

The length of the current bull market and its resilience are setting the stage for disaster. Many young money managers and individual investors are confusing their good fortune of participating in the greatest bull market of all time with their own investing genius.

This bull market has been fueled by nearly continuous rising stock prices as unprecedented amounts of money has flowed from new investors into mutual funds. Today, there are more individual investors participating in the stock market than there have been in decades. Likewise, they have a higher percentage of their household assets in the stock market today than in recent history. As reported in the August 16, 1996 issue of *Investor's Business Daily* stocks represented nearly 27 percent of household assets at the end of 1995 compared with less than 15 percent in the early 1990s, and this percentage is at its highest level since the early 1980s. In the past two and one half years, individual investors have sunk approximately $400 billion into the market, propelling stock prices to new heights.

This tremendous cash inflow from new investors presents several underlying risks. First of all, is the reservoir of individual capital about to dry up, stalling the market? Second, how will these investors react to sharper downside moves and a prolonged stock market decline? Are these 'weak hands' up to facing the bear? Third, the entrance of mass numbers of individual small investors has historically been related to market tops. Will history repeat itself again? Finally, the average age of many money managers on Wall Street is in the low thirties. In other words, they have never experienced the onset and full brunt of a major bear market. How will they react when their 'golden touch' starts to disappear? We received a little sneak preview during the rapid correction of July 1996, and it didn't give me a warm, cozy feeling. The behavior of fund managers was, for the most part, spookier than that of individual investors.

John McGinley, editor of the investment newsletter, *Technical Trends*, sums up the current situation this way, "At times when an individual has a high percentage of assets in stocks compared to recent history, that means he's losing fear of the stock market, he's feeling frisky. And we know when Charlie Ordinary feels bullish, you and I should be heading for the hills...It's a time bomb that's out there. It hasn't gone off yet, but it's ticking."

"Ripeness is all!"

— *Shakespeare*

The Bard is right about ripeness, you don't want to pick and eat a fruit too much before it's time but you also don't want to eat it after it has gone rotten. Right now the stock market is ripe and only history will tell us when it started to rot through to the core. But, only a fool ignores the lessons of history and fails to safeguard against the coming bear.

Harry S. Dent, Jr., author of *The Great Boom Ahead* warns investors, "from late 2000 into 2001, progressively lighten up on stock and move into a strong cash position to await a potential significant correction in the market. Then in mid-to-late 2002, buy stocks again until the market nears its peak between 2006 and 2010...Between 2006 and 2010, the chances of speculation and volatility increase as we begin to move toward what may become the greatest depression of all time. The chances are stocks will continue up into 2010, but I suggest you do not play those final years unless you know what you are doing."

Of course, Dent's predictions are a ways off and the longer you go into the future the harder it is to predict. That's why my timing model uses the intermediate term as its focus. It is geared to capturing 80 percent of market advances and missing 80 percent of market declines. My timing model may signal a number of good intermediate term advances as well as several declines of 10 percent to 20 percent or more before we get to that great depression that Harry Dent is warning us about.

For a nearer-term perspective, consider the following excerpts from *Barron's* "Market Watch" section.

"The price/earnings ratio on the S & P 500 Index is currently 19.3, on the basis of record earnings. Historically, when the S & P 500 P/E ratio has exceeded 19, earnings have been an average 22.4% off their highs. The only other times the P/E has exceeded 19 on peak earnings were January 1962 (stocks fell by 27% over the following six months)

and December 1972 (stocks fell by half over the following two years, even though earnings grew by another 70%)...Given current levels of interest rates, inflation, and other factors, the P/E historically would have been 13.6, not 19.3. The low dividend payout is also food for the bears. Historically, a payout ratio of 43% has been associated with a P/E of 10, not 19.3. The market is fundamentally overvalued..."

— Hussman Econometrics
May 1996

"The ownership of stocks, directly and in funds, is now to a degree not seen since 1973 in the hands of people who have had no opportunity to develop the stomach to ride through more than a few weeks of correction. The long-term relative returns of stocks may be superior to the alternatives after all, but nine months into a correction of 20%-30% looking for all the world like it's on its way to 50%-plus, it won't matter!

There is an awful amount of money in the market that is too important to lose and will leave as injudiciously as it entered. None of us can predict when it will start, but the next correction that goes long enough to convince folks that maybe they shouldn't have bought that dip will likely trigger a series of days giving ways to weeks where each day enough people lose heart and sell/redeem to cause a bunch more to lose heart and sell the next day.

When it's over, and for years to follow, the market will again be dominated by players who have learned how to lose."

— C.L. King's Pep Talk
July 1996

I would alter that to "players who have learned how not to lose by exiting the market on time." Deciding not to invest on dips may be the smartest investment decision you ever make. Hiring a professional member of SAAFTI to advise you on the timing of the next market decline may be a close second.

Please keep in mind, however, that the fact that the market is fundamentally overvalued today tells you nothing about the timing of a major decline, only about the potential magnitude of that decline. Likewise, it doesn't mean that the market can't continue higher and become more fundamentally overvalued. In fact, my studies indicate that for the current bull market to set an all time record, it would have to last until November 1998 and reach a Dow Jones Industrial Average of 9200.

An article by Harry B. Ernst, president of Ernst Institutional Research in Boston, and Jeffrey D. Fotta, chief executive officer of Ernst Institutional Research, in the March 25, 1996 issue of *Barron's* warned that cash flow data indicates that the market may be topping out. As a predictive tool, Dual Cash Flow sports an impressive track record. At the time of the article, none of the Dow Jones Industrial stocks were rated as 'most attractive' while seven were rated 'least attractive.' More importantly, cash flow from operations is dropping at companies all across the spectrum.

An April 1, 1996 *Fortune* article by Richard D. Hylton pointed out that prices, based on several indicators and valuation yardsticks, appear to be getting out of hand. For example, the price to-book-value ratio on the S & P 500 is about 3.5, substantially above its historical average of 1.8 and at the highest level in the past thirty years. Taking a look at dividend yields, they stand at a skimpy 2.2% versus an average of 4.3% over the past seventy years. A spectre of worse things to come, the 2.2% dividend yield is lower than the levels reached before the stock market drops of 1929, 1972, and 1987. Hylton sums up the article as follows," Do you really want to be heavily exposed to stocks when the deluge of money stops? With the stock allocation in your portfolio now much bigger because of the market's winning streak, it's a good moment to take some money off the table." Sounds like market timing to me!

Another *Fortune* article, on April 15, 1996, provided some additional warning signs of a market top. Consider that the 99 favorite stocks of institutions are already selling at P/E premiums of 25% to 50% over historical averages, margin debt is at a fifty year high, and the Leuthold Group's contention that for stocks to be truly cheap again the market would have to fall 49%. That would take the Dow Jones Industrial Average back to the 3000 level. Can your portfolio stand that kind of bear market? I doubt it.

Take a tip from your car's rear view mirror in regard to the next bear market. If you read the small print on the bottom of the mirror it says, "Objects may be closer than they appear." Many of you, indeed most of you, will probably be ecstatic if you somehow get out of stocks reasonably close to the ultimate top and position your account to earn a money market rate of interest during the next bear market. Well, that is the goal of my market timing strategy.

MAKING MONEY IN DOWN MARKETS

"Consider the plight of the (tactical asset allocator or) market timer who knows his system won't add value in bull markets. And even when timing works just the way it's supposed to and shelters investors from the storm of a bear market, even that is an emotional challenge. Some investors are quite comfortable on the sidelines, knowing they have no downside risk. But others are anxious, knowing they'll never make any significant money in a money market fund."

— Paul Merriman
The Fund Exchange

For the more aggressive investor, there may be the desire not only to exit the market at an opportune time, but also to figure out a way to have the opportunity to make more than a money market return in down markets, too! Now there is a practical strategy for taking advantage of downside market moves. It is through the use of what I call an 'inverse' fund, that is, a mutual fund whose investment results are specifically designed to inversely correlate with a major market average, such as the S & P 500.

To test the feasibility of such a strategy, I performed a computer simulation back to 1927. To accomplish this test, I enhanced my basic econometric timing model with an algorithm for timing the use of the inverse fund. I am very encouraged by the results. Over sixty-nine years, using the S & P 500 as the stock fund and the inverse of the S & P 500 as the inverse fund, you could have earned three times as much money as you would without the use of the inverse fund and almost forty times as much as an investor buying and holding the S & P 500 basket of stocks over the same time frame. More importantly, look at the returns in the exceptionally poor market periods. For example, the five worst years since 1927 are shown in Chart 7-1.

PERFORMANCE COMPARISONS

Chart 7-1

Year	S&P Buy-and-Hold	Basic Timing Model	Timing Model with Inverse Fund
1931	-45.4%	-0.9%	+28.4%
1937	-30.5	+7.3	+48.4
1974	-25.4	+15.6	+37.0
1930	-21.8	+0.5	+17.3
1973	-14.8	+6.4	+13.6

See Appendix B for Disclosure Statement.

Chart 7-1 Courtesy of SIMCO

As you can see from the chart, there is a dramatic difference in the performance of the timing model with inverse fund as compared with both the buy and hold strategy and the basic timing model. This comparison is a perfect example of why I strive to continually improve my market timing strategies that reduce risk and deliver superior risk-adjusted performance.

Taking the analysis one step further, I also ran a similar test comparing the NASDAQ against the S & P 500 as the stock fund, using the same inverse fund with twenty years of available NASDAQ data.

The results indicated a clear edge going to the NASDAQ over the S & P 500 and the S & P 500 buy and hold strategy, 22.4 percent, versus 18.4 percent versus 14.3 percent, respectively.

It appears obvious to me that there is great potential for use of this more aggressive growth strategy for certain investors. I use the Rydex Series Trust, a family of no-load mutual fund portfolios, available since 1994 and only offered through investment advisors, that includes a NASDAQ Fund (OTC), an Inverse Fund (URSA), a Government Bond Fund, and a Government Money Market Fund. Be sure to ask for and examine a Rydex prospectus before you invest.

While there is no guarantee that the performance reflected in my computer simulations in late 1995 can or will be replicated by the Rydex Funds using my basic timing model with the inverse fund algorithm, I believe that the potential for making more money in down markets than in a money market fund certainly exists. The results are summarized for the basic timing model with inverse fund (Chart 7-2) as compared to the basic timing model (Chart 7-3) for the period from April 27, 1927 through August 11, 1995 and for the basic timing model with inverse fund using the S & P 500 Total Return Index (Chart 7-4) and the basic timing model with inverse fund using the NASDAQ Composite Index (Chart 7-5) for the period August 29, 1975 through August 11, 1995. For those interested in receiving a full copy of this special research project write to me at 502 N. Travis, Cameron, Texas 76520-2563.

BASIC TIMING MODEL WITH INVERSE FUND

Chart 7-2   04/08/27 to 08/11/95

	Compounded Annual Return	Net Annual Return	$100,000 Inv. Now Worth	Volatility 'Beta'	Risk Adjusted Superiority Index 'Alpha'
MANAGED (SPTR)	17.4%	16.5%	3,398,147,674	0.077	12.284
Buy and Hold (SPTR)		10.4%	84,911,390	1.000	0.000

	Maximum Drawdown (Worst Paper Loss)		Drawdown Beta	Alpha 2
MANAGED (SPTR)	28.70%	02/16/34 – 05/24/35	0.343	10.502
Buy and Hold (SPTR)	83.65%	09/06/29 – 07/08/32		

	Net Returns for Past			Risk Index	STD Deviation	Sharpe Ratio
	1 Yr	5 Yrs	10 Yrs			
MANAGED (SPTR)	22.1%	12.5%	20.1%	0.750	15.30%	0.84
Buy and Hold (SPTR)	23.6%	14.0%	15.1%	1.000	17.82%	0.38

An illustration using SPTR as stock fund, SPIV as inverse fund, GBTP as bond fund, BILL as money market fund,
and SPTR as market index and after all fees
Legend: SPTR = S&P 500 Total Return Indx SPIV = Inverse of S&P "500" TR GBTP = LT Gvt Bds
BILL = U.S. Treasury Bills
See Appendix B for Disclosure Statement.
Chart 7-2 Courtesy of SIMCO

BASIC TIMING MODEL
Chart 7-3 **04/08/27 to 08/11/95**

	Compounded Annual Return	Net Annual Return	$100,000 Inv. Now Worth	Volatility 'Beta'	Risk Adjusted Superiority Index 'Alpha'
MANAGED (SPTR)	15.7%	14.6%	1,086,681,045	0.425	8.052
Buy and Hold (SPTR)		10.4%	84,911,390	1.000	0.000

	Maximum Drawdown (Worst Paper Loss)		Drawdown Beta	Alpha 2
MANAGED (SPTR)	26.51%	05/31/46 – 02/13/48	0.317	8.776
Buy and Hold (SPTR)	83.65%	09/06/29 – 07/08/32		

	Net Returns for Past			Risk Index	STD Deviation	Sharpe Ratio
	1 Yr	5 Yrs	10 Yrs			
MANAGED (SPTR)	25.0%	13.0%	17.9%	0.500	11.61%	0.94
Buy and Hold (SPTR)	23.6%	14.0%	15.1%	1.000	17.82%	0.38

An illustration using SPTR as stock fund, GBTP as bond fund, BILL as money market fund,
and SPTR as market index and after all fees
Legend: SPTR = S&P 500 Total Return Indx GBTP = LT Gvt Bds BILL = U.S. Treasury Bills
See Appendix B for Disclosure Statement.
Chart 7-3 Courtesy of SIMCO

BASIC TIMING MODEL WITH INVERSE FUND
Chart 7-4   08/29/75 to 08/11/95

	Compounded Annual Return	Net Annual Return	$100,000 Inv. Now Worth	Risk Adjusted	
				Volatility 'Beta'	Superiority Index 'Alpha'
MANAGED (SPTR)	20.2%	18.4%	2,925,571	0.472	7.796
Buy and Hold (SPTR)		14.3%	1,433,872	1.000	0.000

	Maximum Drawdown (Worst Paper Loss)		Drawdown Beta	Alpha 2
MANAGED (SPTR)	13.75%	05/07/82 – 08/06/82	0.422	8.146
Buy and Hold (SPTR)	32.57%	08/21/87 – 12/04/87		

	Net Returns for Past			Risk Index	STD Deviation	Sharpe Ratio
	1 Yr	5 Yrs	10 Yrs			
MANAGED (SPTR)	22.1%	12.5%	20.1%	0.857	12.91%	0.86
Buy and Hold (SPTR)	23.6%	14.0%	15.1%	1.000	14.17%	0.49

An illustration using SPTR as stock fund, SPIV as inverse fund, GBTP as bond fund, BILL as money market fund, and SPTR as market index and after all fees
Legend: SPTR = S&P 500 Total Return Indx   SPIV = Inverse of S&P "500" TR   GBTP = LT Gvt Bds
BILL = U.S. Treasury Bills
See Appendix B for Disclosure Statement.
Chart 7-4 Courtesy of SIMCO

BASIC TIMING MODEL WITH INVERSE FUND
Chart 7-5   08/29/75 to 08/11/95

	Compounded Annual Return	Net Annual Return	$100,000 Inv. Now Worth	Risk Adjusted	
				Volatility 'Beta'	Superiority Index 'Alpha'
MANAGED (NCMI)	24.1%	22.4%	5,630,083	0.335	12.755
Buy and Hold (NCMI)		13.6%	1,270,704	0.865	0.245
Buy and Hold (SPTR)		14.3%	1,433,872	1.000	0.000

	Maximum Drawdown (Worst Paper Loss)		Drawdown Beta	Alpha 2
MANAGED (NCMI)	17.01%	06/24/83 – 07/20/84	0.522	11.446
Buy and Hold (NCMI)	35.65%	08/21/87 – 12/04/87		
Buy and Hold (SPTR)	32.59%	08/21/87 – 12/04/87	1.000	0.000

	Net Returns for Past			Risk Index	STD Deviation	Sharpe Ratio
	1 Yr	5 Yrs	10 Yrs			
MANAGED (NCMI)	36.7%	24.0%	23.4%	0.714	12.89%	1.17
Buy and Hold (NCMI)	37.3%	19.7%	12.9%	1.000	14.96%	0.42
Buy and Hold (SPTR)	23.6%	14.0%	15.1%	1.000	14.17%	0.49

An illustration using NCMI as stock fund, SPIV as inverse fund, GBTP as bond fund, BILL as money market fund,
and SPTR as market index and after all fees
Legend: NCMI = NASDAQ   SPIV = Inverse of S&P 500   GBTP = LT Gvt Bds
BILL = U.S. Treasury Bills
See Appendix B for Disclosure Statement.
Chart 7-5 Courtesy of SIMCO

"Portfolio managers should be more concerned with being in cash or short in bear markets than with missing bull markets."

— *A. Gary Shilling*
"Market Timing: Better than a Buy-and-Hold Strategy"
Financial Analysts Journal

MULTIPLYING YOUR MARKET POTENTIAL

Taking the concept of the 'inverse' fund a step further is the objective of one innovative California corporation, Champion Capital. For several years they have been working diligently on creating a new financial asset management system specially designed for asset allocation and market timers. This company's concept is to provide a 'beta' range six times the size of the typical common stock fund 'beta' range. In other words, the new product will be designed to provide a rate of return equivalent to that earned by an investor moving funds between a money market fund and a long or short position in the S &

P 500 Index. Exposure can be increased up to a multiple of three times the investment through the use of a non-recourse line of credit.

Assuming this product does make it to the investment supermarket shelves, it has the potential of providing stiff competition for mutual fund companies. If, in fact, the product can consistently deliver an 'on-track' market multiple of the S & P 500 with reduced transaction costs and the flexibility to trade on the half-hour (rather than once daily on the close), the sky is the limit!

Every market timing professional has had the misfortune of being right about the market but unfortunately positioned in a fund where performance is out of sync with the market in that particular cycle. If this product can eliminate this unwanted but previously unavoidable risk, it definitely has a place in the marketplace.

To satisfy my own curiosity about the potential for such a product, I ran a 25-year computer simulation integrating my timing model with a market multiple strategy as described above. In this study, I limited my beta range from +2.00 to -2.00. The results, shown in Chart 7-6, were impressive. I'm looking forward to having the opportunity to evaluate this exciting new strategy in real time.

Up to now, I have concentrated on how market timing can reduce your risk posture and deliver superior risk-adjusted returns. It is time to take a look at some other investment philosophies and strategies and analyze the rationale behind them.

MARKET MULTIPLE SIMULATION STATISTICS

Chart 7-6

Start Date: 1/2/70   End Date: 3/31/95
Initial Inv.: $100,000

Statistic	Cash	Buy & Hold	Managed
Account Balance	$618,976	$1,464,247	$94,694,283
Compounded Return	7.48%	11.21%	31.17%
Average Return	7.48%	12.46%	34.15%
Standard Deviation	0.16%	14.89%	21.34%
Sharpe Ratio	N/A	0.33	1.25
Beta	0.00	1.00	1.43
Alpha	0.00%	0.00%	20.34%
Ulcer Index	0.00	1.00	0.61

Statistic	Buy & Hold	Managed
1 – Drawdown	44.91%	23.43%
1 – High Date	1/11/73	10/15/80
1 – High Balance	$142,717	$3,176,813
1 – Low Date	10/3/74	3/25/81
1 – Low Balance	$78,617	$2,432,369
2 – Drawdown	32.95%	20.54%
2 – High Date	8/25/87	10/9/89
2 – High Balance	$771,992	$53,225,508
2 – Low Date	10/19/87	1/30/90
2 – Low Balance	$517,603	$42,291,362
3 – Drawdown	24.78%	18.46%
3 – High Date	1/5/70	5/9/82
3 – High Balance	$100,533	$4,130,247
3 – Low Date	5/26/70	8/12/82
3 – Low Balance	$75,619	$3,367,761
4 – Drawdown	19.97%	17.24%
4 – High Date	11/30/80	10/10/83
4 – High Balance	$238,436	$7,148,160
4 – Low Date	8/12/82	7/24/84
4 – Low Balance	$190,828	$5,915,894
5 – Drawdown	19.18%	17.15%
5 – High Date	7/16/90	7/15/75
5 – High Balance	$934,945	$1,038,859
5 – Low Date	10/11/90	10/1/75
5 – Low Balance	$755,638	$860,684

Fees/Income	$ Amount	Annual %*
Interest Income	$26,523,026.81	5.47%
Inverse Credit	3,795,282.27	0.78%
Index Fees	7,011,946.39	1.45%
Admin Fees	2,910,546.48	0.60%
Switch Fees	937,986.98	0.19%

% Time Long	66.44%	Average Long Multiple	+1.67
% Time Cash	13.21%	Average Abs. Multiple	1.52
% Time Short	20.35%	Average Short Multiple	–2.00
Duration (yrs)	25.3	Total Switches	89

Simulation software provided by Champion Capital

Chart 7-6 Courtesy of SIMCO

THE RIGHT SECTOR AT THE RIGHT TIME?

"If you are in the right sector at the right time, you can make a lot of money very quickly."

— *Marshall Schield*
Schield Management Company

If you study the rankings of the best performing mutual funds each year, you will invariably discover a single industry, or sector fund, at or close to the top of the class. Unfortunately, that information is typically little help in selecting a fund for the next year because a different fund usually leads the pack each year.

However, due to the publicity that these high performing sector funds have garnered, many investment advisors have attempted to capitalize on this performance by jumping into the market with 'sector fund rotation' programs. A common marketing thread of the rotation programs that I have looked at is that there is *always* going to be at least one rising sector fund in the market, and they plan to be invested in it. The rotation decision is triggered by a signal from a fund selection algorithm, usually based on relative strength analysis, seeking the best risk/reward ratios at any given time.

Before we go any further, it is appropriate to distinguish between sectors and industries, which are often used interchangeably. However, they are not the same. A sector represents a group of industries that possess similar fundamental characteristics. An industry is a collection of companies with similar primary lines of business.

A major flaw in the sector rotation rationale rests in the fact that these funds did not exist during the last major bear market. Obviously, that leads to the question of how well even the strongest sector funds will really perform and protect your capital in a truly negative market environment.

My research, using S & P industry indices as a proxy for sector funds, studied theoretical sector performance over a quarter of a century and looked at actual sector program performance in 1994 and 1995. The results lead me to conclude that many investors will be disappointed in the performance of always-fully-invested sector rotation programs. They are not likely to fit the title of this chapter,

"Making Money in Down Markets." Based on this analysis, I have not entered that market.

However, my research did point out that combining the market signals of my time-tested econometric model with a sector algorithm (which I call Managed Sectors) delivers the potential to produce superior results. Armed with this knowledge, my goal is to utilize what I believe will be the strongest sector fund(s) during a period when my model forecasts a generally bullish market environment and to stay away from all sector funds when my model forecasts a generally negative, or bearish, market environment.

My study investigated the feasibility of utilizing single industry, or sector funds, to improve investment performance. I used my basic timing model as a benchmark for comparable results over the period December 28, 1986 through December 29, 1995. The six investment strategies analyzed in this research included strategies promoted by sector fund rotation program advisors and several which I believed might possess some merit. The strategies are as follows:

1. Always in the market — active rotation to strongest relative strength funds

2. Always in the market — active rotation to previously weakest relative strength funds on turnaround

3. Active rotation to strongest relative strength funds during periods of my basic timing model showing buy signal

4. Active rotation to weakest relative strength funds on turnaround during periods of my basic timing model showing buy signal

5. Selection of strongest relative strength funds on basic timing model buy signal

6. Selection of weakest relative strength funds on turnaround on basic timing model buy signal

From my research, I made a number of significant conclusions. My first conclusion, that selecting for weakest relative strength on a turnaround appeared to work better than selecting for strongest recent relative strength, differed from conventional thinking in relative strength circles. My second conclusion found that 'always in the market' sector rotation possessed higher risk and probably offered lower long-term returns compared with sector fund rotation only based on a basic timing model buy signal. I caution that this was more difficult to prove since sector funds have not been in existence during a bear market such as experienced during 1973-74. However, looking at Standard & Poor's single industry data going back 25 years and actual results from several sector fund rotation programs that were in existence in 1994 and 1995, led me to this conclusion.

My third conclusion found active rotation to the proper sector funds 'on' a basic timing model buy signal preferable to active rotation among sector funds 'during' a basic timing model buy signal period (see Chart 7-8 versus Chart 7-9). In fact, active sector rotation during a buy signal (see Chart 7-9) does not even appear to be as profitable as traditional timing model results (see Chart 7-7).

In summary, strategy number six (selection of weakest relative strength funds on turnaround on basic timing model buy signal) appears to possess the greatest merit of the ones studied. I will use this in my Managed Sectors Plan (See Chart 7-10). If the results in real-time application since May 1996 are anywhere close to those inferred by the computer simulation of past history, my clients will be very pleased with this program.

TIMING MODEL
12/26/86 to 12/29/95

Chart 7-7

Yearly Return	Year	$100,000 Inv. Now Worth
0.6%	1986	100,600
36.9%	1987	137,714
24.0%	1988	170,832
18.6%	1989	202,543
7.4%	1990	217,600
50.5%	1991	327,540
21.7%	1992	398,724
17.8%	1993	469,593
4.2%	1994	489,150
27.4%	1995	622,969

	Compounded Annual Return	Net Annual Return	$100,000 Inv. Now Worth	Volatility 'Beta'	Risk Adjusted Superiority Index 'Alpha'
MANAGED (NYSE)	24.6%	22.5%	622,969	0.398	13.477
Buy and Hold (NYSE)		17.5%	425,941	0.724	5.674
Buy and Hold (SPTR)		14.2%	330,957	1.000	0.000

	Net Returns for Past		
	1 Yr	5 Yrs	10 Yrs
MANAGED (NYSE)	30.2%	23.9%	N.A.
Buy and Hold (NYSE)	31.9%	26.4%	N.A.
Buy and Hold (SPTR)	37.8%	16.7%	N.A.

An illustration using NYSE as stock fund, GBTP as bond fund, BILL as money market fund,
and SPTR as market index
Legend: NYSE = NYSE Total Return Index   GBTP = LT Gvt Bds   BILL = U.S. Treasury Bills
SPTR = S&P 500 Total Return Indx
See Appendix B for Disclosure Statement
Chart 7-7 Courtesy of SIMCO

MANAGED SECTORS 1
12/26/86 to 12/29/95

Chart 7-8

Yearly Return	Year	$100,000 Inv. Now Worth
1.8%	1986	101,800
62.0%	1987	164,961
12.3%	1988	185,310
48.1%	1989	274,514
14.6%	1990	314,626
56.7%	1991	493,053
24.4%	1992	613,507
22.0%	1993	748,622
2.6%	1994	767,902
52.9%	1995	1,174,170

	Compounded Annual Return	Net Annual Return	$100,000 Inv. Now Worth	Volatility 'Beta'	Risk Adjusted Superiority Index 'Alpha'
MANAGED SECTOR FUNDS	33.9%	31.4%	1,174,170	0.509	21.423
Buy and Hold Sector Funds		14.5%	337,959	0.536	4.290

	Net Returns for Past			Risk	STD	Sharpe
	1 Yr	5 Yrs	10 Yrs	Index	Deviation	Ratio
MANAGED SECTOR FUNDS	53.0%	29.0%	N.A.	0.682	12.80%	2.02
Buy and Hold Sector Funds	29.8%	23.3%	N.A.	1.044	14.96%	0.59

Funds Used During Stock Allocation>0

12/26/86 TO 04/17/87	FBMP	FDPM	FSAG	FSVL	
06/05/87 TO 08/28/87	FBIO	FSEL	HLTH	TECH	
12/11/87 TO 05/13/88	FSPH	FSRB	HLTH		
06/03/88 TO 08/19/88	FSUT	FSVL			
08/26/88 TO 09/15/89	FBIO	FSRB	FSTC	HLTH	
09/29/89 TO 07/27/90	FSAG	FSEN	FSTC		
10/12/90 TO 01/11/91	HLTH	TECH			
01/18/91 TO 06/28/91	FDPM	FIDS	FSAG	FSVL	
07/05/91 TO 11/22/91	FBIO	FIDS	FSPT	FSRB	HLTH
11/29/91 TO 04/03/92	FSRB				
04/10/92 TO 03/05/93	FBMP	FDFA	FSDC	FSRP	
03/19/93 TO 09/24/93	FIDS	FSDC	FSEL	FSPT	FSRP
12/10/93 TO 02/04/94	FBIO	FSCS	FSDC	FSEL	
12/16/94 TO 11/03/95	FSCS	FSEL	FSLE	FSPT	FSRP
12/01/95 TO 12/29/95	FDFA	FSUT	FSVL		

An illustration using GBTP as bond fund, BILL as money market fund,
and SPTR as market index

Legend: GBTP = LT Gvt Bds   BILL = U.S. Treasury Bills   SPTR = S&P 500 Total Return Indx

See Appendix B for Disclosure Statement

Chart 7-8 Courtesy of SIMCO

MANAGED SECTORS 2
12/26/86 to 12/29/95

Chart 7-9

Yearly Return	Year	$100,000 Inv. Now Worth
1.8%	1986	101,800
72.5%	1987	175,623
13.3%	1988	198,996
30.5%	1989	259,717
11.7%	1990	290,183

Yearly Return	Year	$100,000 Inv. Now Worth
44.5%	1991	419,235
−14.0%	1992	360,500
23.1%	1993	443,860
3.1%	1994	457,665
30.6%	1995	597,585

	Compounded Annual Return	Net Annual Return	$100,000 Inv. Now Worth	Volatility 'Beta'	Risk Adjusted Superiority Index 'Alpha'
MANAGED SECTOR FUNDS	24.0%	22.0%	597,585	0.584	11.378
Buy and Hold Sector Funds		14.5%	337,959	0.536	4.290

	Net Returns for Past			Risk Index	STD Deviation	Sharpe Ratio
	1 Yr	5 Yrs	10 Yrs			
MANAGED SECTOR FUNDS	30.6%	15.1%	N.A.	0.897	14.79%	1.11
Buy and Hold Sector Funds	29.8%	23.3%	N.A.	1.044	14.96%	0.59

Funds Used During Stock Allocation>0

12/26/86 TO 04/17/87	FBMP	FDPM	FSAG	FSVL	
12/26/86 TO 03/27/87	FBMP	FDPM	FSAG	FSVL	
04/03/87 TO 04/03/87	FBIO	FBMP	FDFA	FDPM	FIDS	FSAG
04/10/87 TO 04/10/87	FBIO	FBMP	FDFA	FDPM	FSAG	
04/17/87 TO 04/17/87	FBMP	FDFA	FDPM	FSAG	
06/05/87 TO 06/05/87	FBIO	FSEL	HLTH	TECH	
06/12/87 TO 06/19/87	FBIO	FSCS	FSPT	HLTH	
06/26/87 TO 07/03/87	FDPM	FSTC	HLTH		
07/10/87 TO 07/17/87	FDPM	FSTC	FSUT		
07/24/87 TO 08/28/87	FDFA	FDPM	FSTC	FSVL	
12/11/87 TO 01/29/88	FSPH	FSRB	HLTH		
02/05/88 TO 03/25/88	FBIO	FSEN	FSPH	FSRB	
04/01/88 TO 04/08/88	FBIO	FSEN	FSRB	HLTH	
04/15/88 TO 04/15/88	FIDS	FSEL	FSEN	FSPT	FSRB

Funds Used During Stock Allocation>0

04/22/88 TO 05/13/88	FSEL	FSEN	FSPT	FSRB		
06/03/88 TO 08/19/88	FSUT	FSVL				
08/26/88 TO 08/26/88	FBIO	FSRB	FSTC	HLTH		
09/02/88 TO 09/02/88	FDPM	FSAG	FSRB	FSRP	HLTH	
09/09/88 TO 09/09/88	FSEN	FSES	FSRB	FSRP	FSUT	HLTH
09/16/88 TO 09/23/88	FSES	FSRB	FSRP	FSUT	HLTH	
09/30/88 TO 11/11/88	FSRB	FSRP	FSUT	HLTH		
11/18/88 TO 11/18/88	FSAG	FSRB	FSRP	FSUT	FSVL	
11/25/88 TO 12/02/88	FBMP	FSAG	FSCS	FSPT	FSUT	
12/09/88 TO 03/10/89	FBMP	FSCS	FSPT	FSUT		
03/17/89 TO 06/23/89	FBMP	FSES	FSTC	FSUT	TECH	
06/30/89 TO 09/01/89	FBMP	FDFA	FSES	FSRB	FSUT	
09/08/89 TO 09/08/89	FBMP	FSES	FSRB	FSUT		
09/15/89 TO 09/15/89	FIDS	FSAG	FSEL	FSES	FSRB	FSUT
09/29/89 TO 09/29/89	FSAG	FSEN	FSTC			
10/06/89 TO 10/13/89	FDPM	FSEN	FSLE	FSTC	FSVL	
10/20/89 TO 10/27/89	FDPM	FSEN	FSLE	FSTC		
11/03/89 TO 11/03/89	FBIO	FDPM	FSCS	FSEL	FSEN	FSLE
11/10/89 TO 11/24/89	FBIO	FDPM	FSCS	FSEN	FSLE	
12/01/89 TO 12/15/89	FBIO	FDPM	FSCS	FSEN		
12/22/89 TO 01/05/90	FDPM	FIDS	FSAG	FSCS	FSEN	FSPH
01/12/90 TO 01/12/90	FDPM	FIDS	FSAG	FSEN	FSPH	
01/19/90 TO 02/16/90	FDPM	FSAG	FSEN	FSPH		
02/23/90 TO 02/23/90	FSAG	FSEN				
03/02/90 TO 03/16/90	FSEN	HLTH				
03/23/90 TO 03/30/90	FSES	FSVL	HLTH			
04/06/90 TO 04/06/90	FIDS	FSCS	FSES	FSLE	FSPT	FSRB HLTH
04/13/90 TO 04/13/90	FSCS	FSLE	FSPT	HLTH		
04/20/90 TO 04/20/90	FSCS	FSLE	FSRP	FSTC	HLTH	
04/27/90 TO 07/13/90	FSCS	FSLE	FSRP	HLTH		
07/20/90 TO 07/20/90	FSEL	FSLE	FSPT	HLTH	TECH	
07/27/90 TO 07/27/90	FBIO	FSLE	HLTH			
10/12/90 TO 10/12/90	HLTH	TECH				
10/19/90 TO 10/19/90	FDPM	FSAG	FSEN	TECH		
10/26/90 TO 10/26/90	FBIO	FDFA	FSEL	FSPH	FSPT	TECH
11/02/90 TO 01/11/91	FDFA	FSPH	FSPT	TECH		
01/18/91 TO 01/18/91	FDPM	FIDS	FSAG	FSVL		
01/25/91 TO 06/14/91	FDFA	FIDS	FSRP	FSVL		
06/21/91 TO 06/21/91	FDFA	FIDS	FSRP	TECH		
06/28/91 TO 06/28/91	FDFA	FSLE	FSRB	FSRP		
07/05/91 TO 11/22/91	FBIO	FIDS	FSPT	FSRB	HLTH	
11/29/91 TO 12/06/91	FSRB					
12/13/91 TO 12/13/91	FSEL	FSRP	TECH			
12/20/91 TO 01/10/92	FDFA	FSUT				

Funds Used During Stock Allocation>0

01/17/92 TO 02/07/92	FBIO	FDFA	FSPH	HLTH		
02/14/92 TO 02/14/92	FDFA	FSRP				
02/21/92 TO 02/21/92	FDPM	FSCS	FSPT	FSRP		
02/28/92 TO 02/28/92	FSAG	FSCS	FSEL	FSEN	FSES	FSRP
03/06/92 TO 03/06/92	FSCS	FSEL	FSES	FSRP		
03/13/92 TO 03/20/92	FSCS	FSEL	FSRP			
03/27/92 TO 03/27/92	FSLE	FSPT	FSRP	FSVL	TECH	
04/03/92 TO 04/03/92	FIDS	FSRB				
04/10/92 TO 04/17/92	FBMP	FDFA	FSDC	FSRP		
04/24/92 TO 04/24/92	FBMP	FSCS	FSDC	FSPT	FSUT	TECH
05/01/92 TO 05/15/92	FIDS	FSRB	FSRP	FSUT		
05/22/92 TO 05/22/92	FDPM	FIDS	FSCS	FSDC	FSRB	FSTC FSUT
05/29/92 TO 06/05/92	FDPM	FIDS	FSCS	FSRB	FSUT	
06/12/92 TO 06/19/92	FDPM	FIDS	FSRB	FSUT		
06/26/92 TO 06/26/92	FIDS	FSEN	FSLE	FSRB	FSUT	
07/03/92 TO 07/03/92	FIDS	FSES	FSRB	FSUT		
07/10/92 TO 07/10/92	FBMP	FDPM	FIDS	FSRB	FSRP	FSUT
07/17/92 TO 07/17/92	FBMP	FDPM	FIDS	FSUT		
07/24/92 TO 07/24/92	FDFA	FDPM	FIDS	FSEL	FSEN	FSUT
07/31/92 TO 08/14/92	FDFA	FIDS	FSEL	FSEN	FSUT	
08/21/92 TO 10/02/92	FDFA	FSEL	FSEN	FSUT		
10/09/92 TO 10/23/92	FDFA	FSEL	FSES	FSUT		
10/30/92 TO 10/30/92	FBIO	FDFA	FSEL	FSEN	FSUT	
11/06/92 TO 12/18/92	FBIO	FDFA	FSEL	FSUT		
12/25/92 TO 12/25/92	FDFA	FSEL	FSPH	FSUI	HLTH	
01/01/93 TO 01/01/93	FDFA	FSEL	FSUT	HLTH		
01/08/93 TO 01/08/93	FSEL	FSRB	FSUT	HLTH		
01/15/93 TO 01/15/93	FDPM	FSAG	FSEL	FSRB	FSUT	FSVL
01/22/93 TO 02/19/93	FSEL	FSRB	FSUT	FSVL		
02/26/93 TO 03/05/93	FBMP	FSDC	FSPT	FSRB	FSUT	FSVL
03/19/93 TO 03/19/93	FIDS	FSDC	FSEL	FSPT	FSRP	
03/26/93 TO 03/26/93	FIDS	FSDC	FSEL	FSRP		
04/02/93 TO 04/02/93	FIDS	FSDC	FSES	FSLE	FSRP	FSTC
04/09/93 TO 04/09/93	FIDS	FSDC	FSES	FSRP	FSTC	
04/16/93 TO 04/16/93	FIDS	FSDC	FSES	FSTC		
04/23/93 TO 04/23/93	FSDC	FSEL	FSES	FSRB	FSTC	FSVL
04/30/93 TO 06/18/93	FSDC	FSEL	FSES	FSTC		
06/25/93 TO 07/02/93	FSDC	FSEL	FSEN	FSTC	HLTH	
07/09/93 TO 07/16/93	FSDC	FSEL	FSTC	HLTH		
07/23/93 TO 07/23/93	FSDC	FSEL	FSLE	FSRB	FSTC	FSUT
07/30/93 TO 08/13/93	FSDC	FSEL	FSRB	FSTC	FSUT	
08/20/93 TO 09/24/93	FSDC	FSEL	FSTC	FSUT		
12/10/93 TO 12/10/93	FBIO	FSCS	FSDC	FSEL		

Funds Used During Stock Allocation>0

12/17/93 TO 12/17/93	FSCS	FSEL	FSRP	HLTH	TECH
12/24/93 TO 01/21/94	FSAG	FSCS	FSEL	HLTH	
01/28/94 TO 02/04/94	FSCS	FSEL	HLTH	TECH	
12/16/94 TO 01/06/95	FSCS	FSEL	FSLE	FSPT	FSRP
01/13/95 TO 01/20/95	FSCS	FSEL	FSLE	FSPT	
01/27/95 TO 02/17/95	FSCS	FSDC	FSEL	FSLE	TECH
02/24/95 TO 09/22/95	FSCS	FSEL	FSLE	TECH	
09/29/95 TO 09/29/95	FSDC	FSLE			
10/06/95 TO 10/06/95	FSLE	FSPT	FSTC	HLTH	
10/13/95 TO 10/13/95	FSLE	FSVL	HLTH		
10/20/95 TO 10/20/95	FDPM	FIDS	FSAG	FSRP	FSVL	HLTH
10/27/95 TO 10/27/95	FBMP	FSES	HLTH		
11/03/95 TO 11/03/95	FDFA	FSPH	HLTH		
12/01/95 TO 12/29/95	FDFA	FSUT	FSVL		

Legend: FSAG = Fidelity Select American Gold   FBIO = Fidelity Select Biotechnology   FSDC = Fidelity Select Developing Communications   FSEL = Fidelity Select Electronics   FSEN = Fidelity Select Energy   FSES = Fidelity Select Energy Service   FSLE = Fidelity Select Environmental Services   FIDS = Fidelity Select Financial Services   FDFA = Fidelity Select Food and Agriculture   FSPH = Fidelity Select Health Care   FSVL = Fidelity Select Home Finance   FBMP = Fidelity Select Multimedia   FDPM = Fidelity Select Precious Metals/Minerals   FSRB = Fidelity Select Regional Banks   FSRP = Fidelity Select Retailing   FSCS = Fidelity Select Software and Computer   FSPT = Fidelity Select Technology   FSTC = Fidelity Select Telecommunications   FSUT = Fidelity Select Utilities   HLTH = INVESCO Funds – Health   TECH = INVESCO Funds – Technology
See Appendix B for Disclosure Statement
Chart 7-9 Courtesy of SIMCO

MANAGED SECTORS PLAN
Data through December 29, 1995

Chart 7-10 Year	NSYE TR Buy & Hold	Managed Sectors
1987	-2.3%	+62.0%
1990	−13.3%	+14.6%

	Net Annual Return			Volatility 'Beta'	Risk Adjusted Return 'Alpha'
	1 Yr	5 Yrs	10 Yrs		
Managed Sectors	53.0%	29.0%	31.4%	0.509	21.423
Buy & Hold Sector Funds	29.8%	23.3%	14.5%	0.536	4.290
NYSE TR Index	31.9%	26.4%	17.5%	0.724	5.674
S&P 500 Index	34.2%	13.4%	10.7%	1.000	0.000

See Appendix B for Disclosure Statement
Chart 7-10 Courtesy of SIMCO

RANDOM WALK HOGWASH

There are many competing theories of how Wall Street really works. Some investors subscribe to the Efficient Market Theory that the market instantly incorporates all available information into stock prices. On the other extreme, other investors believe in the Random Walk theory that the stock market follows no rhyme or reason.

CNBC's Ron Insana hits the nail on the head in his book, *Traders' Tales*. "There is only one certainty about academic studies of Wall Street...most ivory tower professors haven't a clue as to how the stock market really works."

There are always plenty of naysayers. For years, the experts said that humans could never run a four minute mile. Roger Bannister proved the skeptics wrong. Once Bannister broke the barrier, the four-minute mile became commonplace.

In an interview, Peter Lynch summed up Random Walk as hogwash. "...Wharton professors who believed in it weren't doing nearly as well as my new colleagues at Fidelity. If you believe in Random Walk, you have to believe my Fidelity colleagues' and my success was a fluke. It's hard to support a theory that says the market is irrational when you know somebody who just made a 20-fold profit in Kentucky Fried Chicken and explained in *advance* why it was going to rise."

Demonstrating that stock market moves are indeed predictable, Jeremy J. Siegel reported in his book, *Stocks for the Long Run*, the results of studying the 200-day moving average of stock prices from 1885 through 1993. He used a one percent band around the 200-day moving average to prevent an investor from getting whipsawed with frequent moves in and out of the market. Using the 200-day moving average, an investor is in stocks during all the important bull markets and out of stocks during all the major bear markets. Over the whole period, this simple 200-day moving average timing strategy earned an excess return of 1.52 percent per year over a buy and hold strategy. Most significantly, it allowed the investor to miss the Great Crash in 1929. Siegel concluded that while the 200-day moving average strategy does not raise overall returns dramatically, it does substantially lower risk.

Siegel and others have shown that simple timing methods can and do reduce risk and deserve a good, hard look. I take that one step further and contend that most market timing professionals employ much more sophisticated market timing models than a simple moving average, with the potential to deliver reduced risk plus superior risk-adjusted returns.

Neal Greenberg, a Colorado financial planner, performed a study of forty real world market timers. According to Greenberg, market timing reduced average risk by 65 percent yet delivered an increase in returns by approximately 14 percent.

Peter Lynch is right, Random Walk is pure hogwash, and we have the research and investment results to prove it. To date, the majority of investors have ignored new market timing indicators and computerized analytical methods, leaving the field and the superior investment returns to market timing practitioners. With this book I hope to educate the investing public on the significant benefits of market timing and, in the process of sharing knowledge, also share the fruits of this investment strategy.

DOLLAR-COST AVERAGING DEBACLE

Dollar-cost averaging also sends shivers down my spine if it is not accompanied by a disciplined risk control strategy. It is often touted as a safe way to invest through bear markets as well as bull markets, with almost guaranteed success, without being a math guru or a Wall Street Wizard. It works likes this. Over regular periodic intervals, the individual invests a set amount. According to dollar-cost averaging advocates, over time, the investor tends to purchase shares at a low overall cost basis, which works to increase potential return. The investor purchases fewer shares when stock prices are high and more shares when stock prices are low. By spreading investments out over time, risk is also reduced.

That's the theory. It is a great approach in certain circumstances. For example, it allows beginning investors who only have a small amount to invest each month or quarter to develop a steady pattern of investing. That is a lot better than not putting away any money at all. The real benefit of dollar-cost averaging is that it forces the investor to save regularly.

For people looking to invest a lump sum disbursement or inheritance, it is a different story. If the market is in a relatively steady incline, the dollar-cost investor cannot make enough purchases at low prices to make the strategy worthwhile. Money not invested in stocks while the market is rising is not growing as fast as it could. Likewise, the value of dollar-cost averaging diminishes over time. The amount an individual invested regularly ten or even five years ago won't keep pace with inflation. If you plan to use dollar-cost averaging, you need to increase the amount you invest by at least ten percent each year.

But the real clincher that sinks dollar-cost averaging in my mind is the prospect of a major market decline. As another form of the buy and hold strategy, dollar-cost averaging leaves your portfolio open to significant erosion in the face of a bear market.

Early in a cost averaging investment plan, a bear market does not do that much damage because the investor does not have much to lose. As you know, bear markets can rise up at the most inopportune time. The closer you are to retirement, the more difficult it will be to recover from a bear market. Consider the following example.

You invest $5,000 a year, earning 11.3 percent annually for twenty years. With no bear markets to interrupt the growth of your investment, your $100,000 would grow to $369,826. That's the good news. Let's see what happens if a bear market equivalent to the 1973/74 decline hits early in the life of your dollar-cost averaging plan, such as the first year. Your $100,000 would still grow to $348,456 after twenty years. Not bad. That is because you still had plenty of time to recover from your early loss, and your loss was only on the first $5,000 invested.

Now, take a bear market of the same magnitude in the twentieth year of your investment program, maybe just as you were about to retire. Oops! The value drops to $184,082 because the 44.6 percent drop affects **all** the money you have accumulated over twenty years, not just the first $5,000. Investing another $5,000 under dollar-cost averaging is not going to make up for that $185,000 loss. That's the bad news. See Chart 7-11.

If you want to use dollar-cost averaging to build up your portfolio in your early years, go ahead, but keep in mind that with each passing year the amount at risk increases and your time left to recoup your losses decreases! A person with an established portfolio at or near retirement age must avoid the big losses from which he or she can never recover. That's where a proven risk management market timing strategy proves itself crucial. Market timing provides the potential to grow your financial nest egg through stock market advances while keeping bear market losses to acceptable levels, preserving valuable capital and safeguarding your retirement funds. Remember, Dollar Cost Averaging combined with market timing can be a dynamite combination; but Dollar Cost Averaging alone may blow up in your face.

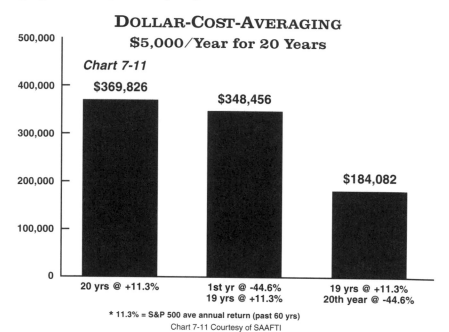

DOLLAR-COST-AVERAGING
$5,000/Year for 20 Years

Chart 7-11

$369,826

$348,456

$184,082

| 20 yrs @ +11.3% | 1st yr @ -44.6% | 19 yrs @ +11.3% |
| | 19 yrs @ +11.3% | 20th year @ -44.6% |

* 11.3% = S&P 500 ave annual return (past 60 yrs)
Chart 7-11 Courtesy of SAAFTI

MAJOR POINT SUMMARY

— Bear markets can be worse than you imagine.

— Market misconceptions can cost you dearly.

— The bull market is exhibiting signs of weariness.

— Continuing to "buy on the dip" could be fatal to your financial health.

— Inverse funds and market multiple products — ways to make money in down markets.

— Investing in the right sector at the right time can be very profitable.

— The stock market does show patterns, it's not a random walk.

— Dollar-cost averaging won't save you from a bear market.

— You need time to recoup from the bear; better yet, avoid the bear.

"It is prudent to keep funds liquid but liquidity often has its price: current taxes."

— *James Sheperdson III, President*
Endeavor Series Trust

CHAPTER 8

Taming the Tax Man

KEEPING MORE OF WHAT YOU EARN

It is one thing to earn a good investment return, it is yet another major accomplishment to keep as much of your earnings as possible sheltered from the tax bite. On average, you work over 120 days a year just to pay your state and federal taxes. Your Tax Freedom Day may be up to twenty days more if you live in a high tax state such as New York while residents of low tax states such as Alabama, Mississippi, and Montana obtain their freedom approximately sixteen days earlier than the average taxpayer. In addition to earning a respectable investment return, you want to gear your investments so that you get to keep more of what you earn.

The value of tax sheltering your investments can be illustrated with a simple example. Assume you invest $2,000 a year in a taxable investment. Chart 8-1 shows the value of that investment at the end of various periods and assuming a variety of investment returns. Interest/dividends are reinvested and an effective tax rate (combined federal and state) of 35 percent is applied to earned interests/dividends.

TAXABLE INVESTMENT

Chart 8-1	Value at this Rate of Return		
Years	4%	7%	10%
5	$ 10,820	$ 11,492	$ 12,216
10	$ 23,146	$ 25,930	$ 29,149
15	$ 37,186	$ 44,070	$ 52,619
20	$ 53,179	$ 66,861	$ 85,151
25	$ 71,397	$ 95,496	$130,244
30	$ 92,150	$131,473	$192,748

Chart 8-1 Taxable Investment. Assumes interest/dividends reinvested and a 35 percent combined effective tax rate.

As you can see from the chart, your $2,000 annual investment with a 4 percent rate of return would have grown to $53,179 by the end of twenty years. Boosting your rate of return to 7 percent and keeping your money invested for twenty-five years would raise the value of your investment to $95,496. Earning a 10 percent return for thirty years bumps the value of your portfolio up to $192,748.

It does not take long for a relatively small annual investment ($2,000) to build up to a sizeable nest egg. That is the beauty of reinvesting your interest and dividends and compounding your investment gains. In other words, put your investment earnings back to work for you. You can magnify the value of your investment portfolio even more by reinvesting more of your investment earnings.

How can you accomplish reinvesting more of your money? That's a fair question and one easy enough to answer. It's as simple as keeping the tax man at bay. In other words, combining the miracle of compound interest with the incredible power of tax deferral! If there is a 'secret' to investing, this is it! There are a number of tax-deferred options to fit any investment budget. You can choose from such tax-deferred investments as individual retirement accounts (IRA's), simplified employee pension plans (SEP's) for the self-employed, company sponsored retirement plans such as 401(k)'s, and variable annuities, just to name a few. The first three; IRA's, SEP's, and 401(k)'s; provide for tax-deductible contributions within certain limits, as well as tax-deferred earnings. Variable annuities are usually funded with after-tax contributions, all earnings are tax-deferred, they have virtually no contribution limits, and no requirement to begin withdrawals at a certain age. Of course, you can employ as many of these tax-deferred investment options as your circumstances dictate.

Now, let's take a look to see what happens when you take your annual $2,000 investment and place it in a tax-deferred investment vehicle. Just as before, interest/dividends are reinvested to compound your investment gains. The only difference is that taxes are postponed until after you start withdrawing money from your tax-deferred investment for use during retirement. Comparing the same holding periods and investment rates of return, we see a significant difference in the value of your investment portfolio. The results are shown in Chart 8-2.

TAX-DEFERRED INVESTMENT

Chart 8-2	Value at this Rate of Return		
Years	4%	7%	10%
5	$ 11,286	$ 12,374	$ 13,580
10	$ 25,057	$ 29,880	$ 35,834
15	$ 41,861	$ 54,647	$ 72,298
20	$ 62,364	$ 89,687	$132,049
25	$ 87,382	$139,262	$229,958
30	$117,909	$209,398	$390,394

Chart 8-2 Tax-deferred investment. Assumes interest/dividends reinvested.

Using a tax-deferred investment increases the value of your investment portfolio to $62,364 for an investment earning a 4 percent rate of return for twenty years. That compares with the $53,179 portfolio value for the taxable investment. The difference is even more dramatic when the investment earns a higher rate of return over a longer time period. Consider the investment earning 10 percent over thirty years. In this case, the tax-deferred portfolio grows to $390,394 versus only $192,748 for the taxable portfolio, over twice as much!

BENEFITS OF VARIABLE ANNUITIES

Without a doubt, keeping the tax man at bay can pay tremendous benefits in the form of higher portfolio values. It's appropriate here to review the benefits of one form of tax-deferral that anyone can use...variable annuities, an investment you should not overlook, especially if you are approaching your retirement years.

If you got a late start on saving for retirement or have decided that the amount of money you have accumulated to date is not going to last you through your retirement years, one means of increasing the potential return on your investments and the amount of financial assets you will have available at retirement is the variable annuity.

Baby boomers, looking ahead to retirement, are taking this message to heart. Variable annuity sales have skyrocketed over the past several years, bolstered by the coming of age of the baby boom generation. According to the VARDS Report, variable annuity sales reached a record $51.5 billion in 1995. In fact, the more than $148 billion in variable annuity sales during the period 1993 through 1995 is over 60 percent more than the $92 billion in variable annuity sales for the previous seven years combined. See Chart 8-3.

A number of factors are behind this explosive growth. To be sure, the sustained bull market has drawn new investors. Likewise, the growth of mutual funds have expanded investment choices while 401(k) plans have taught investors the value of tax-deferred investing. Enhanced variable annuity products have also played a role in attracting new customers.

INDUSTRY VARIABLE ANNUITY SALES

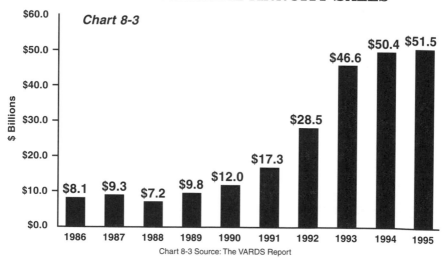

Chart 8-3

Chart 8-3 Source: The VARDS Report

Finally, the coming of age of the baby boom generation represents a prime market for variable annuities. Baby boomers are using variable annuities as a way to grow their retirement assets efficiently while taking advantage of their tax-deferral benefits.

A variable annuity is an insurance contract with a different twist. This tax-deferred retirement vehicle is issued by an insurance carrier that offers mutual fund-type investment options and includes life insurance protection. Unlike its distant cousin, the fixed annuity, the variable annuity does not guarantee a minimum rate of interest over the contract lifetime. However, it does permit investment in equities

> **"Mutual funds and annuities are complementary, not mutually exclusive investments. The only significant difference between the two is that in variable annuity contracts, mutual funds are called sub-accounts."**
>
> *— Bruce F. Wells*
> **All about Variable Annuities**

through a variety of investment options, thereby giving the investor an opportunity to participate in the stock market which has traditionally outperformed other forms of investments over the long-term. The variable annuity value is determined by the changing value of the underlying portfolio of debt and equity securities.

The underlying portfolio typically looks and performs just like a family of mutual funds. Today, many mutual fund companies offer variable annuities in conjunction with an insurance company, where the underlying investments mirror well-known funds and are, in fact, managed by the same portfolio managers.

Under the fixed annuity contract, the insurance company assumes the investment risk while variable annuity investors shoulder the market risk in anticipation of enhancing their investment return and boosting their retirement distribution amount. The purchase of a variable annuity can be tailored to the individual's financial situation offering either a lump sum payment or a series of installment payments. As indicated earlier, the range of available investment options continues to expand. Investors can opt between a number of investment choices including money market, balanced, fixed income, index, and equity funds. There is even a variable annuity in registration today that plans to include an inverse fund such as we discussed in Chapter 7, "Making Money In Down Markets." This could really have exciting potential.

Other investment options increasing the degree of diversification available beyond traditional growth and income funds include mortgage securities funds, global and international equities funds, and gold and natural resources funds. Like mutual fund families, variable annuities allow investors to move between these portfolios with no or minimal cost. Obviously, the investment return and principal value will fluctuate and an investor's shares in a mutual fund or a variable annuity, when redeemed, may be worth more or less than the original investment.

The growth of the multi-fund manager concept also provides for greater diversification and investment choices. Investors can choose from a variety of professionally managed funds with a range of investment goals and strategies. In addition, variable annuities are drawing a great deal of attention due to a number of distinct advantages over investing in mutual funds or individual securities.

The ability to move from one investment vehicle to another as economic realities change provides a great deal of flexibility. This market timing element can reduce risk and produce superior risk-adjusted returns. The investor can take as aggressive or conservative a stance as he or she desires in order to achieve his or her investment goals within the context of his or her investment strategy and risk posture.

This flexibility is enhanced by the variable annuity's tax-deferred status. It allows you to postpone paying taxes on your investment gains until you start to withdraw funds. Investment gains are free to earn additional returns without being diminished by the tax bite. Deferring taxes can dramatically increase the earning potential of your money. For example, a $100,000 investment earning 10 percent annually and taxed at a rate of 31 percent, would be worth $194,884 at the end of ten years. That same investment, tax-deferred, would grow to $259,374. Of course, the IRS still gets its piece of the gains. At the 31 percent rate, the total taxes would amount to $49,406, leaving the investor with $209,968...an increase of $15,084 or 16 percent more earnings than in the taxable account.

The longer your money is invested in a variable annuity, the greater the benefit of tax-deferral. At the end of twenty years, a $100,000 investment returning 10 percent annually and taxed at 31 percent would have grown to $379,799. Tax-deferred, that same $100,000 would have grown to $672,750. After paying 31 percent in taxes, you would still have $495,197 left, an increase in earnings of 41 percent. If you look at the same investment after thirty years, the taxable investment would have grown to $740,169 versus a value of $1,235,009 for the tax-deferred annuity after payment of 31 percent in taxes. That's a 77 percent greater gain.

Another tax saving attribute of variable annuities is the ability of investors to switch investments between subaccounts (investment options within the annuity) without triggering a taxable event as it would in a regular mutual fund. Within multi-manager annuities, you can even change fund families without any current tax consequences. The tax-free exchanges of investment assets also permits the contract holder to utilize asset allocation techniques and market timing without setting off a taxable event. Talk about having your cake and eating it, too! IRS regulations provide for even greater flexibility. Under IRS Section 1035, variable annuity holders may even switch insurance carriers while maintaining the tax-deferral.

Compared with other retirement vehicles such as individual retirement accounts (IRA's), simplified employee pension plans (SEP's), and 401(k)'s, investors are not limited to minimal amounts of annual contributions nor do contributions have to be made from earned income. $1 million or more annually can be contributed to most variable annuities.

Expanded death benefit features represent another attraction of variable annuities. Greater annual step-ups of the minimum death benefit provides a fail-safe value no matter how aggressive an investment stance the annuity holder takes. Think of it as another form of insurance against the onset of a bear market.

In general, minimum death benefits guarantee the contract holder with a minimum payout in case of death, no matter how poorly the investment portfolio may be performing at the time of death. Thus, it protects against downward market fluctuations by locking in a minimum payout. The minimum death benefit is typically calculated as the greater of the contract value at the time of death, the highest account value on any contract anniversary (plus subsequent investments), or the amount contributed plus an effective annual yield. A stepped-up death benefit is reset to equal the account value, typically every seven years, while the rolled-up death benefit is increased by a certain percentage, typically 4 or 5 percent, every year regardless of fund performance. Variable annuity death benefits also avoid probate by passing directly to the named beneficiary.

Variable annuities provide a degree of security not afforded to owners of fixed annuities. Unlike fixed annuities which are general insurance company assets, variable annuity investments are separate assets held by a trustee and cannot be attached by creditors in the event the insurance company fails. And in some states, variable annuities are also judgment proof and cannot be attached by the creditors of the owner of the annuity.

Variable annuities are geared toward investors with a long-term focus on retirement planning. Surrender charges for early withdrawal of funds discourage redemptions and encourage letting the money perform its job of building retirement funds. Like retirement accounts, except under certain circumstances, you cannot withdraw variable annuity funds prior to age 59 1/2 without incurring a 10 percent tax penalty. However, you can delay beginning withdrawals from the annuity until age 90 or longer, compared to age 70 1/2 with tax-deferred retirement accounts. Depending on your personal financial situation, this could be a very important feature.

Surrender charges can amount to as much as 9 percent in the early years with a downward sliding scale to zero after seven years. Obviously, incurring surrender charges can entirely wipe out or substantially reduce investment returns. Therefore, it's important you invest with a long-term perspective.

The annuity aspect comes into play when you decide to start withdrawing your retirement funds. A variety of payout options gives investors the ability to plan their retirement income the way they want to receive it. At that time, you can either make irregular or systematic withdrawals while leaving your investment in the variable annuity account, or you can annuitize the account. For most investors, I would not recommend annuitization.

Among annuity payout options are a single lump sum payment, lifetime annuity (you receive income for the remainder of your life), joint lifetime annuity (you and your spouse receive income as long as either of you is alive), and a lifetime annuity with a minimum number of payments guaranteed. Should you die before you receive the prescribed minimum number of payments, your beneficiary will receive the balance. With a variable annuity, if your heir is also your spouse, he or she can opt to continue the annuity and further postpone withdrawals and taxes.

It's easy to get into a variable annuity. Typically, only a $1,000 minimum initial investment is required. Subsequent investments can be as low as $50. However, the average initial investment totals $20,000.

Of course there are some trade-offs to consider. First of all, variable annuities usually carry higher fees than a typical mutual fund; however, the gap has been narrowing in recent years. Be sure to take into account all fees including the management fees, contract maintenance fee, and an assessment to cover mortality and expense risk and administration. Shop around for the best deal in terms of overall product and fees. Carefully examine the prospectus for all costs, fees, and terms. These fees typically total 2.24 percent annually on a $25,000 investment, compared to an average 1.4 percent for a mutual fund. For this reason, annuities work best with fairly aggressive growth stock funds that offer the higher potential long-term returns. In these funds, the additional fees are often offset by superior performance. I believe this occurs because funds under the variable annuity umbrella are often smaller and thus more nimble than their retail counterparts. In addition, variable annuity investors typically take a longer term investment focus and cause less turnover problems for the portfolio manager.

When comparing variable annuities, determine what other features are available such as electronic funds transfer, dollar-cost averaging, account rebalancing, number of transfers allowed per year, any transfer charges, flexibility of distribution options, and adequacy of account valuation statement.

The stiff surrender charges can be a significant drawback should circumstances force the withdrawal of money during the early years of the contract. Finally, depending on the annuity chosen, the choice of investment options may be limited or the presence of top performing fund managers may be absent. Investigate the number of subaccounts and the range of investment options. Likewise, evaluate the fund performance in light of your investment goals and risk posture.

As baby boomers continue to move toward retirement age, look for growing interest in variable annuities as an excellent vehicle to fund their retirement dreams. Chart 8-4 illustrates the tax benefits of investing in a variable annuity versus a mutual fund. The early year results of the variable annuity are hampered by the deferred sales charge and the 10% tax penalty if the annuity was surrendered early. If you can stick it out for

TAX-DEFERRED VARIABLE ANNUITY
VS. MUTUAL FUND

Chart 8-4   **Tax-Deferred Variable Annuity Contract**

Year	Age	Contract Value *	Deferred Sales Charge	Income Tax	Tax Penalty	Net After Taxes
1995	59	$100,000	$7,000	$0	$0	$93,000
1996	60	117,600	6,000	4,524	0	107,076
1997	61	138,298	5,000	12,986	0	120,312
1998	62	162,638	4,000	22,869	0	135,769
1999	63	191,262	3,000	34,422	0	153,840
2000	64	224,924	2,000	47,941	0	174,984
2001	65	264,511	1,000	63,769	0	199,742
2002	66	311,065	0	82,315	0	228,750
2003	67	365,813	0	103,667	0	262,146
2004	68	430,196	0	128,776	0	301,419
2005	69	505,910	0	158,305	0	347,605
2006	70	594,950	0	193,031	0	401,920
2007	71	699,661	0	233,868	0	465,703
2008	72	822,802	0	281,893	0	540,909
2009	73	967,615	0	338,370	0	629,245
2010	74	1,137,915	0	404,787	0	733,128
2011	75	1,338,188	0	482,893	0	855,295
2012	76	1,573,709	0	574,747	0	998,963
2013	77	1,850,682	0	682,766	0	1,167,916
2014	78	2,176,402	0	809,797	0	1,366,605
2015	79	2,559,449	0	959,185	0	1,600,264
2016	80	3,009,912	0	1,134,866	0	1,875,046
2017	81	3,539,656	0	1,341,466	0	2,198,190
2018	82	4,162,636	0	1,584,426	0	2,578,208
2019	83	4,895,260	0	1,870,151	0	3,025,108

* This assumes a 17.60% before-tax rate of return. This was the average return of S&P '500' for 1980-89. Of course, past performance is no guarantee of future results. A 39.00% marginal tax bracket is used.

Mutual Fund

Year	Age	After Tax Fund Value	Deferred Sales Charge *	Net After Taxes	Net Difference In Favor Of Annuity
1995	59	$100,000	$5,000	$95,000	$(-2,000)
1996	60	110,736	4,000	106,736	340
1997	61	122,625	3,000	119,625	687
1998	62	135,790	2,000	133,790	1,980
1999	63	150,368	1,000	149,368	4,472
2000	64	166,511	0	166,511	8,472
2001	65	184,388	0	184,388	15,354
2002	66	204,184	0	204,184	24,566
2003	67	226,105	0	226,105	36,040
2004	68	250,380	0	250,380	51,039
2005	69	277,261	0	277,261	70,344
2006	70	307,027	0	307,027	94,892
2007	71	339,990	0	339,990	125,804
2008	72	376,491	0	376,491	164,418
2009	73	416,911	0	416,911	212,334
2010	74	461,671	0	461,671	271,457
2011	75	511,236	0	511,236	344,059
2012	76	566,122	0	566,122	432,840
2013	77	626,901	0	626,901	541,015
2014	78	694,205	0	694,205	672,400
2015	79	768,735	0	768,735	831,529
2016	80	851,266	0	851,266	1,023,780
2017	81	942,658	0	942,658	1,255,532
2018	82	1,043,862	0	1,043,862	1,534,346
2019	83	1,155,931	0	1,155,931	1,869,177

* If a no-load fund is used, the breakeven in favor of the annuity will take several years longer.

Chart 8-4 Courtesy of SIMCO

10 years or more, the after-tax differences in favor of the variable annuity are potentially so huge that you can't ignore them.

It is important to note that this illustration assumes that the entire annuity contract is liquidated at once, an unlikely event. If withdrawals are scattered over time, the comparison would favor the variable annuity even more over the mutual fund.

Einstein believed that compound interest was one of the great wonders of the world. Tax-deferred investing takes that one step beyond, putting all the dollars to work many times over instead of being diminished by the tax bite.

The "Rule of 72" puts the benefit of tax-deferred investing into a time perspective. The "Rule of 72" states that in order to determine how long it takes money to double in value divide 72 by the expected return to arrive at the number of years it will take. For example, an investment earning a return of 9 percent will take eight years to double.

72/9 = 8 YEARS TO DOUBLE

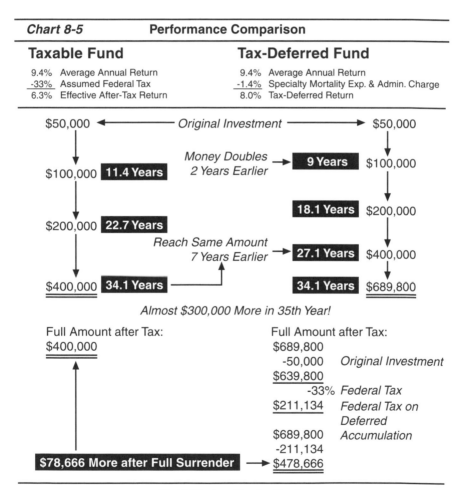

Chart 8-5   **Performance Comparison**

Taxable Fund   **Tax-Deferred Fund**

9.4% Average Annual Return   9.4% Average Annual Return
-33% Assumed Federal Tax   -1.4% Specialty Mortality Exp. & Admin. Charge
6.3% Effective After-Tax Return   8.0% Tax-Deferred Return

$50,000 ◄——— *Original Investment* ———► $50,000

Money Doubles 2 Years Earlier → **9 Years** $100,000

$100,000 **11.4 Years**

18.1 Years $200,000

$200,000 **22.7 Years**

Reach Same Amount 7 Years Earlier → **27.1 Years** $400,000

$400,000 **34.1 Years** ——— **34.1 Years** $689,800

Almost $300,000 More in 35th Year!

Full Amount after Tax: Full Amount after Tax:
$400,000 $689,800
                                 -50,000 *Original Investment*
                                $639,800
                                  -33% *Federal Tax*
                                $211,134 *Federal Tax on Deferred Accumulation*
                                $689,800
                                 -211,134
$78,666 More after Full Surrender → $478,666

Chart 8-5 Courtesy of American Skandia

Chart 8-5 compares the performance of a taxable mutual fund versus a tax-deferred fund. As you can see, the $50,000 initial investment is doubled to $100,000 over two years earlier in the tax-deferred investment. Likewise, the tax-deferred fund reaches a value of $400,000 after twenty-seven years, seven years before the taxable investment. Of course, tax-deferral does not equate to tax-free investing. The tax-deferred account will have to eventually pay income tax, in this case $211,134, on the deferred investment gains. However, the investor is still better off by nearly $79,000. In real life, most investors will not surrender their entire annuity at once and pay taxes; therefore, the balance of the $689,800 after withdrawals and fees will be left to continue to earn income and defer taxes.

Chart 8-6 shows the difference in annual retirement income based on the accumulated retirement portfolio.

DIFFERENCE IN RETIREMENT INCOME

Chart 8-6

$400,000	Take Assumed Rate as Annual Income	$689,800
9.4%	Do Not Invade Principal	9.4% - 1.4% = 8%
$37,600	**47% Greater Income** ⟶	**$55,180**

Chart 8-6 Courtesy of American Skandia.

The tax-deferred annuity encompasses three distinct phases, each with its own level of importance. Chart 8-7 illustrates the three phases. During the Investment Phase you make one or more premium payments which are allocated to one or more separate accounts invested in portfolios of stocks, bonds, money market instruments, and/or other securities. The sooner you begin your retirement plan the better because your money will have more time to work for you. It is important to recognize the impact of inflation that erodes the value of your retirement fund's purchasing power. It is a good idea to increase your contributions by an inflation factor to compensate for the higher cost of living in years to come.

During the Accumulation Phase, your annuity premiums immediately begin accumulating on a tax-deferred basis. Unlike taxable mutual funds, earnings are reinvested and compound to build a larger retirement nest egg. As mentioned earlier, you can utilize a market timing strategy and shift investments between portfolios without triggering a taxable event. As the market environment changes, you can adapt your financial portfolio without incurring a tax liability.

The Payout Phase gives you a wide variety of payout options that we've previously discussed, including an option of income you cannot outlive. The payout can be tailored to your own personal financial situation.

ANNUITY PHASES

Chart 8-7

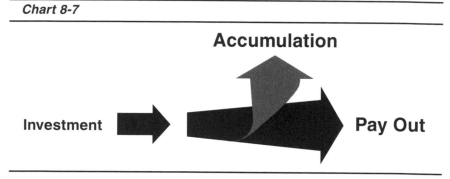

Chart 8-7 Courtesy of American Skandia

Finally, keep in mind that while a variable annuity contract is a great investment tool, it is not the total solution. To realize your full investment potential utilizing a variable annuity, you must still protect yourself from bear market ruin through a disciplined risk management strategy such as market timing.

A WORD ABOUT VARIABLE LIFE INSURANCE

The simplest way I can describe variable life insurance is that it is a permanent life insurance policy allowing the owner of the policy to direct the cash value into and among the different investment options. In a traditional life policy, the insurance company controls the rate of growth of cash value.

Many experts believe variable life offers investors a better deal than traditional whole life insurance, but it is not as cost effective as buying term insurance and investing the difference on your own. However, some investors choose variable life, because if funded in at least four substantially equal payments over a seven year period, it allows investors to borrow tax-free, rather than withdraw from the policy. The loans are repaid before the cash value plus the remaining profits are paid tax-free to your heirs.

Maintaining a variable life policy in compliance with all applicable regulations can be a complex task and should not be attempted without the guidance of an experienced life insurance expert. And, just as with a variable annuity contract, a variable life policy will not reach its full potential without utilizing its equity investment options coupled with a disciplined risk management or market timing strategy.

MAJOR POINT SUMMARY

— Keeping more of what you earn takes tax planning.

— Tax-deferred investments enhance your return.

— Variable annuities combine the miracle of compounding with tax deferral.

— Variable annuities have no limits on contributions and no withdrawal requirements.

— Variable annuities offer flexible investment options.

— Variable annuities can benefit from market timing with no tax consequences.

— Variable annuity death benefits provide bear market insurance.

— Flexible payout options can be tailored to your situation.

— Variable annuity subaccounts can outperform mutual funds.

— "Rule of 72" shows how tax-deferral reduces the time necessary to double your money.

— Variable life insurance can provide for tax-free borrowing and tax-free inheritance, too!

> **"I never knew an early rising, hard working prudent man, careful of his earnings, and strictly honest, who complained of bad luck!"**
>
> *— Joseph Addison*
> *English poet*

CHAPTER 9

Investing for The 21st Century

A MESSAGE FOR KORI'S GENERATION

The future belongs to the young...but only if they sufficiently plan for it. This principle is what I am trying to instill in our daughter, Kori, in her early twenties. Creating wealth in America is within anyone's reach. Keeping it is another matter altogether, as we have discussed throughout this book.

Use this chapter as a primer to help set your goals and establish solid plans to secure your financial future. I recommend that all young people take to heart the following common denominators of successful people:

1. Maintain a desire to excel.

2. Be punctual and develop good work habits (look for work after you have landed your job).

3. Make a good first impression. Have spring to your stride.

4. Write down specific goals.

5. Keep your priorities in order (God, family, career).

6. Learn to communicate effectively both orally and in writing.

7. Work on a lifetime program of self-improvement (love of reading).

Dear Kori:
It's not important that you be the best. What's
important is that you do your best. If you do that,
your mother and I will be proud of you and, more
importantly, you'll be proud of yourself.

— Love,
Dad

To the above, I would add the secrets of the really rich:

1. Put money to work. Start early and stick with a regular savings and investment program throughout your lifetime. Use your money and that of others through partnerships, joint ventures, etc. On any business venture, obtain a large portion of the "seed money" up front and borrow as little as possible (be very conservative here), but be aggressive in the areas of planning, operations, and marketing.

2. Put people to work for you. Go into business for yourself. Leverage yourself by building a team, motivating each member to his or her full potential. Learn to delegate.

3. Keep working yourself. Get out there and talk to the troops. Learn how to lead, not push.

4. Develop the ability to rebound. Recognize that adversity and major mistakes are part of life. The key is to learn how to overcome them and to use that experience to prevent future mistakes.

On the other side of the coin, pay heed *to the following traps that can put you in the poor house*:

1. Continuing to borrow and increase debt load during periods of prosperity. Putting off paying down debt.

2. Assuming that a new investment will not go sour.

3. Co-signing or guaranteeing notes for others.

4. Paying for work before it is completed to your satisfaction.

"The bitterness of poor quality outlasts the sweetness of low price."

— *Author Unknown*

REAL WEALTH 101

Seeking "real wealth" first requires an understanding of what constitutes real wealth. Use the following definitions and comments as a solid framework for developing your plan and strategies to create lasting wealth.

Budget. A spending plan for living "below your means." Target spending as little as necessary on consumption items (entertainment, vacations, etc.) and things that depreciate in value (clothing, cars, consumer electronics, etc.) by comparing prices and ferreting out discounts. This way you can save and invest as much as possible in items that can appreciate (mutual funds, stocks, real estate, art, antiques, etc.) to increase your net worth.

Use credit cards only for convenience and never as a way to obtain credit, because the exorbitant interest charges will eat you alive. For example, assume you charge $2,500 on your credit card at 19.8 percent APR and pay only the required minimum payment of 2 percent of the balance due. It would take you 53.4 years to pay off the balance and over that 53 years you would have paid a total of $13,057. That amounts to $10,577 in interest on purchases of $2,500. Not a very savvy way to accumulate wealth.

One way to boost your net worth is to budget and live below your means. Shopping at discount stores, purchasing less flashy automobiles, clipping coupons, and taking sack lunches to work versus eating at trendy dining establishments all put money in the bank and to work in investments, compounding your income This habit requires creating a mental attitude of saving and investing over spending.

Compound Interest. The process of earning interest on interest over time (a miracle) or paying interest on interest over time (a curse). For example, if you invested $400 a month for 30 years at 8 percent interest, your nest egg would grow to $596,144 due to the miracle of compounding. Likewise, paying $400 per month for 30 years for a home mortgage at 8 percent interest would result in total payments of $144,400, of which, $89,486 would represent interest charges.

Income. The money you receive each week, month, or year from employment or investments. Income is taxed, net worth is not. Which makes more sense to try to maximize?

Net Worth. Also considered real wealth. The difference between what you earn and what you spend each year (i.e. what you save) represents your annual addition to net worth. You can invest this difference in assets such as CDs, stocks, bonds, mutual funds, etc. and ultimately make yourself rich through the miracle of compounding. You calculate net worth by deducting total liabilities from total assets.

Concentrate on building net worth. One savings and investment formula recommends saving 5 percent of after-tax income until age 40. At that point, you add 1 percentage point annually until age 45. From then on, you save at least 10 percent annually and continue to build up your savings and investments, even into retirement.

Obviously, these regular savings require putting into action a financial plan. Put your retirement plans such as 401(k)'s, IRA's, and SEP's to work for you on a tax-deferred basis. Investigate other financial planning options such as insurance, variable annuities, and direct investments such as stocks, bonds, and mutual funds.

Many people fail to take full advantage of their tax-deferred 401(k) plans. Adding $1,000 per year to your contribution only costs you $720 (assuming you are in the 28 percent tax bracket). Over 25 years, that amounts to $18,000 (25 x 720) out of your spending money. However, assuming an 8 percent compounded rate of return, you will retire with an extra $52,600 after 25 years.

As a guide, Thomas J. Stanley and William D. Danko, authors of *The Millionaire Next Door*, devised the following net worth equation. Multiply one-tenth of your age by your annual income to determine the approximate level of your desired net worth. For example, if you are currently 25 years of age and earn $40,000 annually, your net worth should be $100,000 (25 x .1 x $40,000). The difference between your target net worth and actual net worth lets you know how much more you need to save to close the gap.

Rich. The circumstance of possessing enough assets (bank deposits, investments, income producing property, etc.) to generate enough income to live comfortably without having to work to supplement your income. As a single person today, assume that $2,000 a month is sufficient to live comfortably. If so, you might need $800,000 in capital to generate enough income to maintain your purchasing power by the time your working years are over.

Project yourself 20 years into the future. You are now married with three children. In the meantime, inflation has increased at 4 percent annually. At that rate, your income level must increase to around $7,000 per month just to keep up with the higher cost of living and the additional costs of raising a family. In order to generate that level of income and protect against future inflation, you will need approximately $2.5 million in assets. At retirement age, it would take even more, an estimated $3.5 million to $4 million.

Success. The achievement of finding something you like to do so much that you would be happy to do it for nothing. Learn how to perform your work so well that others will pay you for doing it...then you are a success. Utilize all your potential...be all you can be.

When considering your first job, follow your heart, not your pocketbook. Search for the career that you truly love. Don't worry about low initial compensation. Look to the future and look for ways to improve yourself and, in the process, achieve greater job satisfaction and higher compensation.

Here's a three-minute quiz, or what I call Real Wealth 101, that every young person should take. It gets you thinking about the difference between income and real wealth. Take a few minutes and determine how well you understand real wealth. Circle the best answer.

1. A   B   C   People who live in expensive homes and drive luxury cars
                 A. are rich.
                 B. may have a high income.
                 C. are always heavily in debt.

2. A   B   C   If I save 10 percent of my income from now until I retire and invest it wisely,
                 A. I will miss out on a lot of fun.
                 B. I will never be able to take a neat vacation.
                 C. I will accumulate real wealth.

3. True   An NBA All-Star making an income of $4
    False   million per year is rich.

4. A   B   C   Which of the following is a good investment?
                 A. Clothes
                 B. Stock
                 C. Automobile

5. A B C   Compound interest is
                A. so complicated to calculate that it's a
                   miracle that anyone can figure it out.
                B. earning interest on interest over time.
                C. interest paid to make compounds.

6. True   Rich people have sufficient assets to generate
   False   enough income to live comfortably without
                working.

7. A B C   Building real wealth begins with
                A. investments.
                B. budgeting.
                C. savings.

8. True   Keeping your credit cards charged to the
   False   maximum is smart because it lets you buy
                things that you could not afford otherwise.

9. A B C   A rich person always has
                A. high debt.
                B. high income.
                C. high net worth.

10. A B C   Each of the following is a common denomi-
                nator of a successful person except
                A. driving a luxury car.
                B. being punctual with good work habits.
                C. being able to communicate effectively.

Bonus

11. A B C   Suppose you had a choice of two jobs, each
                lasting 35 days. Which one is best?
                A. Job A pays $1,000 per day.
                B. Job B pays 1 cent on day one and
                   doubles the pay each day.

See answer key at the end of the chapter.

Accumulating lasting wealth takes a concerted effort and advance planning. I recommend the following steps for a more satisfying retirement.

1. Develop a reasonable long-term plan and stick with it. View proper planning for worry-free retirement from a long-term perspective. Set your objectives and employ an asset manager. Make changes only in response to significant changes in your circumstances or consistent underachievement of objectives over a complete economic cycle (five or more years). By instituting a plan, you will be less likely to be tempted to react emotionally to short-run fluctuations in investment markets.

2. Be honest in assessing your ability and willingness to take risk. In order to beat taxes and inflation, you must accept some risk. But do not let greed outweigh good investment judgement in determining the proper reward/risk ratio for your financial situation and desired risk posture.

3. Cultivate living habits that favor saving, and ultimately investing, over spending.

4. Let the miracle of compound interest work over time. The market timing risk management approach to investing has proven that it can generate superior returns versus both risk-free investments and the overall market over the long-term, especially on a risk-adjusted basis.

5. Entrust your retirement assets to investment professionals. Unless you possess the experience, personal self-discipline, and willingness to manage your retirement assets full time, I strongly suggest that you hire a professional investment advisor, registered with the SEC under the Investment Advisors Act of 1940. The roster of SAAFTI (address and phone number are located in Chapter 1) is a good source of potential candidates.

   Why worry about day-to-day market fluctuations when you have an experienced, full-time professional tracking market moves for you? Keeping your investment plan on track is like keeping your car finely tuned...for most people, you can't do it yourself anymore. You need to go to the professionals for expertise. Like the automobile repair advertisement says, "You can pay me now or pay me later." If you don't take care to fine-tune your investments, you could pay dearly in poor performance and devastating bear market losses at an inopportune time.

What you need is a good independent mechanic (your local financial planner or investment advisor) who uses the best diagnostic tools (market timing) and the best available parts (top mutual fund families) to give you high performance (superior risk-adjusted returns by participating in 80 percent of the market's advance) and help you steer clear of any accidents (avoiding 80 percent of bear market declines).

FINDING THE RIGHT ADVISOR FOR YOU

Finding the right investment advisor for you plays an important role in your financial planning. More and more individuals are turning to financial advisors for help with their investments. Part of the reason lies in the increasing complexity in the world of investing. Today there are more than 6,000 stock, bond, and money market funds from which to choose, double the number in existence in 1990. In addition, corporations have passed on more of the responsibility to individual employees for selecting among the investment choices for their 401(k) and other retirement plans.

It's unrealistic to expect an individual working to keep the income flowing and trying to build net worth also to be able to track 6,000 mutual funds, to stay on top of multiple asset classes and their relative valuations, and to follow rapidly expanding global opportunities (the U.S. only accounts for 20 percent of the world's economy) in order to effectively manage his or her own money over the long-term.

With more money to invest and a greater dependence on the results of those investments for their retirement nest egg, people are seeking financial advice in record numbers. Some estimates place direct purchases, without a broker or financial advisor, by investors in the $2.8 trillion mutual fund industry accounting for as little as 15 percent of the total.

Every person has a circle of competence...things that they do well. If you make your living as a product development manager in a computer software company, you are probably going to be hard pressed to make a living being a concert pianist. If you need brain surgery you don't attempt it yourself, moonlighting as a brain surgeon. Instead, you find the best brain surgeon available. You have probably heard the old adage, a person serving as his or her own lawyer has a fool for a client. Successful people operate within their own circle of competence and hire outside professionals to work for them in areas outside of that circle of competence. Likewise, you need a full-time, experienced, professional, disciplined investment advisor to take the emotions out of your investment decisions.

Building a good relationship with a financial advisor, however, isn't always easy. To accomplish this, it is helpful to understand the feelings you might experience when you meet with an advisor. First of all, trust needs to form a key aspect in the relationship. It is normal to initially worry that the person across the table is just giving you a line in hopes of trying to sell you something and take your money.

It is also very difficult for many people to openly discuss their financial situations. Talking about money remains a taboo in our society thus exposing your financial situation feels uncomfortable. To add to this discomfort, your advisor is required by law and regulation to ask a number of questions, which you may consider to be very nosy, to determine the suitability of different investment options for you.

You may also fear looking foolish in front of the advisor. As a respected professional in your field, it can be difficult to admit that you have not managed your money as well as you have managed other aspects of your life such as your career. The reality is that very few people have the time or inclination to be experts at many different subjects. Finally, even relatively well-off individuals often don't believe that they have enough money to interest a professional financial advisor.

You need to overcome those fears and uncertainties to make the relationship with your advisor work. First and foremost, ask your advisor questions. The only dumb question is the one that doesn't get asked. You need to establish a comfort level with the advisor by gaining an understanding of his or her background and financial expertise. Don't be afraid to ask uncomfortable questions such as how he or she has invested money for their own account or what investments they have found most profitable or least successful. Inquire why he or she became an investment advisor and what professional background and experience led them to this position.

Make sure you understand the advisor's investment approach and what the worst case scenario might be using that approach. Is that a risk you could accept? Does your investment time frame fit the advisor's investment methods? How is the advisor compensated for managing your money? Does the advisor have access to your funds and under what circumstances? Could your money end up in the advisor's office decorations or seaside condo? If you are not comfortable with the responses to your questions, look elsewhere for an advisor. Remember, your gut feelings or instincts with people often prove right. Find somebody you can work with comfortably.

Time represents one of the most important elements of a successful investment strategy. You must be willing to give the strategy and the investment advisor adequate time to make it work for you.

> **"You can't expect to see calves running in the field the day after you put the bull in the pasture."**
>
> — *Texas rancher*

Constantly changing advisors in search of the perfect fit will end up hurting performance more than it helps. There are many different investment advisors and investment approaches from which to choose. Take the time up front to find one who fits your financial needs and goals and don't be afraid to tell a prospective advisor that you don't think it would be a good fit. If the person gets insulted by your comment, take that as a good indication that he or she is definitely not right for you.

If this is your first venture with a financial advisor, you don't have to trust all of your funds to your new investment advisor. While most advisors charge a sliding scale of fees that benefits the client who has more money under management, it may make sense for you to start with a smaller initial investment and later add to that amount as your confidence in the advisor and his or her strategies increases.

You get what you pay for, so don't base your investment advisor decision on fees alone. Look at the total picture. While it is unwise to pay too much, it can be a disaster to pay too little and lose a major part of your investment or even everything.

BUILDING REAL WEALTH OVER TIME

A final word about time and the young. Young people possess one of the greatest success factors of all...time. The sooner you put your savings and investment plan into action, the longer your money goes to work for you, compounding your investment returns into a substantial nest egg. Accumulating a million dollars by age 65 is not nearly as difficult as it looks, especially if you start early. Over the past 70 years, common stocks have averaged a return of 10.5 percent per year as we learned in Chapter 2. At that rate of return, you double your money in a little less than 7 years. Working backward, it looks like this:

Age	Portfolio Value
65	$1,000,000
58	500,000
51	250,000
44	125,000
37	62,500
30	31,250
23	15,625
16	7,813

Adaptation of Scott Burns' "Missing Margarita Plan"

If your parents invest only $7,813 on your behalf when you turn sixteen, instead of buying you a used car the day you get your driver's license, your retirement is virtually assured. If you just can't get along without that car in high school, you still have the opportunity to earn that $1 million by investing $15,625 by age 23 or $31,250 by age 30. Putting that into perspective, it's only about one year's worth of income for a college graduate with a few years of work experience under his or her belt.

Obviously, a million dollars may not be what it once was, and may not be enough for you to achieve your financial goals 40 or 50 years down the road, but it is still an impressive amount of money, far more than most working people accumulate in a lifetime.

Real Wealth 101 Quiz Answer Key: 1. B, 2. C, 3. F, 4. B, 5. B, 6. T, 7. B, 8. F, 9. C, 10. A, 11. B.

> **"I have a premonition**
> **That soars on silver wings,**
>
> **A dream of your accomplishments**
> **And other wondrous things,**
>
> **I do not know beneath what sky**
> **Nor where you'll challenge fate,**
>
> **I only know it will be high**
> **I only know you will be great!"**
> — *Author Unknown*

MAJOR POINT SUMMARY

— Creating lasting wealth requires planning.

— Develop your success characteristics.

— Put money to work regularly.

— Avoid pitfalls that lead to the poor house.

— Understand the definitions of real wealth and success.

— Concentrate on building net worth.

— Entrust your retirement assets to investment professionals.

— Find an advisor that matches your disposition and financial goals.

— Time and timing can be an unbeatable combination.

"He was at the right place at the right time!"
— *Denis Waitley*

CHAPTER 10
Epilogue

SUMMARIZING THE ALTERNATIVES

I trust that I have made a solid case in this book for the importance of maintaining a healthy percentage of your investment assets committed to equities, even during your "Golden" years of retirement. If this concept needs to be reinforced, refer back to the tale of Connie Conservative in Chapter 1.

With regard to stock market investing, I have tried to show you that the individual investor basically has four alternatives:

1. Buy and Hold Investing — Has theoretically provided enough return to offset taxes and inflation, but very few investors have the emotional strength to ride out all the ups and downs of the stock market. As we showed with Peter Hope in Chapter 1, this strategy can literally wipe you out if a bear market occurs after you retire and are making regular withdrawals.

2. Dollar Cost Averaging — Can be a valuable tool for disciplining a young person to save and invest regularly. However,

as I showed in Chapter 7; it does <u>not</u> offer protection against bear markets and, therefore, is a dangerous and risky strategy in a mature portfolio, unless coupled with market timing.

3. Passive Asset Allocation — Can provide some reduction in risk by spreading your investment among a variety of different asset classes, but also sacrifices significant return potential in the process (See Chapter 4). Furthermore, the risk protection aspect of passive (strategic) asset allocation is highly overrated. After all, 60% of a 50-percent bear market decline is still a 30% loss, much higher than most investors will tolerate.

4. Disciplined Risk Management/Professional Market Timing — Has historically kept bear market losses low enough to keep investors committed to equities and, as a by-product, given investors a superior risk-adjusted return. I believe that it is the only one of the four alternatives that is likely to save our generation and future generations from irreparable financial damage over the long term.

Obviously, I believe with all my heart that market timing is the best strategy you can use to reduce the risks of stock market investing. Yet, I realize that some of you may have read elsewhere that market timing does not work. The contradiction may be confusing, and you may feel that you still do not know what to do!

I offer this suggestion. When I have found myself in a similar dilemma, I found it helpful to list each possible outcome and the likely end result for me personally. Let's go through this exercise with market timing and see if it benefits you.

POSSIBLE OUTCOMES	LIKELY END RESULTS
1. Market timing works/you use it.	Great, you will probably be rich.
2. Market timing does not work/ you use it.	You will make less return than if you did not use it; however, your risk should also be lowered.

MORE OUTCOMES	MORE LIKELY RESULTS
3. Market timing does not work/ you don't use it.	So what!
4. Market timing works/you don't use it.	You may be completely wiped out, especially if you have to make withdrawals during the next bad bear market.

What option will you choose to take? My bet is that you are thinking that you would be nuts *not* to use a disciplined risk management strategy. It's a pure case of reward versus risk. Compare the end results. The worst case scenario while using market timing (2.) means you might earn a little less return. On the other extreme, the worst case of not using market timing (4.) could mean you end up flat broke. You don't have to be a genius to conclude that you need to find a good professional market timing advisor today.

Consider the following comparison. Paying your advisory fee for timing advice is like paying an insurance premium, except that it's for protection against a catastrophic event in the stock market. That's probably a good analogy. However, just like an insurance policy with its deductibles and depreciation calculations, this protection is not 100 percent perfect either. And just like an insurance policy, you don't fail to pay your premium for your next year of coverage because your house did not burn down this year.

If you made it this far in the book, congratulations! You are a winner, because you are now one of those special people who understands why *Lasting Wealth Is A Matter Of Timing*!

Appendix A
Disclosure Statement

SUMMARY

The timing model is based on a set of proprietary indicators and calculations used to project major market movements. This model was originated by John K. Sosnowy in 1970. The timing model is used to determine when to change the allocations in, and/or exchange into and out of various funds having different investment objectives within families of mutual funds.

PARAMETERS

The results of "buy" and "sell" signals generated by the timing model are shown in the illustrations in relation to the movement of the specific portfolios and/or indices utilized. These results would have to be considered hypothetical prior to 1979, since actual account records prior to that date are not available. Sosnowy and his former partner issued a joint sell recommendation in conflict with the model on 11/10/82; however, steps have been taken to insure that such recommendations in conflict with the model will not be issued in the future.

These illustrations are net of all charges, expenses and fees, and assume the reinvestment of all dividends and capital gains. Nothing has been taken out of taxes. Money market funds were not widely available prior to 1975; therefore, we use short-term T-Bills as our money market investment on any illustration going back prior to 1975. All prices are the weekly close nearest to the actual exchange date. The stock, bond, and money market portfolios used in this illustration are not necessarily from the same fund family, as would normally be the case in an actual account.

The NYSE TR Index represents all stocks on the New York Stock Exchange, with dividends reinvested. It is an unmanaged index. You cannot actually invest in the NYSE TR Index.

RISKS

The volatility of the portfolios and/or indices used in these illustrations may be materially different from the mutual fund and/or annuity portfolio actually utilized by a client. Additionally, the portfolio composition of the funds used by clients having similar investment objectives may materially differ from each other, as well as, the portfolios used in this illustration. Therefore, the actual results which could be obtained by an investor would, of course, vary depending on the performance of the particular investments chosen by him and the costs and expenses associated with such investments. The investment return and principal value of an investment will fluctuate so that an investor's shares, when received, may be worth more or less than their original cost. Also, an investment using variable annuity contracts will involve additional expenses and limitations.

The performance data quoted represents past performance. *Past performance should in no way be construed as a guarantee of future return.*

Appendix B
Disclosure Statement

SUMMARY

The timing model is based on a set of proprietary indicators and calculations used to project major market movements. This model was originated by John K. Sosnowy in 1970. The timing model is used to determine when to change the allocations in, and/or exchange into and out of various funds having different investment objectives within families of mutual funds.

Sosnowy is committed to state-of-the art applications of modern portfolio theory utilizing historical simulation techniques. As a result of this ongoing quantitative research, modifications and improvements have been made to the timing model over the years and are expected to be made in the future. We believe it is not only important for an investor to know the actual results that our model existing at the time generated, but also the results that today's timing model would have generated. We have historical data on the key variables in our model all the way back to 1927. Therefore, we can and do run computer simulations back-testing today's model as far back as 1927. This gives us a much greater comfort level about the decisions we made for model improvements than if we based them only on data back to 1970.

PARAMETERS

The results of "buy" and "sell" signals generated by the timing model are shown in the illustrations, in relation to the movement of the specific portfolios and/or indices utilized. These illustrations are hypothetical and do not necessarily represent actual trading.

These illustrations are net of all charges, expenses and fees, and assume the reinvestment of all dividends and capital gains. Nothing has been taken out for taxes. Money market funds were not widely available prior to 1975; therefore, we use short-term T-Bills as our money market investment on any illustration going back prior to 1975. All prices are the weekly close nearest to the actual exchange date. The stock, bond, and money market portfolios used in this illustration are not necessarily from the same fund family, as would normally be the case in an actual account.

The NYSE TR Index represents all stocks on the New York Stock Exchange, with dividends reinvested. It is an unmanaged index. You cannot actually invest in the NYSE TR Index.

RISKS

The volatility of the portfolios and/or indices used in these illustrations may be materially different from the mutual fund and/or annuity portfolio actually utilized by a client. Additionally, the portfolio composition of the funds used by clients having similar investment objectives may materially differ from each other, as well as, the portfolios used in this illustration. Therefore, the actual results which could be obtained by an investor would, of course, vary depending on the performance of the particular investments chosen by him and the costs and expenses associated with such investments. The investment return and principal value of an investment will fluctuate so that an investor's shares, when received, may be worth more or less than their original cost. Also, an investment using variable annuity contracts will involve additional expenses and limitations.

The performance data quoted represents past performance. *Past performance should in no way be construed as a guarantee of future return.*

Glossary

Accreted. The process of earning or growing gradually. For example, the interest on zero coupon bonds is accreted.

Active Asset Allocation. An asset allocation strategy involving continuous monitoring and periodic rebalancing of the portfolio as needed among multiple asset classifications, usually done in increments. See also dynamic asset allocation.

Adjustable Rate Preferred. A preferred security with its dividend payment pegged to a specific index or indices.

AIMR Standards. Performance presentation standards mandated by the Association for Investment Management and Research.

Alpha. The difference between portfolio return and expected return. A positive alpha means a portfolio has earned a premium over what is expected given the level of risk-free return, market index return, and the volatility of the portfolio as expressed by beta.

American Depositary Receipt (ADR). A negotiable receipt for shares of a foreign corporation held in the vault of a United States depositary bank.

Annual Report. The Securities and Exchange Commission required report presenting a portrayal of the company's operations and financial position. It includes a balance sheet, income statement, statement of cash flows, description of company operations, management discussion of company financial condition and operating results, and any events which materially impact the company.

Annuity. A series of payments continuing until death. An annuity contract, issued by an insurance company, provides a series of payments for the life of the annuitant or for an agreed-upon number of years. See also Fixed Annuity and Variable Annuity.

Arbitrage. The process of attempting to profit from small discrepancies in price between securities and/or between markets.

Artificial Intelligence. The field of computer science dedicated to producing software that attempts to mimic the processes of the human brain.

Asset Allocation. Investment strategy of reducing risk and increasing return potential by investing in a variety of asset types. Also known as strategic or passive allocation because changes in allocation are made very infrequently.

Asset Play. A stock investment that value investors find attractive due to asset undervaluation by the market.

At The Money. The situation when the underlying security's market price equals the strike, or exercise price.

Back End Load. A sales charge that is only deducted at redemption of fund shares. The charge typically decreases to zero over time. Also known as deferred sales charge.

Back Testing. An important tool in model building. A strategy is tested on historical data, and then the strategy is applied to new, or out-of-sample data to determine whether the results are consistent with the sample.

Basis Point. Gradation of fixed income yields based on a 100-point scale representing one percent. For example, the yield difference between 7.75% and 7.95% is 20 basis points.

Basis Price. The cost of an investment used to determine capital gains or losses.

Bear Hug. An unsolicited acquisition offer submitted to management or the board of directors of the target company. The offer is designed to force the target to publicly disclose the offer and enter into negotiations with the bidder.

Bear Market. A period of time during which stock prices decline over a period of months or years. It is usually defined by a fall in prices in excess of 20 percent on the major benchmark indices.

Beta. A measure of volatility comparing the returns of an individual investment relative to the market. Securities with a beta of 1.0 are equal in risk to that of the overall market. Stocks with betas greater than 1.0 possess more risk than the market while stocks with betas less than 1.0 have less risk than the market.

Bond. A long-term debt security which obligates the issuer to pay interest and repay the principal. The holder does not have any ownership rights in the issuer.

Bond Ratio. The measure of a company's leverage comparing the firm's debt to total capital.

Bottom Up Investing. Investment strategy starting with company fundamentals and then moving to the overall economic and investment environment.

Bull Market. A period of time during which stock prices advance over a period of months or years. It is usually defined by a rise in prices in excess of 25 percent on the major benchmark indices.

Busted. A convertible whose underlying common stock value has fallen so low that the convertible provision no longer holds any value.

Buy and Hold. A strategy of purchasing a portfolio of securities and riding out all of the ups and downs of the market over the long-term.

Call Option. A contract providing the holder the right to buy the underlying security at a specific price for a specified time period.

Call Provision. A provision allowing the security issuer to recall the security before maturity.

Capital Gains. The profits received and distributed from the sale of securities within the portfolio.

Capitalization Weighted Index. A market average such as the S & P 500 that takes into account the market value of each security in the index.

Cash Equivalent. An asset type with maturities of less than one year. Also known as a money market security.

Cash Flow. The flow of funds in and out of an operating business. Normally calculated as net income plus depreciation and other non-cash items.

Cash Flow/Debt Ratio. The relationship of free cash flow to total long-term indebtedness. This ratio is helpful in tracking a firm's ability to meet scheduled debt and interest payment requirements.

Cash Flow/Interest Ratio. How many times free cash flow will cover fixed interest payments on long-term debt.

Cash Flow Per Share. The amount earned before deduction for depreciation and other charges not involving the outlay of cash.

Cash Ratio. Used to measure liquidity. It is calculated as the sum of cash and marketable securities divided by current liabilities. It indicates how well a company can meet current liabilities.

Closed-End Fund. An investment fund with a fixed number of shares outstanding and trades on exchanges like stock in regular companies.

Cluster Investing. Method of diversification recommending investing in stocks from different clusters or groups.

Collar. In a stock-for-stock acquisition, a provision for the adjustment of the exchange ratio in order to guarantee that the target company's shareholders will receive securities having a specified minimum market value.

Common and Preferred Cash Flow Coverage Ratios. How many times annual free cash flow will cover common and preferred cash dividend payments.

Common Stock Ratio. The relationship of common stock to total company capitalization.

Contrarian. An investor seeking securities out-of-favor with other investors.

Convertible. A security that is exchangeable into common stock at the option of the holder under specified terms and conditions.

Correction. A price decline with the market retracting some of its previous gains, but not enough to be defined as a bear market.

Cost-Benefit Analysis. A review of the incremental costs and benefits associated with a specific trading strategy.

Covered Call. An option in which the investor owns the underlying security.

Cross-Correlation. Analysis of investment returns of different asset classes to determine whether or not they move in conjunction with or counter to other asset classifications.

Crown Jewel. A company's most attractive asset or line of business.

Cumulative. As it relates to preferred stock, any unpaid preferred dividends accrue and must be paid prior to resumption of common stock dividends.

Current Ratio. A liquidity ratio calculated by dividing current assets by current liabilities.

Cycles. Repeating patterns of business, economic and market activity. The length of a cycle is measured in trading days from bottom to bottom. The end of one cycle is the beginning of the next. See also market cycle.

Cyclical. Industries and companies that advance and decline in relation to the changes in the overall economic environment.

Day. A trading day, weekends and holidays excluded.

Debt-To-Equity Ratio. The relationship of debt to shareholder's equity in a firm's capitalization structure.

Defensive Investments. Securities that are less affected by economic contractions, thus offering some downside price protection.

Definitive Agreement. A legally binding agreement which explicitly sets forth the representations, obligations and rights of each party, including the conditions under which the merger can be terminated.

Discount Rate. The interest rate the Federal Reserve charges on loans to member banks.

Discretionary Account. An account in which trades are effected without prior client approval, usually through the use of a limited power of attorney.

Diversification. The spreading of investment risk by owning different types of securities, investments in different geographical markets, etc.

Dollar Cost Averaging. Investment strategy of investing a fixed amount of money over time to achieve a lower average security purchase price.

Dow Jones Industrial Average. Market index consisting of 30 U.S. industrial companies. Used as a measure of market performance.

Dow Theory. Investment theory that the market moves in three simultaneous movements, which help forecast the direction of the economy and the market.

Drawdown. The reduction in account equity (or value) as a result of a trade or series of trades over a defined period of time. Maximum drawdown can be best expressed as the worst paper loss over the period.

DRIP. Dividend reinvestment plan in which stockholders can purchase additional shares with dividends and/or cash.

Dynamic Asset Allocation. An asset allocation strategy involving continuous monitoring and periodic rebalancing of the portfolio as needed among multiple asset classifications based on an analysis of the current reward/risk ratio in each class as well as changes in investor circumstances. Rebalancing is usually done in increments. See also active asset allocation.

Earnings Per Share. Net after-tax income divided by the number of outstanding company shares.

Economic Series. The complete cycle of economic periods such as from expansion to slowdown to contraction to recession/depression to increased activity back to expansion.

Economic Value. With respect to stock, the anticipated free cash flow the company will generate over a period of time, discounted by the weighted cost of a company's capital.

Efficient Market. A market that instantly takes into account all known financial information and reflects it in the security's price.

Emerging Markets. Securities markets in countries other than those, such as the United States, England, Germany, Japan, etc., which are considered to be established, developed markets.

Exchange Offer. An offer made directly to the target company's shareholders soliciting the exchange of their shares for the bidder's securities. No shareholder vote is required.

Exercise Price. The price at which an option of futures contract can be executed. Also known as the striking price.

Expected Return. The return one should have expected given the risk taken, overall market returns, and the level of risk-free returns.

Expected Value. An anticipated value of a strategy based on probability.

Expert System. A rule-drive artificial intelligence trading system requiring an expert to interpret the indicators. An expert system possesses the advantage of being able to outperform many mechanical systems.

Expiration Date. The last day on which an option or future can be exercised.

Fairness Letter. An opinion, usually written by an investment banker and addressed to the board of directors, as to the fairness of a proposed reorganization from the standpoint of the company's shareholders.

Fed. Short for Federal Reserve.

Federal Funds. Also known as Fed Funds. They are the legal reserves required to be held by banks and often borrowed and lent between banks overnight. The interest rate charged on Fed Funds is known as the Fed Funds Rate.

Federal Reserve. The national banking system consisting of 12 independent federal reserve banks in Atlanta, Boston, Chicago, Cleveland, Dallas, Kansas City, Minneapolis, New York, Philadelphia, Richmond, St. Louis and San Francisco.

Financial Intermediary. A financial institution such as a trust company or an investment manager who directs other people's money into investments.

Financial Planner. One who prepares investment, tax, estate, and/or insurance plans and may provide advice as to the implementation of such plans.

Fiscal Year. The 12-month accounting period that conforms to the company's natural operating cycle versus the calendar year.

Fixed Annuity. A contract issued by an insurance company guaranteeing a particular rate of interest for a certain period of time, after which the guaranteed rate is reset.

Forecasting. Making projections about the future direction of the economy and the markets, usually based on fundamental analysis.

Formula Investing. An investment strategy that shifts portfolio assets from one asset classification to another based on predetermined factors.

401(k) Plan. A defined contribution retirement plan that allows employees to contribute part of their salary before taxes. Many plans offer a variety of investment options, including stock, bond and money market funds.

Free Cash Flow. Determined by calculating operating earnings after taxes and then adding depreciation and other noncash expenses, less capital expenditures and increases in working capital.

Free Cash Flow/Earnings Ratio. The percentage of earnings actually available in cash. It is the percentage of free cash available to company management for investments, acquisitions, plant construction and dividends.

Front End Load. A mutual fund sold to the public at the offering price. The difference between the offering price and net asset value represents a sales charge on each investment in the fund.

Fundamental Analysis. Investment strategy focusing on the intrinsic value of the company as evidenced by a review of the balance sheet, income statement, cash flow and operating performance. Can also be applied to the market as a whole.

Fund Timing. Moving in and out of stock funds based on a technical signal, often based on the price of the fund moving above or below a moving average. Also known as fund conversion or fund switching.

Gap. A trading pattern when the price range from one day does not overlap the previous day's price range.

Global Depositary Receipt (GDR). Similar to ADR. Depositary receipt issued in the international community representing shares in a foreign company. Other designations include International Depositary Receipt (IDR) and European Depositary Receipt(EDR).

Greenmail. A corporate repurchase of a block of stock at a premium price in order to remove the threat of an unfriendly takeover attempt by the seller.

Growth Investments. Companies or industries with earnings projected to outpace the market consistently over the long-term.

Hedging. The use of derivative securities such as options or futures in an attempt to reduce or eliminate the risk of holding another security.

High-Tech Stock. Securities of firms in high-technology industries such as biotechnology, computers, electronics, lasers, medical devices and robotics.

High Yield Bond. Also known as a junk bond.

Hybrid Security. A security that possesses the characteristics of both a stock and a bond, such as a convertible bond.

Indenture. The legal contract spelling out the terms and conditions between the issuer and bondholders.

Index. Compilation of performance for specific groupings of stocks or mutual funds such as the Dow Jones Industrial Average and S & P 500.

Index Fund. A mutual fund whose objective is to mirror the performance of a popular index such as the S & P 500.

Index Option. An option on a specific market index such as the S & P 100 (OEX). Also known as a cash settlement option.

Indicator. A measurement of the economy or securities markets used by economists and investment analysts to predict future economic and financial moves and direction. Indicators are classified as leading, coincidental or lagging. This can be based on fundamental, monetary, sentiment, or momentum factors. Indicator examples include interest rate changes, price-to-earnings ratios, and number of unemployment claims, etc.

Individual Retirement Account (IRA). A tax-deferred retirement account for wage earners. An IRA account holder must begin taking distributions by April 1 of the year after reaching age 70 $1/2$.

Inflation. A general rise in the prices of goods and services. The Consumer Price Index and the Producer Price Index are two measures of inflation.

IPO (Initial Public Offering). The first public offering of a company's stock.

Insider. Anyone having access to material corporate information. Most frequently used to refer to company officers, directors and top management.

Institutional Investor. Investor organizations, such as pension funds and money managers, which trade large volumes of securities.

In The Money. The situation when the price of the underlying security is above the exercise price.

Internal Rate Of Return. Also known as Dollar Weighted Return; so called because it gives greater weight to those time periods when more money was invested. Not suitable for determining the relative skill of a manager.

Intrinsic Value. The difference between the current market price of the underlying security and the striking price of a related option.

Inverse Fund. A mutual fund whose investment results are designed to inversely correlate with a major market average such as the S & P 500.

Investment Manager. One acting as an investment advisor to other people. The arrangement may or may not involve discretionary authority to make trades on behalf of the client. See also registered investment advisor.

Investment Style. The predominant investment philosophy of an investment manager, such as a value investor, momentum player, earnings driven, market timer, etc.

Junk Bond. A bond with ratings below investment grade.

Leading Indicator. An economic measurement that tends to accurately predict the future direction of the economy or stock market.

LEAPS. Long-term equity participation securities. Long-term options with maturities up to two years.

Leverage. The use of debt to finance a company's operations. Also, the use of debt by investors to increase the return on investment from securities transactions.

Leveraged Buyout. A reorganization in which a group of investors, usually acting in conjunction with management, purchases control of the target company with borrowed funds that are secured by the target's assets.

Life Cycle Investing. Developing an investment strategy based on where you are in your life cycle.

Liquidation. A reorganization in which a company's assets are sold piecemeal to various buyers and the net proceeds distributed to shareholders.

Liquidity. The degree of ease in which assets can be turned into readily available cash.

Listed. Investment securities that have met the listing requirements of a particular exchange.

Load. Denotes a mutual fund's initial or deferred sales charge. See also back end load, front end load, and no load.

Lock-Up. A provision of a merger agreement which gives the proposed bidder certain advantages over other potential acquirers.

Maintenance Margin. The minimum equity value that must be maintained in a margin account. Initial margin requirements include a minimum deposit of $2,000 before any credit can be extended. Current Regulation T rules require maintenance margin equal at least 50 percent of the market value of the margined positions.

Margin. The capital (in cash or securities) that an investor deposits with a broker to borrow additional funds to purchase securities.

Margin Call. A demand from a broker for additional cash or securities as collateral to bring the margin account back within maintenance limits.

Market Cycle. A variation in prices that comes full-circle, usually consisting of a decline in excess of 20 percent and a subsequent advance of at least 25 percent.

Market Risk. The uncertainty of returns due to fluctuations in the overall market.

Market Timing. Measuring the direction of a market or a market index and moving funds in or out of the market based on those measurements. A method of reducing risk exposure to the market. Classic market timing usually involves 100 percent moves between stocks and cash. See also tactical asset allocation.

Mechanical System. A trading system that automatically generates buy and sell signals when a set of conditions have been reached.

Momentum Indicator. A market indicator using price and volume data to predict strength or weakness and possible turning points.

Monetary Analysis. The study of money flows into and out of the economy. Useful in predicting interest rates and market direction.

Money Markets. Short-term low-risk investments such as T-Bills, bank CDs, commercial paper, and bankers acceptances.

Moving Average. A mathematical procedure used to smooth out fluctuations in data.

Municipal Bond. A bond issued by a local or state government or government agency.

Mutual Fund. An investment company that sells shares in itself to the investing public and uses the proceeds to purchase individual securities.

NAFTA. North American Free Trade Agreement.

Naked Option. An option written when the investor does not have a position in the underlying security.

NASD. The National Association of Securities Dealers, Inc. The self-regulatory body for the broker/dealer community.

NASDAQ. National Association of Securities Dealers Automated Quotation System, providing computerized quotes of market maker for stocks traded over the counter.

Net Asset Value (NAV). The quoted market value of a mutual fund share. Determined by dividing the closing market value of all securities owned by the mutual fund plus all other assets and liabilities by the total number of shares outstanding.

Net Worth. Assets minus liabilities.

Neural Network. An example-based artificial intelligence system that can automatically test and update a knowledge base or set of rules or facts.

No Load Fund. A mutual fund sold to the public at net asset value (NAV), with no sales charges.

OPEC. The Organization of Petroleum Exporting Countries.

Open-End Fund. Also known as a mutual fund. Distinguished from a closed-end fund by a continuous offering of shares and a commitment to repurchase outstanding shares at net asset value.

Option. A security that gives the holder the right to purchase or sell a particular investment at a fixed price for a specified period of time.

Out Of The Money. A call option whose striking price is higher than the underlying security's current market price; a put option whose striking price is lower than the current market price.

Overbought. Market prices that have risen too far and too fast, overextended.

Oversold. Market prices that have declined too far too fast, overextended.

Participating. As it relates to preferred stock, the preferred stockholder shares in additional dividends as the earnings of the company improve.

Payout Ratio. The percentage of a company's profit paid out in cash dividends.

Poison Pill. A security issued by a target company to its shareholders which has special provisions that would make an unfriendly takeover extremely expensive for the acquirer.

Policy Asset Allocation. An asset allocation strategy with a long-term "normal" asset allocation mix.

Portfolio. The investment holdings of an individual or institutional investor; including stocks, bonds, options and money market accounts.

Portfolio Manager. The individual or individuals responsible for overall investment strategy, as well as, the buying and selling decisions for the securities in the portfolio.

Preferred. A security with preference to dividends and claim to corporate assets over common stock.

Price/Earnings Ratio. Determined by dividing the stock's market price by its earnings per common share. Used as an indicator of company performance and in comparison with other stock investments and the overall market.

Price-Weighted Index. A market average such as the Dow Jones Industrial Average that takes into account only the price of each security in the index, thus is unduly influenced by a high priced stock.

Prime Rate. The interest rate charged on loans by major banks to their best commercial customers.

Private Placement. The placement of a security directly with a person, business, or other entity without any offering to the general investing public.

Program Trading. Transactions based on signals from computer programs, usually entered directly from the trader's computer to the market's computer system.

Prospectus. The SEC required printed summary of the registration statement. The prospectus contains critical information about the security offering such as business, management, financial data and risks.

Proxy Fight. An attempt to gain control of a target company by voting out the existing board of directors and replacing it with a new slate supported by the insurgents, often for the purpose of pursuing a reorganization of the company.

Put Option. A contract giving the holder the right to sell the underlying security at a specific price over a specified time frame.

Qualified Plan. A retirement plan approved by the I.R.S. and eligible for favorable tax treatment. Earnings on plan assets are not taxed until they are withdrawn or distributed.

Quick Ratio. Current assets less inventory divided by current liabilities. Used to measure corporate liquidity, it is regarded as an improvement over the current ratio, which includes the usually not very liquid inventory.

REIT. Real Estate Investment Trust.

Raider. An individual or corporation with a reputation for attempting unfriendly takeovers.

Random Walk. Investment theory implying that market moves follow no rhyme or reason.

Range. The high and low prices over which the security trades during a specific time frame such as day, month and 52-weeks.

Rating. Independent ranking of a security in regard to risk and ability to meet payment obligations. Major ratings services include Moody's, Standard & Poor's, and Duff & Phelps.

Rebalancing. The process of adjusting a portfolio mix to return to a desired asset allocation level.

Registered Investment Advisor. One who has registered with the SEC to provide investment advice or analysis on securities. Also known as an investment counselor or money manager.

Relative Strength. Comparison of a security's price movement in relation to its competitors, its industry, or the entire market.

Risk. The financial uncertainty that the actual return will vary from the expected return. Risk factors include inflation, deflation, interest rate risk, market risk, liquidity and default.

Risk-Adjusted Return. Presentation of performance results to account for risk incurred to achieve such results. Puts performance comparison on an equivalent-risk basis.

Risk Management. An investment strategy designed to reduce the exposure to market risk when the probability of loss is high. See also, active, dynamic, and tactical asset allocation, and market timing.

Rule Of Eight. Diversification strategy that contends a minimum of eight stocks is necessary to properly diversify a portfolio.

SAAFTI. The Society of Asset Allocators and Fund Timers, Inc.

Schedule 13D. The required notification form filed with the Securities and Exchange Commission by a person or group who acquires more than five percent of a company's outstanding equity securities. Among the items included in the form are the identity and background of the acquirer, the amount and source of funds used to make the purchases and a general statement regarding the purpose of the transaction.

Scorched-Earth Defense. An attempt by a target company to make itself less attractive to an unwanted acquirer. Actions may include selling off prime assets and making acquisitions that use up excess cash.

Seasonality Trading. A strategy for effecting trades during seasonally favorable periods such as first of the month and around holidays.

SEC. The United States Securities and Exchange Commission. The legislatively-mandated regulatory body for the broker/dealer and investment advisory communities.

Secondary Market. Market where previously issued securities trade such as the New York Stock Exchange.

Sector Fund. A mutual fund that focuses the majority of its investments in a single industry.

Security. An investment that signifies an ownership or creditor position in a corporation.

SEP-IRA. A simplified employee pension plan, where contributions are made directly to an employee's IRA account. Much simpler to administer than a 401(k).

Shark Repellent Clauses. Amendments to a company's charter and/or bylaws designed to discourage unwanted suitors.

Sharpe Ratio. A classic risk/return measure, expressed as portfolio return minus risk-free return divided by the portfolio's standard deviation.

Short Against The Box. Investment strategy of selling short while holding a long position in the security.

Short Interest Ratio. A calculation that indicates the number of trading days required to repurchase all of the shares that have been sold short.

Short Sale. Sale of a security not yet owned in order to capitalize on an anticipated market price drop.

Short Squeeze. Rapid price rise forcing investors to cover their short positions. This drives the security price up even higher, often squeezing even more short investors.

Show-Stopper. A substantive violation of law by an acquirer which would justify an injunction against the offer.

Size-Weighted Composite. Mandated by AIMR in constructing a portfolio composite for presenting performance results, as opposed to equal-weighted.

Special Situation. An undervalued security with special circumstances such as management change, new product and technological breakthrough, favoring its return to better operating performance and higher prices.

Specialist. A trader on the floor exchange assigned to make a market in a specific stock.

Spin-Off. Shedding of a corporate subsidiary, division or other operation via the issuance of shares in the new corporate entity.

Split. A change in the number of outstanding shares through board of directors' action. Shareholder's equity remains the same, each shareholder receives the new stock in proportion to his holdings on the date of record. Dividends and earnings per share are adjusted to reflect the stock split.

Spread. In a stock quotation, it's the difference between the bid and ask price. In mergers and acquisitions, it's the difference, either in dollars or as a percentage, between the current market price of the target company's securities and its expected value upon completion of the transaction. In trading, it's a transaction in which two related contracts/stocks/bonds/options are traded to exploit the relative differences in price change between the two.

S & P 500. A broad-based stock index composed of 400 industrial, 40 financial, 40 utility, and 20 transportation stocks.

Standard Deviation. A measure of the fluctuation in a security's price over time. The lower the standard deviation, theoretically, the less the risk.

Standstill Agreement. A negotiated settlement between a target company and a potential unfriendly acquirer which sets a limit on the number of shares that the acquirer may purchase over a specified period of time.

Stock Index Futures. A futures contract that uses a market index as the underlying instrument.

Stop Loss. The risk management technique in which the security is liquidated to halt any further decline in portfolio value.

Strategic Asset Allocation. Very similar strategy to passive asset allocation. Uses principles of modern portfolio theory and the efficient frontier to set dedicated allocation percentages or targets. Rebalancing back to the target is performed periodically to adjust for differences in performance (usually ±5% or more).

Striking Price. The price at which an option or future contract can be executed according to the terms of the contract. Also called exercise price.

Style. See investment style.

Switching. Selling one security and purchasing another.

Synthetic Securities. Securities created by buying and writing a combination of options that mirror the risk and reward profile of a security.

Tactical Asset Allocation. A version of market timing. It can utilize more than just the two asset classes of classic market timing (stock and cash), but employs the same principles of market measurement and risk control in response to changing economic and market conditions. The risk tolerance of the investor is assumed to remain constant.

10K,10Q. Annual and quarterly reports required by the Securities and Exchange Commission. They contain more in-depth financial and operating information than the annual and quarterly stockholder's reports.

Target. The company that is the object of an acquisition proposal or tender offer.

Technical Analysis. Investment strategy that focuses on market and stock price and volume patterns.

Time-Weighted Return. The preferred performance presentation mandated by AIMR. A calculated return that gives the same weight to time periods, regardless, of the amount of money invested. The time periods are linked geometrically.

Top-Down Investing. Investment strategy starting with the overall economic scenario and then moving downward to consider industry and individual company investments.

Total Return. The return achieved by combining both the dividend/interest and capital appreciation earned on an investment.

Total Return Index. A market average such as Market Logic's NYSE TR Index that gives equal weighting to the daily price changes of every issue in the average.

Trading Range. The spread between the high and low prices for a given period of time.

Treasuries. United States Government guaranteed securities. Among them, from shortest to longest, are Treasury Bills, Treasury Notes, and Treasury Bonds.

Trend. The prevailing tendency or price movement of a set of data as related to time.

Trend Following. Moving in the direction of the prevailing price movement.

Turnaround. A positive change in the fortunes of a company or industry. Turnarounds occur for a variety of reasons such as economic upturn, new management, new product lines, and strategic acquisitions.

12b-1. An annual charge deducted from fund assets to pay for distribution and marketing expenses. Often, after a certain period of time, funds charging a 12b-1 allow shareholders to convert to a class of shares without this fee.

Ulcer Index. A measure of price volatility over time that attempts to disregard upside volatility and measure the relative pain of downside volatility.

Underlying Security. The security which may be bought or sold under the terms of an option agreement, warrant, etc.

Undervalued Situation. A security with a market value that does not fully value its potential or the true value of the company.

Uptrend. Upward movement in the market price of a stock.

Value Averaging. An investment purchase method that concentrates on the investment's value, not its cost.

Variable Annuity. An insurance company contract providing for tax-free buildup of earnings, but whose return is not fixed, but variable, depending on the value of the underlying investments.

Venture Capital. Funds provided by individuals or groups, as startup or expansion capital, typically for an ownership percentage of the enterprise.

Volatility. A measure of a security's tendency to move up and down in price. Beta and standard deviation are measures of volatility.

Volume. The number of units of a security traded during a given time frame.

Warrant. An option to purchase a stated number of shares at a specified price within a specific time frame. Warrants are typically offered as sweeteners to enhance the marketability of stock or debt issues.

Whipsaw. Losing money on both sides of a price swing.

White Knight. A third party which, by offering a higher price in a friendly transaction, saves a target company from being acquired by an unwelcome bidder.

Working Capital. The difference between current assets and current liabilities.

Yield. An investment's return from its interest or dividend paying capability.

Yield To Maturity. The yield of a bond to maturity based on its current market price. The yield to maturity is greater than its stated yield if the bond is selling at a discount from face value and less than its stated yield if the bond is selling at a premium to face value.

Zero Coupon. A bond selling at a discount to maturity value and earning interest over the life of the bond but paying no cash dividend until maturity.

Index